connect™ plus+

LESS MANAGING.
MORE TEACHING.
GREATER LEARNING.

What Is *Connect Plus*?

McGraw-Hill *Connect Plus* is a revolutionary online assignment and assessment solution providing instructors and students with tools and resources to maximize their success.

Through *Connect Plus*, instructors enjoy simplified course setup and assignment creation. Robust, media-rich tools and activities, **all tied to the textbook's learning outcomes**, ensure you'll create classes geared toward achievement. You'll have more time with your students and less time agonizing over course planning.

Connect Plus Features

McGraw-Hill *Connect Plus* includes powerful tools and features that allow students to access their coursework anytime and anywhere, while you control the assignments. *Connect Plus* provides students with their textbook and homework, **all in one accessible place.**

▶ *Simple Assignment Management*
Creating assignments takes just a few clicks, and with *Connect Plus*, you can choose not only which chapter to assign but also specific learning outcomes. **Videos, animations, quizzes**, and many other activities bring **active learning** to the forefront.

▶ *Smart Grading*
Study time is precious and *Connect Plus* assignments **automatically provide feedback** to you and your students. You'll be able to conveniently review class or individual student knowledge in an online environment.

▶ *Connect Plus eBooks*
McGraw-Hill has seamlessly **integrated eBooks** into their *Connect Plus* solution with **direct links to the homework, activities, and tools**—students no longer have to search for content, allowing them more time for learning.

McGraw-Hill provides live instructor orientations for *Connect Plus* to guarantee you will have a worry-free experience.

 McGraw Hill

connect™ plus+

To learn more about *Connect Plus*, go to **www.mcgrawhillconnect.com** or contact your local representative.

Your Campus Resources

	Name of Office on Your Campus	Phone Number	Location	Hours	Email Address
Career Placement Office					
Learning Center					
Campus Security					
Student Center/Student Services					
Bookstore					
Library					
Academic Advising					
Financial Aid					
Other _____					

Choosing Success
in Community College and Beyond

RHONDA ATKINSON
Valencia Community College

DEBBIE LONGMAN
Southeastern Louisiana University

McGraw Hill

Connect
Learn
Succeed™

ISBN   978-0-07-337518-2
MHID 0-07-337518-7

Vice president/Editor in chief: *Elizabeth Haefele*
Vice president/Director of marketing: *John E. Biernat*
Senior sponsoring editor: *Barbara Owca*
Director of development: *Sarah Wood*
Developmental editor: *Danielle McCumber*
Senior marketing manager: *Keari Green*
Lead digital product manager: *Damian Moshak*
Digital development editor: *Kevin White*
Director, Editing/Design/Production: *Jess Ann Kosic*
Project manager: *Marlena Pechan*
Buyer: *Susan Culbertson*
Senior designer: *Srdjan Savanovic*
Lead photo research coordinator: *Carrie K. Burger*
Media project manager: *Brent dela Cruz*
Cover design: *Srdjan Savanovic*
Interior design: *Maureen McCutcheon*
Typeface: *11/13 Minion Pro*
Compositor: *Aptara®, Inc.*
Printer:*Quad/Graphics*
Credits: The credits section for this book begins on page 301 and is considered an extension of the copyright page.

Library of Congress Control Number: 2010938044

www.mhhe.com

about the authors

▶ RHONDA **ATKINSON** Rhonda Holt Atkinson is originally from Arkansas. She taught first-year students at Louisiana State University (LSU) in Baton Rouge for 20 years, at Central Missouri State University (CMSU) for about 7 years, and is now a professor of education at Valencia Community College in Orlando, Florida. In addition to this textbook, she has written many other college textbooks in reading and study skills with Debbie Guice Longman and worked on a variety of other writing projects, such as workplace learning in industrial construction trades, ESL health curricula for low-literate adults, after-school programs on museums in Louisiana for middle school students, and curriculum evaluation projects for the U.S. Army and Northrop Grumman.

▶ DEBBIE **LONGMAN** Debbie Guice Longman hails from Louisiana. She taught first-year students at Louisiana State University (LSU) in Baton Rouge for about 10 years, where she met Rhonda Holt Atkinson. She is currently a professor at Southeastern Louisiana University in Hammond, Louisiana, about 45 miles from New Orleans, where she has taught for almost 20 years. In addition to this textbook, she and Rhonda Atkinson have co-authored many other college textbooks in reading and study skills and consulted on a variety of other projects, including high school and university curricula, workplace learning in industrial construction trades, and career school in-service. Dr. Longman is a certified Quality Matters (QM) Master Trainer.

Dedication

To those we teach and learn from on a daily basis:
Tom, Rachel, Yvonne, and Anthony;
Richard, Jacob, Christopher, Mara, and Danielle.

brief contents

contents

CHAPTER **TWO**

Interacting with Your College Community 26

CHAPTER **THREE**

Deciding to Know Yourself 54

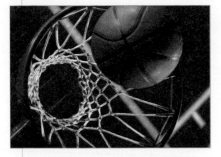

CHAPTER **FOUR**

Choosing Goals for College and Life 82

CHAPTER **FIVE**

Decisions for Managing Time 102

CHAPTER **SIX**

Choices for Succeeding in Class and Online Courses   130

CHAPTER **SEVEN**
Choosing to Read Actively   152

CHAPTER **EIGHT**

Decisions about Study and Test Taking 174

CHAPTER **NINE**

Making Choices about Today's Technology   202

CHAPTER **TEN**

Making Financial Decisions 226

CHAPTER **ELEVEN**

Choosing Health and Wellness 246

CHAPTER **TWELVE**

Exploring Career Options and Opportunities 276

Choosing Success in Community College and Beyond

First Steps to Choosing Success

College opens many doors to your future. What are some of the doors you see college opening to you? What factors will you use to decide which to open and which to close?

YOU DECIDE

To *wonder* means to think or have curiosity about. Things and ideas you wonder about often mask a need for a decision. Check the items below that apply to you.

In terms of my new community college environment, I've been wondering . . .

- ☐ 1.1 Now that I'm in college, what's next?
- ☐ 1.2 What's so different about being a college student?
- ☐ 1.3 How will I know what to do in college?
- ☐ 1.4 What's the best way for me to learn?
- ☐ 1.5 What does this book have that can help me?

Each of these decision points corresponds to the numbered modules that follow. Turn to the module for immediate help.

Congratulations! You are a college student! As a college student, you may find you have more choices and greater responsibility for the decisions you make. That's why this text is titled *Choosing Success in Community College and Beyond.* It provides a way for you to recognize your options and make conscious choices to get the outcomes you want in college and in life.

COLLEGE SUCCESS BEGINS NOW ❯

Now that I'm in college, what's next?

The First Week of Class

I need new skills for my job—that's why I am here. . . . I did well in high school, but I can already tell that classes here will be different. . . . As a dual-credit student, I'm still in high school—but I want to fit in here. . . . I came here but I really want to go to the state university so I've got to make grades that will transfer. . . . I planned to go to work after high school. After looking at the job market, I decided to come to college but I am undecided about a career. . . . I dropped out of high school and got a GED. I know how important an education is to me.

Notice anything in common in these statements? All reflect typical feelings and concerns of new students. All colleges are in the business of **retention.** They want students to stay in school until they meet their goals or finish a degree or program. Their goal is student success. Thus, your college provides resources like this course to help you and other students address college concerns and succeed. This text gives you strategies for thinking through decisions on topics from career decision making to wellness. Your course instructor will help you apply what you learn to your specific college.

> **retention**
> Keeping students in school until they meet their goals or finish a degree or program.

College is a lot to take in at once. That's OK. Take a look at the table of contents of this book. Read through the twelve tips for week 1. Together they form the big picture of what you need to know. Thus, if you need information before it's covered in class, you'll know which chapter focuses on it. But you need to decide to be proactive. The twelve tips for week 1 help you get started.

▶ Twelve Tips for Week 1

Get oriented. You probably already know where your classes meet. It's also a good idea to know how to find your instructors outside of class. You need phone and office numbers as well as e-mail addresses for them. Instructors that are **adjunct** faculty often don't have offices of their own. But they probably have mailboxes in departmental offices where you can leave messages, and they have their own e-mail addresses.

> **adjunct**
> Part-time faculty.

- Also, make sure you know where to find basic campus services. Depending on what's available at your campus, this might include the student center, food services, recreation facilities, financial aid office, and library.

- Try to find out what other activities or services are on hand. You may want to find where to use a computer, obtain services if you have a disability, cash a check, print papers, or get tutoring if you need help.

It's OK if it takes some time to adjust to school. Everyone was once a new student.

- Your campus website serves as a good reference for general services. These include campus security and administrative offices like academic offices and student services. Call campus information if you need help finding a specific department.

- Finally, ask for help if you need it. Some students don't ask questions because they think they'll "sound dumb." Nothing could be further from the truth. Everyone at your college—student, faculty, or staff—was once new to the campus. Stop in offices and ask for directions. Ask students you meet for help.

- Still, know that your campus is like any other place. Some people will be patient, helpful, and kind. Others might not. Don't take it personally. The first few weeks of a term are demanding for both students and faculty. If the first person you talk to isn't helpful, talk to someone else. And keep in mind that you don't need to know everyone and everything at once.

Mix and mingle. Make a decision to meet new people. Choose to get to know the people in your classes right away.

- Even though you may feel a little uncomfortable doing so, try to introduce yourself to at least one person in each class. If that feels too strange, start by nodding and smiling at the students around you.

- If your campus has a newspaper, plan to read it regularly. Most newspapers have a calendar section that lists campus activities, meetings, or other events. You might also look at what's on the bulletin boards in each building. They often give helpful information and insights into your college's culture. (*See Chapter 2 to find out more about your campus's community.*)

Open up. Make choices that open your mind to learning more about yourself. Figure out how you learn best. Become aware of your options and the way you make decisions. (*Chapter 3 shows you how your aptitudes and abilities, interests, values, and learning preferences can contribute to your academic success.*)

Get the big picture. Once you get a **syllabus** from each class, make a term planner. Your term planner will help you prioritize choices throughout the term.

- To make your term planner, get a cheap monthly print calendar or a digital calendar with large blocks for each day and then get your school's **academic calendar.** It is often found at your college website.

- Using the academic calendar, first record all holidays, school vacations, and academic due dates. Second, using your syllabus, record test dates

syllabus
Outline of course content for a term.

academic calendar
Calendar of the school year starting in August or September rather than in January; shows information such as registration and drop dates or exam periods.

If you record all important events and assignments for the term in a monthly planner, you will be less likely to miss a crucial deadline.

and due dates for papers, exams or projects. Third, set up intermediate deadlines for completing phases of lengthy projects. For instance, for a major paper, you can set deadlines for completing the research, first draft, and last draft. Fourth, record important personal events. These would include fun and family activities, medical appointments, and so on.

- Now, remove or print all the pages for the term. Post where you can see all the months—the whole term—at the same time. Seeing your commitments all at once will help you make better decisions about time management. (*See Chapter 4 for more time management tips.*)

Network. As you meet new people, tell them about your interests, needs, and goals. Faculty, staff, and other students may know someone or something that can help you. This helps you create a network of support. (*Chapter 5 provides more information about ways to achieve your goals.*)

Prepare to think differently. College is about the process of thinking as well as the product of thinking. Although you will have much to learn, the focus is less on memorizing ideas and more on thinking critically about them when it comes to taking exams. (*You'll learn more about critical thinking as well as ways to prepare for and take tests in Chapter 6.*)

Go to class. Starting with the first day of class, decide to attend your classes each time they meet even if your instructors don't take attendance. You're the one going to college. You want to get the most from your classes.

- When possible, choose to sit at the front of the classroom. Studies show students who sit in the front do better than those who sit in the back.

- Be sure to take notes. As soon as you can after class, try to spend three to five minutes reviewing your notes. (*Chapter 7 provides more information about listening and notetaking.*)

- Attendance is just as important in an online class. Log into your online course daily to check e-mail and announcements.

Work for yourself as well as for grades. As a college student, you're working for yourself and your future. Learning is not a spectator sport. Just as regular workouts exercise your body, regular completion of assignments and readings exercises your mind and skills.

- Faculty assume students know to read the chapters listed on the syllabus. As a result, instructors may never actually assign them. They just expect you to read them. This is even more important in online courses where you have more autonomy for completing assignments.

- Choosing to read, or at least **preview,** the text before class helps you make sense of lectures. To "preview" is to read a chapter's introduction, headings, subheadings, boldfaced terms, and summary before a full reading. (*You'll learn more about reading and learning from textbooks and online materials in Chapter 8.*)

preview
Reading a chapter's introduction, headings, subheadings, boldfaced terms, and summary before a full reading of the content.

Get (tech) help. **Technology** is an integral part of learning in today's colleges. Some students, and you may be one of them, have concerns or fears about using it. That's OK. Whatever your technology skills, you'll need to know how technology is used on your campus.

technology
Computers and the digital resources accessed by them.

- This means that there are aspects of technology that are new to everyone. College staff know this. They provide resources and assistance to help, but it's up to you to choose to use them. Know where to find these on your campus and when they are available. Most colleges provide quick links or references on their websites.

- If you cannot easily use a computer to find information, use e-mail, access campus information, or navigate a **course management system,** be sure to get help now. Look for workshops and orientation sessions to show you how to use your campus's online systems.

- Your instructors should explain how to use the technology required in their courses. Take notes for future use. Try using the course technology on your own or check with your campus help services. If you still have questions, ask other students in the class or make an appointment to see your instructor. (*Chapter 9 describes how to maximize your skills as a learner in the information age.*)

course management system
Software used by faculty and students to deliver on-line learning (e.g., Angel, moodle, Blackboard).

Don't worry yet. If you haven't chosen a career goal, don't worry. Most first term courses are basic classes that apply to most programs. Focus on getting to know your campus and maximizing your academic success. Make plans to visit your advisor or career-planning office to explore options. (*Chapter 10 provides information about career decision making.*)

Watch your money. Make a budget for the rest of the term. The first week of classes is generally the most costly. That's because you pay tuition and buy books and other supplies. Analyze your remaining funds. Then, divide the amount by the number of weeks in the term. Don't forget to plan for financial emergencies. Remember that everything you buy—from coffee to college supplies—represents a choice you make about how to spend your money. (*Chapter 11 provides additional suggestions for college money management.*)

Stay healthy. New academic experiences—and less time—may cause you to eat and worry more and sleep and exercise less. Pay attention to what you eat and the amount of rest and exercise you get. What you eat and do are choices you make each day. (*Chapter 12 gives information about ways to handle these and other wellness issues.*)

Top 10 Things to Do the First Week of School

Check each task as you complete it.

☐ 1. Find basic campus services both on campus and online. Save phone numbers on your phone and bookmark links to services. There is also a place to record this information on page ii of this book.

☐ 2. Make a term planner.

☐ 3. Get names and phone numbers or e-mail addresses for one person in each class. Save this information in your cell phone or in your notebook for each class.

☐ 4. Get a college catalog and/or bookmark the catalog link on your computer.

☐ 5. Find two people you want to add to your network of support.

☐ 6. Sit at front of room in each class and check in to online classes daily.

☐ 7. Learn the features of any course management software used in your classes. Get a zip or flash drive to save electronic information.

☐ 8. Buy a notebook or folder for each class and create class folders on your computer or flash drive. Get or download a syllabus for each class and put it with the corresponding notebook or folder.

☐ 9. Even though they are expensive, buy your books right away. They are your tools for the courses you take. Be sure you have the right books and materials for each course.

☐ 10. Decide to make the most of your college experience.

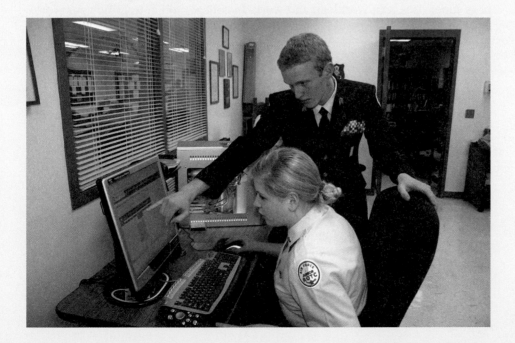

What's so different about being a college student?

How College Is Different

If you're like most students, you'll find that higher education differs from high school and work experiences. Why?

First, you are an unknown. In terms of academics, your new instructors don't know if you graduated top in your class or dropped out of school. They don't know if you like, dislike, or fear their subjects.

Second, in high school, you had a year for most subjects. Now you must complete more work in less time than ever before. You have only yourself to oversee your workload. You may have hundreds of pages to read with only two or three exams during the term. There may be no assignments due one week, and something due each day the next. Also, you—not your instructors—hold the responsibility for learning. Instructors give you information and assignments, but you'll more often learn on your own rather than in class.

That's why most colleges consider 12 hours of credit a full-time load. It's not that they think 12 hours of time per week in class is a full-time job. Instead, they assume the work you must do outside class added to the time you're in class equals a full-time job.

Your college experience differs from work as well. For instance, at work, your boss supervises your workload and work. In college, you determine your workload. If you take too many classes, you alone are responsible for the results. And instructors may not see your work until you submit a completed assignment.

Where and when you learn differs from where and when you work. You rarely get to choose a worksite. Where you study, however, is your choice. A work day is a specific period of time, usually 8 hours. If you work overtime, you get paid extra for that time. Class time is hardly ever 8 hours straight. Study time, as well as most online classes, has no specific hours. Studying "overtime" may—or may not—pay benefits in better grades.

A key difference in any college experience involves choices and the decisions you make about them. Unlike high school in which most students took many of the same courses on a daily basis, college courses provide more options. You get to choose your major. Although there are requirements such as math, English, and science courses, you often get some choice (e.g., chemistry versus geology) depending on your major. You decide where and when to take courses (onsite, online, evening, weekend, daytime) and how many courses to take at one time.

You decide how you approach each course and how you will prove yourself each term. You can choose to be interested or bored. You can decide to give it all you've got or just give up. You also decide how to handle your workload. You can choose to attend classes or skip them. You can decide to plan ahead and work hard on assignments or do them at the last minute. You also make choices about if, when, and where to study as well as how and what to study. You choose which organizations to join, which opportunities to accept, and what campus resources to use.

You can also decide how to respond to the experiences, interests, and attitudes of people around you. So, if your peers, friends, family, co-workers, or former teachers/counselors value higher education and financially or emotionally support you, you can choose to rely on them in order to maximize your success. But if friends, family, or co-workers view college as a waste of time or if former teachers/counselors viewed you as "not college material," then you can decide to look elsewhere for support.

Some decisions are clear. In general, going to class is better than not going to class. However, what if an emergency arises—a friend needs a ride to work, a relative needs help, or sick children need your care? Your choice suddenly becomes more difficult as you weigh options.

Some choices have lasting or life-changing effects. Should you pursue a two-year certification program or go on for a four-year degree? Will you major in information technology or in nursing? Will you love one person or another? Should you take this job or that one?

Other decisions, like what to eat for lunch or what to wear, are less important because of their short-lived effects. Still, some people seem to give the same kind of attention to both types of decisions. Indeed, some students seem to spend more time choosing *when* to take a course than they spend in deciding *which* course to take. As a result, they often struggle with the minor decisions of life while failing to give important choices the consideration they deserve. Because the important choices are not thought out, they often don't work out.

The decisions you make now affect your future. For instance, some students decide to take the first semester easy. Their grades are average at best. Then, a course sparks their interest. They decide that this is what they want to major in. But they discover that this degree is a competitive program. It only takes the students with the highest **GPAs.** Even if students don't choose competitive programs, average grades still affect their futures. After they complete their programs or degrees, they will compete for jobs. Just having a degree or certification is no longer enough in today's job market. The best (and sometimes only) jobs go to students that show they can work well with others, write and communicate well, and act honestly. Some students don't see the long-term consequences of the choices they make on a day-to-day basis. The rest of this chapter helps you avoid this mistake. You already know how higher education differs from other situations. Next, you'll learn a strategy for making choices. You'll also learn how to manage the changes you face. Moreover, the rest of this text provides you with chances to think through the decision-making process in different situations.

GPA
Grade point average.

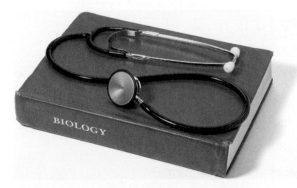

activity 2

What Do *You* Need to Know? Ask the Experts!

Your instructor will provide an in-class panel of "experts" from your college either in person or on video. They may be students, other faculty, staff, and/or administrators.

PART 1:   The Experts

The experts will respond to the following questions and/or any other prompts your instructor creates. Your instructor may also ask you to create a list of questions you want answered. Take notes on what they say.

I feel the biggest challenge students face is . . .

The biggest decision I see students as having to make is . . .

The question I get asked most often is . . .

Students tell me they (and/or I) like . . . about college.

Students tell me they (and/or I) dislike . . . about college.

The thing that surprised me most about this college when I first arrived here was . . .

I think the biggest difference between college, work, and high school is . . .

My advice to new students would be . . .

PART 2:   Summarize Your Findings

_____

_____

_____

PART 3:   Your College Future

Now that you've heard from college "experts" and other new students, what do you need to learn or do in order to be successful at your community college?

_____

_____

_____

GROUP APPLICATION: In small groups of 3–5 students, answer the following questions and compare answers.

1. What do you like best about this college?

2. What do you like least about this college?

3. What surprised you about this college when you first arrived here?

4. What do you think is the biggest difference between college, work, and high school?

5. What helped you get oriented here?

6. What piece of advice would you offer to someone new to this college?

7. What do you think contributes to a student's success on campus?

8. What do you think is the biggest cause of failure on campus?

5C Approach for Decision Making

How do *you* make decisions? The choices some people make seem to be little more than a roll of the dice. Decision making is the very core of this text. You'll learn to use a basic five-point process for making decisions. Each point begins with the letter **C.** You can recall the points by remembering the **5Cs**—Define the <u>C</u>hallenge; Identify the <u>C</u>hoices; Predict the <u>C</u>onsequences; <u>C</u>hoose an option; <u>C</u>heck your outcome. You can also visualize the points on a star. See Figure 1.1.

5C
Five-point decision-making process.

Each chapter helps you identify how to make decisions that will affect your success at your college . . . and in life. Your decisions then result from conscious choices rather than unconscious responses. You will use the 5Cs throughout this text to think critically through a variety of topics and issues. While you might not always think through every choice you make, knowing and using the 5Cs gives you a concrete strategy for making important decisions.

Define the <u>C</u>hallenge

Solving a problem involves first clearly defining what the problem is. To do so, consider the context. What issues or actions surround the problem? What other people are involved and what part do they play? Second, determine the relevant

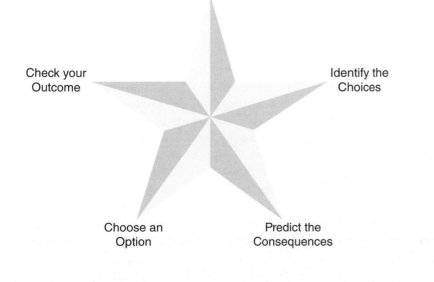

Define the Challenge

Check your Outcome

Identify the Choices

Choose an Option

Predict the Consequences

Figure 1.1 The 5C Model for Decision Making.

importance of the problem and long-term effects of the decision. Will this still be important tomorrow, next week, next month, or next year? Third, talk to others about the situation. Different viewpoints help you become more objective. Finally, as clearly as possible state your problem, or challenge, verbally or in writing. If you can't clearly state it, you don't have enough information to make a decision.

For instance, choosing a major is a problem that many students face. Issues that affect the choice might include your prior high school experiences and grades, your aptitudes and abilities, the time you have to devote to classes, the amount of time and money needed to achieve that career goal, job opportunities, and potential salary. If you have a family, your decision affects their future as well as yours.

Choosing a career is an important decision with long-term effects. Perhaps you've discussed your situation with family and friends as well as college advisors. They've helped you assess your interests and needs. You describe your challenge as "a need to choose a major that will result in an interesting career that provides job security and matches my lifestyle needs."

Identify Choices

Unlike math problems that have a single right answer, many possible right answers exist when making decisions. Thus, the first step in making a decision is finding out what choices you face. At first, you might consider all options from the most logical to the most unlikely. Although each might have value, you'll probably find that some can be quickly discarded. Your goal might be to identify three to five choices that you want to explore further.

Next, you identify workable options—in the case of choosing a major, one that will lead to a career that will get you where you want to go. For instance, in thinking about majors, you might decide that, as a practical matter, your options consist of those programs available at your school. You visit the campus career center. You check course requirements in the college catalog. You search for information on the Web. The outcome is a list of your possible choices.

Predict Consequences

Once you make a short list of choices, your next task is to consider the consequences of each one. To do so, you think of the negative and positive results of each choice by reviewing your personal experiences and preferences and through research (e.g., talking to others, looking up additional information). This helps you make a kind of balance sheet.

A balance sheet gives you only your odds. For instance, suppose your choices are nursing, elementary education, and computer programming. You decide that completing an elementary education program will take too long—a minus. Your research tells you that there are few jobs for computer programmers in your community—another minus. The nursing program has two plusses. One, you could get a degree in a two-year program. Two, jobs are available in your community right away. These are items you'd put on a balance sheet to help you predict the consequences of your choice.

You may be able to add a lot more items to your balance sheet. In the end you may see that the logical choice would be to pursue a particular major. Perhaps employees in that field make a lot of money, or get their choice of jobs, or attain prestigious status. It might be something you do well. It might be something others urge you to do. Still, if you know you could never be happy in that field, that would go on your balance sheet, and it would never be your best choice. So, no matter the results of your balance sheet, the choice remains yours. You decide how much risk you're willing to take in your choice or the level of safety or comfort you need about this choice. As you make college decisions, you weigh your choices against the context of your institution and your values (*see Chapter 3*).

Your attitude toward the choices you must make also plays a part. For instance, some people are overwhelmed by their choices and get stuck in a situation. They think that maintaining their current status helps them avoid making a choice. Not so. Staying in the same situation is a choice whether you realize it or not. Or some people think of themselves as being in no-win situations. But you can just as easily think of your challenge as win-win.

In other words, each choice has benefits. Each presents opportunities. In deciding what major to pursue, you may be thinking about what you'll miss by choosing one curriculum over another. Instead, focus on the opportunities and remind yourself that, either way, you won't lose. Remember that separating a good choice from a bad one isn't usually difficult. The results are obvious. The difficult decision is when you have to choose between two or more good options.

Choose an Option

After you've considered your choices, it's time to choose one and put your decision into effect. How do you do that? First, *set a deadline for enacting your decision*. This gives you a target to reach.

Second, *think of your decision in positive instead of negative terms*. In other words, phrase your decision so that you anticipate opportunities for success rather than threats of failure. For instance, a decision to make the dean's list at the term's end is more motivating than the decision *not* to be placed on probation at the end of the term.

Third, *make the outcome of your choice dependent solely on you*. Forming a study group the week before the final exam seems like a good goal—unless the members of the group get sick or otherwise fail to show up. If you depend only on the group for success on the test, you may be disappointed with the results.

Fourth, *use others for support*. This seems like a contradiction of the previous tip. But, there is a big difference. Instead of making a decision contingent on others, you use others only for help and assistance. This kind of network provides information, advice, and friendship.

Fifth, *visualize success*. Most people tend to replay mentally their personal errors. They end up rehearsing them so well that the same mistakes happen again and again. You avoid some problems by visualizing and rehearsing the success of your decision instead of its failure.

Last, *become aware of self-sabotage*. Set yourself up for success. For instance, if your decision is to study for an exam rather than socialize with friends or family, avoid places (noisy student center, busy kitchen, etc.) in which you might be unable to focus. Instead, find a quiet place with few distractions.

Consider again the example of choosing a major. Suppose, after careful thought, you decide to start the nursing program. You arrange for care for your children during class. You take learning skills workshops to brush up on notetaking and test taking. You go to tutoring for help in math and science. You have good grades at the end of the first term. Things appear to be fine. What's next?

Check Your Outcome

Congratulations! You identified several choices. You looked at the consequences and selected what you thought was the best choice. But did experience prove you out? Checking your outcome helps you see if your decision is working. Luckily, most decisions can be rethought. Even major decisions often can be altered.

For instance, you chose to major in nursing because you thought it was a career in which you would always be able to find a job. But at the end of the first term, you find that majoring in nursing isn't working out. Maybe you found that you didn't like science as much as you thought. Labs interfered with time with your family. The sight of blood made you ill. You may still feel you must stick with your decision though. Why?

If you made a choice that didn't work out, what's better now—being unhappy or rethinking your decision and making another choice? Was it really the best choice, or did it only seem so based on the information available at the time?

How do you know, and when do you know, if the choice you made is a good one?

First, find out if you are satisfied with the outcome. At the very least, the situation you wanted to resolve should be improving. Next, check to see if your choice has had enough time to work. Look to see if there were any choices that you failed to consider, and if you successfully predicted the outcomes and/or risks of the choice you made.

activity 3

Applying the 5Cs to a Problem

You can use the 5C approach to help you make decisions about a variety of problems. Identify a problem in your life and respond to the following prompts. Use additional paper if needed.

PROBLEM:				
Step	**Action(s)**	**Your Response**		
STEP 1: Define the **C**hallenge.	Describe the problem you face.			
STEP 2: Identify **C**hoices.	Make a list of options for consideration			
STEP 3: Predict **C**onsequences.	Identify the positive and negative outcomes for each option or for the best two or three options. Create a balance sheet that shows the plusses and minuses for the good and bad consequences of each option.	PLUSSES		MINUSES
STEP 4: **C**hoose an option.	Set a deadline for putting the choice into effect. Be sure that you described your choice in positive terms (what you will do instead of what you won't do). Identify what you need to do to implement the choice. Make a list of people who will support your choice. Imagine what life will be after your option has been put into effect. How do you like the picture you see? Think of any thoughts or behaviors that might sabotage your efforts and identify ways to control them.			
STEP 5: **C**heck your outcome.	Determine when and how you will know if your option proved to be successful.			

Learning as an Active Decision

As a college student, learning is your priority, and learning is not a spectator sport. It's an active practice. You get from learning what you put into it. The way you approach coursework—in class, online, and on your own—is an ongoing choice. Thus, you have a pressing need for effective learning strategies as well as chances to practice them regularly. The key is deciding to change your approach from a passive to an *active* one. Active learning is an ongoing process of thinking and doing that you purposefully control. Such new ways of thinking require new tools and strategies to help you absorb the process.

SQ3R is one of these strategies. SQ3R helps you read print materials more actively. It also helps you remember more about what you read. You'll learn other active learning strategies throughout this text.

> ## SQ3R: A Plan for Active Learning from Print Materials

Survey. A survey is your preparation for learning. When you survey a chapter, you purposefully **skim** it. You can use the title to capture the main idea. Skimming the chapter introduction, outline, headings, and visual content adds details. This forms the "big picture" of what the chapter contains. It creates a framework for your next in-depth reading. You also think about what you already know about the topic and what information will be new to you. Thus, right away, you are making reading more active because you are making conscious decisions about content and your role in learning it.

Question. Once you gain a general sense of the content through your survey, you can be more purposeful about what you want to learn from it—your learning goals. As you read

SQ3R
An active reading strategy developed by Francis Robinson consisting of five steps: Survey, Question, Read, Recite and Review.

skim
Read quickly for key ideas.

SURVEY

Before reading this chapter, prepare for learning. Purposefully skim the title, introduction, headings, and graphics. As you survey, decide what information you already know and what information is new to you.

◀ **CHOOSING TO BE AN ACTIVE LEARNER**

QUESTION

Change each module section's heading into a question. This forms your learning goal for reading.

you can set learning goals about the content by asking questions about each section. You can do so by turning a heading into a question. For instance, in reading this text right now, the module heading above, *Learning as an Active Decision,* might be rephrased as the question: *How can learning be an active decision?* or *What can I do to make learning an active decision?* Ask questions about other aspects of the chapter text as well, as it strikes you to do so (e.g., key terms, photos or exhibits). Questions make learning more active because they create a need for finding their answers.

CHOOSING TO BE AN ACTIVE LEARNER >

READ

Read each module in the chapter without marking. Reread and mark key information that answers your question.

RECITE

Stop after reading each module and make sure you understood the content. Organize or summarize content and make notes.

Read. Read each section of text to answer your questions and achieve your learning goals. Some people find that their attention wanders as they read. Before they realize it, they've marked (highlighted or underlined) an entire section or read to the end of the page without really paying attention to any of it. You can avoid this by adding purposeful action to the reading process. As you read the section, do not mark anything. After you've read the section, skim through it again and mark only key words and details. Avoid marking whole sentences.

Recite. Check your understanding after each section before continuing. You should now be able to answer the question you asked at the start of the section. If you can't, review your marked content or reread the section. To make this step more active, organize or summarize ideas that answer your question and make notes. Deciding how to organize or summarize the content makes this step more active. Putting it in your own words in notes increases retention. And rather than rereading what you marked to recall its importance in future study sessions, your notes will serve as study cues.

CHOOSING TO BE AN ACTIVE LEARNER >

REVIEW

Skim the notes you made throughout the chapter. How does the content fit together? What information is still unclear? Were your learning goals met? Can you answer the review questions and define terms?

Review. Most people close their books at the end of a chapter. Instead, spend five or ten minutes quickly thinking through the chapter from the beginning. Now that you have all the information, the "big picture" you created should have more detail. This review solidifies your understanding as you put all the pieces together. Make notes of sections you still have questions about or ideas that are still unclear to you.

The rest of the chapters in this text include prompts at their beginnings and ends to remind you of this process. At the start of each chapter, you will find the Survey, Question, Read, and Recite prompts. At the end of each chapter will be the Review prompt. This will help you practice the process. By the end of the text, SQ3R will be a natural part of your learning strategies.

Maximizing Your Use of *Choosing Success in Community College and Beyond*

Each chapter of this text helps you look at yourself and your college environment from a decision-making viewpoint. To this end, each chapter begins with a reminder to use the first four steps of the SQ3R process to approach your reading; this feature is called *Choosing to Be an Active Learner.*

You'll also find at the beginning of each chapter a list of *Learning Outcomes,* key concepts within the chapter. These fulfill two goals. One, by reading them, you learn about chapter content. Two, they tell you what you need to grasp from the chapter. You will also find a kind of self-assessment—called *You Decide*—at the start of each chapter. *You Decide* consists of questions that give you a chance to see what choices and decisions about the chapter topic are most important to you. Each question you check represents an aspect of your new learning environment. Each is tied to a module of the chapter, a self-contained unit on the specific issues it involves. You can turn to the numbered module for immediate help, or you can pay special attention when you get to that module as you read the chapter in its entirety.

Each module in each chapter contains useful information and practical tips for building your skills and most also include an *Activity* that allows you to practice what you've learned. Many of the activities also include *Group Applications*, in which you will work with others to achieve results. *Key terms* in the chapter discussion are marked with boldfaced text; definitions for these terms appear in the margin.

At the end of each chapter you will find a *Chapter Review*. These review questions help you recall and apply what you have learned. You'll also have a chance to rethink your responses to *You Decide* at the start of the chapter in a revised form—*Did You Decide?* This time you will mark the areas in which you feel you've gained skills or strength since starting the chapter and record how you have done so. This will help you see where you've made progress and where you still need to do some work. If you save your answers from each chapter, you'll eventually have a portfolio of ideas and strategies that you can use in all of your courses.

One of the chapter ending features is a journal activity, *Reflecting on Decisions,* that asks you to think about decisions you have made or need to make in terms of the subject of that chapter. At the end of each chapter, *Perspectives* is written by people who work or learn at two-year colleges. Each *Perspectives* section includes questions to consider as you read as well as another opportunity to think through the 5C process. You will also find a *Choosing to Serve* feature at the end of each chapter. It identifies ways in which you can decide to serve and learn while in college.

Finally, you will find another SQ3R prompt (*Choosing to Be an Active Learner*) to remind you to *review* the chapter in its entirety.

Don't forget, this textbook has a website that accompanies it. There you'll find study tips and review materials to help you be successful in this course and in college.

chapter review

Respond to the following on a separate sheet of paper or in your notebook.

1. Review the tips for the first week of class in module 1. Put a check by the ones you were already planning to use. Which of the other items was most surprising to you? Why?

2. Review the italicized statements at the beginning of Module 1. List one that you identify with. Why?

3. How does it feel to be a new student at your community college? List three feelings you've had since arriving on campus and the situation that caused them. What does your campus do or provide to orient students? Have you decided to take advantage of any orientation services or activities? Why or why not?

4. Which of the differences between your community college and high school or your community college and the work world have you

already noticed? What effect is that having on your decision to attend community college?

5. Describe a decision you made as the result of your adjustment to life as a community college student. How did you make the decision? How satisfied are you with the outcome of that decision at this time?

6. Review your response to the previous question. How is the decision-making process you used like the 5C process? How is it different?

7. What text feature of this book do you think will be most useful to you? Why?

8. What changes do you think you face or will face as a community college student? How do you plan to adjust to those changes? List three strategies that may help you make a smooth transition to your community college.

did you decide?

Did you accomplish what you wanted to in this chapter? Check the items below that apply to you.

Review the *You Decide* statements that you identified at the beginning of the chapter, but look at them from a new direction. If you didn't check an item below, review that module until you feel you can confidently apply the strategies to your own situation. However, the best ideas are worthless unless they are put into effect. Decide what information you found helpful in the chapter and how you plan to use it. Record your comments after the statements below.

☐ 1.1 I know what it takes to be successful in college.
_____

☐ 1.2 I know where on campus to get help if I need it.
_____

☐ 1.3 While college is still new to me, I know and accept my role as a learner.
_____

☐ 1.4 I know that active learning is the best way to learn information.
_____

☐ 1.5 I understand how to use information in this textbook.
_____

perspectives

As a community college student, you will encounter new people, places, and ideas as you navigate your new environment. The decisions you make about each one depend on how you view yourself and the world around you. In this passage, Mark David Milliron, president and CEO of the League for Innovation in the Community College, reflects on the backgrounds of learners who decide to attend community colleges and what they face when they arrive. He also discusses the role of choices in college coursework and in life.

The questions you need to answer precede the passage. Why? As you now know from the SQ3R process, questions make reading a more active process. They provide clues to what is important. They provide reasons to read. Thus, whether questions about a passage come before or after it, skimming them before reading makes reading a more effective and efficient process.

Respond to the following after reading the passage:

1. What is your reaction/feeling to the passage?
2. What are some of the pressures YOU face?
3. How would you describe your personal or academic background?
4. What do you see as the main idea of the last three paragraphs?
5. What effect does this article have on you?
6. Choose ONE of the issues/problems described in the passage (e.g., finding child care, not knowing how to navigate the college environment, recent high school graduate, older adult student). Describe how the 5C decision-making process applies.

   A. What problem situation did the individual need to solve?

   B. What key **C**hoices might be open to the individual?

   C. What would be the major **C**onsequence(s) of each choice?

   D. What would you recommend that this individual **C**hoose?

   E. How might the individual **C**heck the outcome of the decision?

Your courage astounds us. We probably don't tell you this enough. You see, we too are pushed and pulled by classes, calendars, and the constant press of our work in education. But when we slow down, look around, and soak in all of your stories, we are humbled.

Many of you will be the first in your family to set foot on a college campus. At times it can feel as though there is no one who really understands how strange and awkward your first steps are. You fill out our forms, meet our advisors, take our placement tests, piece together a schedule, step into our classrooms—whether they're online or on campus—and enter a new world. Sometimes it's hard for us to remember how overwhelming our rules and procedures seem

to you. And we should remember. What you may not realize is that many of us started our higher education journey at a community or technical college. We've just been in this world so long that we sometimes lose touch with how we felt *our* first day. Be patient with us.

Some family and friends don't know much about the journey you're on. Their ideas about college are shaped by movies and TV. Nonetheless, they truly want you to succeed. Some of them have fought, struggled, begged, and borrowed to give you this opportunity. While you are so happy to have their support, you sometimes feel pressured by the weight of their expectations.

You may have different pressures. We've seen some of you suffer through unsupportive, angry, or abusive parents, spouses, or friends. This inner circle plays out their fears or insecurities by discouraging you at every turn, trying to convince you that you too will fail. Some are afraid that your success will take you away from them, so they subtly sabotage your journey. Many of you struggle with uncooperative supervisors or job schedules that make attending class difficult or impossible. Weekend or night courses are a must, even though you're mentally tired and physically worn out. Some of you have major family responsibilities. You search to find good child care and wrestle with the guilt of being away from your kids even though you're going to college to better *their* lives. Still, others must strive to care for parents, nieces, nephews, cousins, and grandchildren. We know that at times it feels as though a higher power is working to keep you from taking this new path. But have faith, because nothing could be further from the truth.

"Will there be people who look like me?" You worry you won't see familiar faces when you look at the students, teachers, and leaders on campus. Or you are differently labeled and wonder whether we'll understand your needs. While we may not be perfect, we work hard to serve and connect with you and your communities. More than almost anywhere in higher education, the diversity that strengthens us and inspires you will be there.

For many of you, beginning with us fresh out of high school makes perfect sense because of where we're located, our cost, our size, or a host of other reasons. You hit the ground running in our honors programs or jump into our student activities. Some of you share your strengths as peer tutors, student leaders, or community volunteers. You are models of service and learning for us all.

Many of you, however, come through our open doors later in life. You may have reached a turning point in your life—the kids are getting older, your job is getting colder, or your dreams are getting further away. It's time for a radical shift. But you wonder what to expect and what will be expected of you as you move into this new world. You're going from waiting tables to mastering computer networking, or from working in a factory to spending sleepless nights pursuing a nursing degree. Others are simply right sizing, training for a job closer to home or one that will allow you to slow down and enjoy life in a different way. More and more of you are coming back for short courses, certifications, or degrees after already achieving a bachelor's degree or higher. For you, it's about staying up to speed and giving yourself new options.

But no matter where you start, you can finish well. Some of you start with us in programs to learn to read and move on to complete a GED; you move through math, reading, and pre-college writing; you complete certifications and degrees on your way to jobs or a university. Along the way, you strive with each passing day, month, and year to get better. Remember, "better" is not about how you compare to others. Better is about how *you* compare to how *you* were yesterday.

Your persistence in getting better teaches us that the time it takes to complete a course or program isn't really the issue. That time will pass either way. What matters is whether you remain at a dead end or move to a place where new learning opens up different pathways for your career and life. With each passing day, you continue on, riding with the ebbs and flows. Obstacles of all sorts flood your way from semester to semester or quarter to quarter: births, deaths, marriages, divorces, getting jobs, losing jobs, and just about every other kind of life experience you can imagine. Some of you need to step out for a time to take care of these situations; but you dive back in, and we welcome you with open arms.

What do you do when it's all said and done? What happens after you move on to work or other education? Some of you go on to run multinational corporations, fly through space, star in movies, run statehouses, and map the human genome. Others target your talents closer to home: raising families, serving communities, creating new businesses, fighting fires, saving lives, or teaching children. In short, you throw yourself into the pool of humanity and the positive ripples cascade out.

And it all begins with a choice—an incredibly courageous choice. You choose to try, to walk through the open doors of our college and begin. You make this choice again and again as you take each step along the journey. You choose to stay, to engage, to give it your best. This choice can and will change your life forever. All because you have the courage to learn.

reflecting on decisions

What have you learned about college and decision making that can help you decide which opportunities to pursue?

◄ CHOOSING TO SERVE

JUST SAY **THANKS**

Who contributed to your decision to start college? Many students point to family, friends, employers, coaches, teachers, or others that affected the decision to go to college. Perhaps you can't point to a person that affected your choice. Rather, it was the result of an interest or experience. For instance, perhaps therapy after a broken leg resulted in an interest in allied health careers. Or, your love of cars created an interest in a technical degree. Even though specific people weren't involved, people were behind that experience. So, in almost every case, people that you know and people that you'll never know affected your choice to go to college. If you haven't already done so, you might think about contacting those people and letting them know that what they did made a difference in your life.

Like you, members of the military joined for a variety of reasons. And like you, their choices were often affected by people they know as well as people they never knew. You can choose to thank them by logging on to Let's Say Thanks (http://www.letssaythanks.com/Home1280.html). This site, sponsored by the Xerox Corporation, lets people select cards drawn by schoolchildren and add a message. The cards are printed and delivered to military personnel around the world.

CHAPTER **TWO**

In this chapter you will learn

2.1 How to use your college catalog and website

2.2 How to access resources and services on your campus

2.3 Who is in your college community

2.4 How to identify which organizations at your college fit your needs

2.5 How to communicate effectively with your faculty

2.6 How to better communicate with others and resolve conflicts when they occur

CHOOSING TO BE AN ACTIVE LEARNER

S U R V E Y

Before reading this chapter, prepare for learning. Purposefully skim the title, introduction, headings, and graphics. As you survey, decide what information you already know and what information is new to you.

Q U E S T I O N

Change each section's heading into a question. This forms your learning goal for reading.

R E A D

Read the section without marking. Reread and mark key information that answers your question.

R E C I T E

Stop after each section and make sure you understood the content. Organize or summarize content and make notes.

Interacting with Your College Community

A **community** is a social network of people who interact within a specific place. At your college, this network includes campus resources, faculty, students . . . and now, you. You not only need to know with *whom* to interact, but you also need to know *how* to interact with them to maximize your success. What campus resources and individuals have you already visited on your campus? What made you decide to go to them?

YOU DECIDE

To *wonder* means to think or have curiosity about. Things and ideas you wonder about often mask a need for a decision. Check the items below that apply to you.

In terms of my new community college environment, I've been wondering . . .

☐ 2.1 How can catalog and website content help me understand the language of my campus community?

☐ 2.2 How do I find offices, resources, and services I need on campus?

☐ 2.3 What diverse groups exist on my campus?

☐ 2.4 What organizations are on my campus and what are the advantages of joining them?

☐ 2.5 How can I become more comfortable talking to my instructors?

☐ 2.6 What's the best way to communicate with others and resolve any problems with them?

Each of these decision points corresponds to the numbered modules that follow. Turn to the module for immediate help.

A community is more than a network of people. It also implies a sense of identity—the feelings and expectations related to it. How does your sense of community at this school compare with what you thought it would be?

Perhaps you expected to explore the mysteries of the universe as part of a group of interesting classmates led by fascinating professors. Instead, you've found yourself in the back of the classroom, reviewing what you already know. Maybe you imagined yourself effortlessly balancing work, family, and school only to find yourself overwhelmed and exhausted. In many ways, your expectations may have failed to match reality.

The best way to avoid such surprises is to learn, understand, and adjust. In order to interact effectively, you need to know the language of your school. Your campus catalog and website are good sources of information. You will also need to learn about campus services and resources, as well as faculty, organizations, and your fellow students. Finally, you need effective communication skills and conflict resolution strategies for times when communication fails.

Understanding the Language of Your School: Catalog and Website Content

Even when two groups of people speak the same language, differences exist among them. For instance, in Great Britain, *queue* refers to what we call *line*. Their *biscuits* are our *cookies*. A British *chemist* would be called a *pharmacist* in the U.S. Such language differences often result in misunderstandings. Thus, it's important to know the language of your college community. The two most important resources for doing so are your campus website and college catalog.

Your first introduction to your college may have been a virtual one if you explored its website before ever visiting the campus. Most colleges have specific links for prospective or future students that give them information before they are admitted. But now you are a member of the college community. Your needs have changed. You need specific and current information about interacting with your campus community on a day-to-day basis.

> Key Parts of Your Campus Website

Information Management System. Collegewide system for e-mail and other announcements. Faculty, staff, and campus office use this to inform or contact you. Get into the habit of logging in and checking it daily.

Academic Calendars. Schedules of deadlines and events. The most important calendar is the academic calendar which identifies exam schedules, enrollment, withdrawal, and other key deadlines.

QuickLinks. Short list of the most important links on the site. These often include the library, computer services, degrees/departments, catalogs, class schedules, directories of phone numbers and e-mail addresses, and financial aid.

Academics. Information about specific departments in terms of their degree and certification programs, course descriptions, and faculty. Advising, tutoring, and learning assistance resources may be listed here as well.

Student Services/Campus Life. Information about nonacademic resources and services. These include campus activities and organizations, career services and internships, student government, and information for students with disabilities.

Key Parts of the College Catalog

The **college catalog** forms a key source for understanding the language of your college community. Revised each year, the catalog you use in the year you first enroll is your contract with the college. This means that if program requirements change in the future, you will still meet requirements as stated in your governing catalog. Thus, your college catalog is your first resource for identifying and understanding the language of your college community as well as the rules and policies that guide interactions within it.

> **college catalog**
> Book describing services, curricula, courses, faculty, and other information pertaining to a postsecondary institution.

- **Academic classification.** Describes how the number of completed credit hours translates into freshman, sophomore, or other status. Credit-hour value is approximately equal to the number of hours per week of in-class instruction (lab, studio, or performance courses often involve more hours of in-class instruction than are reflected in credit-hour value). Course-load requirements describe the maximum and minimum hours required to be at full-time status.

- **Academic policies and regulations.** Describes certification or degree requirements, academic standards, and registration regulations.

- **Academic standards.** Lists the rules governing student conduct, including disciplinary sanctions, academic disciplinary actions, and appeal procedures. These rules apply in cases of academic dishonesty (cheating or plagiarism) or other institutional infractions.

- **Admissions information.** Explains criteria for admission to the institution, regulations for the transfer of credits, and availability of special programs.

- **College degree requirements.** Outlines the required and elective courses needed for completion of a degree. These are often divided by semester/quarter or academic year.

- **Course descriptions.** Summarizes the content of each course, which is usually identified by a number and title.

- **Student services.** Identifies nonacademic activities and services available to students, including campus organizations, internships, career planning, and food service information.

- **Tuition and fees.** Lists in-state and out-of-state costs, including tuition, room and board, fee schedules, student health fees, parking fees, and lab fees. May also identify financial aid opportunities (scholarships, grants, loans, campus jobs).

- **Glossary.** Provides meanings of higher education terms as defined by your college.

activity 1

Using Your Campus Website and College Catalog

PART 1:   Campus Website

Answer the following questions:

1. List three items you can find on the **campus homepage:**

    1. _____
    2. _____
    3. _____

2. Locate the following information from your **academic calendar** and record on the inside cover of this text for quick reference:

    1. When is the last day to withdraw from courses?

    2. What holidays occur this term?

    3. What is the last day of classes?

    4. When do finals begin? end?

3. List three items you can find on **campus library** page:

    1. _____
    2. _____
    3. _____

    Does the library have an online catalog that you can use to see if a particular book is in the library?

    _____ YES   _____ NO

4. Find the list of degree or certification programs. List three that interest you.

    1. _____
    2. _____
    3. _____

5. Find the calendar of campus events. List one event that you would like to attend and its date/time

    _____

6. Find the student handbook. List three topics within it.

    1. _____
    2. _____
    3. _____

7. Find a list of student organizations. List one that you would be interested in joining.

    _____

8. Find information on financial assistance. Identify one type of financial assistance on your campus.

    _____

9. What is the name of your campus information system? _____

10. Find information about any other campus office or service that interests you. List the office or service and describe why it interests you. _____

11. Choose from items 1–10. Use the 5C approach to identify a challenge you might face on campus and help you make a decision that would solve this problem.

PART 2:   College Catalog

Use your college print or online catalog to complete the following.

1. Find and record information about two scholarships/loans for which you might be eligible.

_____
_____
_____

2. Find the curriculum in which you plan to major.

   a. Compare/contrast courses suggested for your first term with those suggested for your final term. How do you account for similarities/differences?

_____
_____

   b. Examine the curriculum carefully. Locate two courses in your major area and read their descriptions. Which will you find more enjoyable? Why?

_____
_____

   c. Read the description for each of the courses in which you are now enrolled. How do the descriptions compare to the actual content of the course? What conclusion(s) might you draw about the courses and descriptions you identified in *b*?

_____
_____

3. Using your college catalog glossary or other campus resource, define each of the following terms in your own words:

Academic calendar _____

Drop _____

Withdrawal _____

Residency _____

Elective _____

Syllabus _____

Transcript _____

Prerequisites _____

Transfer credit _____

Credit hour _____

GROUP APPLICATION: Identify three to five additional words or phrases you've heard around campus but aren't sure you understand on a piece of paper. Don't sign your name to the paper. After all of the pages are collected, your instructor will randomly select several words or phrases for discussion by the group.

Campus Offices, Resources, and Services

Have you ever heard someone say, "It's not what you know, but who you know?" Although what you know is vitally important in college, who you know in your campus community can be just as worthwhile. You'll find the people you need to know in offices around campus. They can help you locate the resources and services you need.

While every campus is different, all college communities share some common offices and services. Knowing the location of each one and the services it offers helps you become better oriented to your new environment.

❯ Key Places on Campus

- **Registrar's Office.** Also called Office of Records or Registration. Tracks courses you take and grades you get. Evaluates advanced, transfer, or correspondence work. Provides transcripts. May have the responsibility to determine if you meet graduation requirements.

- **Business Office.** Records student financial transactions, such as tuition, fees, fines, or other payments.

- **Financial Aid Office.** Also called Student Aid and Scholarship Office. Provides assistance in locating and distributing supplemental funds such as grants, loans, scholarships, and on-campus employment.

- **Advising Office.** May also be called Academic Advising or Academic Counseling. Provides information and assistance in life, career, and educational planning as well as help in preparing for university transfer or workforce development.

- **Dean's Office.** Academic "home" for courses and degree programs (e.g., Liberal Arts, Basic Sciences, Business, Technology, Allied Health).

- **Student Development.** Source for services and programs outside of academics. Includes student government, campus clubs and organizations, career counseling.

- **Library.** Contains online and print materials for reference and recreation, including books, magazines, newspapers, journals, DVDs, and reference books. May also contain computer lab, tutoring, and photocopying facilities. Workshops or classes may be available to familiarize you with library services and holdings.

- **Campus Bookstore.** Since you are reading this textbook, you've probably found the campus bookstore, but did you notice that the bookstore also sells notebooks, art supplies, and other materials? Many also carry over-the-counter drugs and toiletries, snack foods, and school-related clothing and gear.

- **Campus Security.** Also called Campus Police or Public Safety. Provides parking and traffic guidelines. Many campus security offices maintain an escort service to ensure the safety of students walking across campus late in the evening.

- **Learning Center.** Also called Learning Resource Center, Learning Assistance Center, and Learning Lab, among other names. Offers assistance in study skills or specific content areas through workshops or individualized lessons, tutoring, and/or taped, online, or computerized instruction.

activity 2 | Identifying Campus Resources

PART 1: Campus Chart

Complete the chart of offices and contact information located on the inside back cover of this text.

PART 2: Campus Resources

What's on your campus? Go to each of the following locations on your campus and find out what it offers in order to answer the following questions:

1. College Bookstore. Other than textbooks, what does the bookstore sell?

   _____

2. Library. Other than books for checkout, what other materials and/or services are available at your library?

   _____

3. Student Center/Student Services. What's available at your student center? If your campus doesn't have a student center, go to the student services office and find out what it offers.

   _____

4. Career Services. What resources are available at your campus career services office?

   _____

5. Learning Center. What resources are available at your campus learning center?

   _____

Experiencing Campus Diversity

Diversity characterizes today's typical college campus. Students come from different academic backgrounds. People of every age, ethnic identity, and socioeconomic level have found a place on campus. Students with learning and other disabilities are attending college in greater numbers. International students and U.S. students from urban, suburban, and rural communities share classrooms and ideas. Faculty and staff are also members of diverse groups representing different academic backgrounds, viewpoints, geographic areas, and cultural backgrounds. Although many people think of individual aspects of diversity (e.g., race or gender), diversity is more a complex combination of factors that come together in each individual. Although these aspects may be used to identify people, no individual is—or should be—defined by a single aspect.

Diversity in theory is one thing. Diversity in terms of people sitting next to you or teaching you might be quite a different experience. You—or they—may hold preconceptions about people whose race, gender, culture, religion, political views, age, clothes, sexual orientation, or other factor differs from your own. You—or they—may harbor thoughts and feelings of dismay, distrust, and even discrimination. Awareness of such thoughts and feelings is a first step toward change. Maybe you realize that the person that sits next to you in math makes you feel uncomfortable because of the clothes she wears. Recognition of stereotypical characteristics rather than individual ones is a second step. Now you think about why clothes—rather than the individual—could make you feel uncomfortable. Choosing to have an open mind is a third step. You decide to talk to the student and find that both of you are majoring in the same thing. This leads to a conversation about your shared interest in the field. Being more open-minded and ready to interact with others, then, allows you to learn more about who people are as individuals rather than who you perceive them to be as members of a specific group. Part of the college experience is to provide you with information and courses from which you can better understand and appreciate the world around you. Diversity in the classroom allows you to move beyond theory to firsthand experience . . . if you decide to do so.

> **diversity**
> Variety in the academic environment as the result of individual differences.

Finding Commonalities in Our Differences

PART 1:   True or False?

For this activity create a list of four statements about yourself that you wouldn't mind sharing. Three of the statements should be true and one should be false. The statements should reflect some aspect of the diversity that describes you but that is not clearly obvious from looking at you (e.g., age, home state/country, interests/hobbies, background, political view, academic or personal accomplishment, jobs, degree/career interests and so on) rather than a superficial aspect of yourself (current address, favorite color, name of pet).

Example Statements: I am 25 years old. I am from Texas. I worked as the Mickey Mouse character at Disneyland for a summer. I enjoy playing guitar.

PART 2:   True or False?

Divide into small groups. After a person shares his/her statements, the other members of the group should guess which one is false and, as appropriate, discuss any stereotypes that might be involved (e.g., all Texans are cowboys/girls and you don't look like a cowboy/girl).

The person reveals which statement is false. Members of the group that share one of the aspects or a similar aspect should provide that information (e.g., I am also from Texas/I visited Texas on a vacation; I'm also majoring in a health field).

PART 3:   "Who Are You?"

Form groups of three. Student 1 will ask the question, "Who are you?" Student 2 will answer the question with one or more descriptive sentences. Student 3 will observe the interaction. However, after Student 2 responds, Student 1 repeats the question, "Who are you?" and Student 2 must provide additional information. Student 3 continues to observe. In total, Student 1 will ask and Student 2 will respond to the same question five times, with each response being a different answer. Each member of the group takes turns as the person who asks, responds, and observes. At the end of the three rounds of questions, the group should discuss the following: What was difficult about answering the questions? What did you observe about the person asking the questions? What did you observe about the person answering the questions? How did the answers change? What did you learn about the other two students? What did you learn about yourself?

Getting Involved: Joining Campus Groups

All work and no play can be almost as bad as all play and no work. Academics is clearly your main goal. Your classes should, and do, take much of your time. But friendships and campus life are important, too. They foster important interpersonal and leadership skills. Even if you are a full-time student who works and has family responsibilities, check with your student services office to see what options might be available to you. Online groups and campus pages on social networking sites can provide you with similar opportunities to network and contribute.

Students who actively participate in an extracurricular or community group or who have other campus interests tend to remain in school longer than those who have no such ties. This is because they don't just go to college; they are part of college life. In addition, job recruiters and employers like candidates who are well-rounded with a variety of interests. In today's job market, everyone they see has a degree. They want to see students who set themselves apart. They are looking for people that can handle a diverse range of activities while remaining academically successful.

What group(s) should you join? Your needs, values, and interests determine which groups suit you best. For instance, if you like outdoor activities, you might join a club that schedules hiking and camping trips. In general, it really doesn't matter which group you choose, as long as you become involved in campus life. There's really no substitute.

Name of Group	Eligible Members	Purpose of Membership	Advantages of Membership
Intramural sports	Students who are not part of school-sponsored athletic teams	To organize teams and play various athletic games against others	Encourages teamwork, fair play, leadership, health, and fun
Special interest groups	Any student	To meet and share ideas about a topic or mutual interest	Provides opportunities to meet others with similar interests or to develop new interests
Service organizations	Any student	To volunteer time for the benefit of others or to gain experience in a particular field	Provides various opportunities to work for the common good of your institution or community
Social organizations	Any student	To have fun and make friends	Affords greater assimilation into the institution
Campus employment	Any student	To get involved in campus life while getting paid	Offers the opportunity to work within area of study and chances to meet and know students, faculty, and staff
Noncredit or leisure classes	Any student	To learn more about an interest or gain practice or expertise without the cost or stress of grades in credit courses	Provides ways to gain information (e.g., conversational version of a foreign language) or practice skills (choral groups; exercise classes)

Students participating in Habitat for Humanity.

How Do You Want to Grow?

Under the first heading below, list the personal characteristics you feel you need to develop—this is your *Challenge*. For example, perhaps speaking in front of groups, working with others, improved health, and stress management might be areas you feel you need to develop. Then under the next heading (to the right), identify and list several *Choices* on your campus that might help you develop these characteristics. What would be the *Consequences* of participating in each group (e.g., time, cost, effort)? List these next. Which do you think you would *Choose*? What plan do you have to *Check* the outcome? Briefly describe.

Challenge: *Characteristics Needing Development*	Choice: *Organization/Activities to Support These Characteristics*	Consequences: *How Will You Check?*

GROUP APPLICATION: After completing the activity, share individual answers with your group. What similarities and differences do you discover among your group's answers? What factors might contribute to these similarities and differences?

How can I become more comfortable talking to my instructors?

Working with Faculty

A popular urban legend tells of an instructor whose students changed his behavior. Whenever he walked to the left side of the room, they seemed to lose interest in what he said. They yawned, wrote notes, whispered, and paid little or no attention. When he moved to the right, they sat up straight. They listened carefully, took notes, and asked questions. The instructor soon began to lecture only from the right side of the class. Is it true? According to urban legend website www.Snopes.com, maybe not. What is true, however, is that you *can* influence the behavior of your instructors. Instructors try to be fair and impartial, but they are people, too.

Think about the people you meet. Some act in ways that make you want to know them better. Others do not. Instructors feel the same way about students. When they meet a new group of students, they react to and with each one. Whether in class or out of class, your behavior determines if their reactions to you are positive or negative. You control whether or not you are a student worth knowing better.

▶ Classroom Behavior

To obtain and keep an instructor's goodwill, you need to be polite and respectful. Arriving on time and dressing appropriately make a good first impression. Prompt and consistent attendance proves your commitment to the course. Avoiding the inappropriate use of technology (e.g., texting or talking on your cell phone) during class shows respect and commitment. The quality of your work also reveals your regard for the instructor and the course. Your work is, after all, an extension of you. Only work of the highest quality in content, form, and appearance should be submitted.

Sitting near the front of the room in about the same seat for each class gives the instructor a visual fix on you. Although the instructor may not keep attendance records, he or she will subconsciously look for you and know you are there. Sitting near the front of the room also helps you maintain eye contact with the instructor. This too registers positively on an instructor.

Your apparent interest in the lecture is often reflected in your *actions*. **Body language,** such as sitting straight, facing the instructor, arms uncrossed, shows your openness and desire to learn. Body language includes facial expressions, like smiling, and movements, nodding your head, raising your eyebrows in

body language
Nonverbal communication.

recognition. The opposite of this is also true. Nonverbal responses of skepticism or boredom clearly show through body language (yawning, reading the newspaper, texting on your cell phone, sighing, looking out the window, rolling your eyes, frowning).

Body language is especially important when you read your instructor's comments on returned assignments in class. Constructive criticism is part of the academic process and should be a learning experience. An instructor's critical comments are not a personal attack. Your body language should reflect your ability to accept those comments in the spirit in which they are given.

Inappropriate use of technology is a recent form of nonverbal communication. If you can see your instructor, your instructor can see you. Your instructor can see who is paying attention and who is sending text messages on cell phones. Your instructor can also see who is taking notes on a computer and who is playing games, checking e-mail or Facebook, or simply surfing the net. Although you may be able to multitask while listening to a lecture, your instructor may perceive it as a lack of interest or rudeness.

Some students fear speaking aloud in class. Often they think their questions will sound "dumb" to either the instructor or other students. Still others feel too shy to speak up in class. Maybe they've had embarrassing experiences in the past and speaking in class frightens them. Generally, however, if something in the lecture confused you, it confused other students, too. Others are often waiting for someone else to make the first move. That person can be you.

Speaking in class is less stressful if you know how to phrase your questions or comments. Be relevant and respectful. Nothing frustrates an instructor more than rude questions, long, unrelated stories, or questions whose answers were just discussed. Preceding your question with what you *do* understand helps the instructor clarify what confuses you. By briefly stating what you think was just said, you aid the instructor in finding gaps in your knowledge. Be sure to be precise about the information you need. For example, in a math class, instead of saying, "I don't get it," you would say, "I understand the first two steps of the problem, but I don't know how to get to the next step."

Active participation in class discussions proves your interest. If you ask questions or make comments about the lecture topic, you show your attention. But if you feel you simply cannot ask a question in class, then see your instructor before or after class or make an appointment.

If you have to be late for class, enter as discreetly as you can. After class, wait for your instructor and apologize. If you are often late, make an appointment to see your instructor to explain your tardiness. If your instructor is sympathetic and accepts your excuse, thank him or her. If your instructor indicates that your continued lateness will negatively impact your grade, you have three choices: get to class on time, accept the penalty, or drop the class.

Out-of-Class Behavior

Getting to know an instructor personally involves special effort. Smiling and saying hello when you see an instructor outside of class is a friendly opening gesture. Positive, sincere feedback about course content, exams, and so on often opens lines of communication. Visiting an instructor's office often and for long time periods also affects how an instructor feels about you but, unfortunately, in a negative way. Instructors maintain office hours so students with valid problems can reach them. They also use that time to grade papers, prepare lectures, complete paperwork, and conduct research. Thus, many instructors resent students who—without reason—constantly visit them. This does not mean that instructors do not like to talk to you and other students. They do. Talking to you helps them understand your problems and learning needs. It gives them an opportunity to interest you in their content areas.

Today's faculty are also available via e-mail, and many of the same rules apply. Don't overload your instructor's e-mail box with forwarded information (e.g., good luck chain letters or jokes). When you do write your instructor, include your full name in the body of the e-mail as well as the class and section in which you are enrolled. This helps a busy instructor respond more efficiently and effectively. When you ask questions, be specific. Rather than writing, "I'm having a problem in your course," you could write, "I'm unsure of what you mean in assignment 3 in terms of the content of the essay." Also, asking for assistance well before a due date makes a better impression than last-minute pleas. Asking for clarification of a grade is another good reason to contact your instructor. However, you should convey a sincere interest in improving future papers rather than pleading for a change on the grade you received. Your tone should be inquisitive rather than accusing.

Although faculty appreciate student friendliness, address your instructor in the same manner that you would in class. Mr./Mrs./Ms./Dr. are the safest choices. Refrain from calling your instructor by first name unless he or she specifically asks you to do so. Do not address your professor informally—leave Dude, Lady, Man, Buddy, Bro, and Girlfriend for your friends. Use standard formats, spelling, and punctuation.

Your best bet is to e-mail your instructors only when you have a serious issue—filling their inboxes with e-mails with many questions and comments is not a good idea. Also, while it may seem easier to e-mail and ask questions and favors, instructors tend to look less favorably upon these long-distance requests. Rather, visit an instructor's office and make it personal.

What do you do if you think a grade was unfairly or incorrectly assigned? First, you should contact your instructor for clarification, especially if your concern is about a final grade. If, after discussing a grade with an instructor, you feel you have been unfairly treated, you have the right to an appeal. This appeal involves, first, meeting with the professor and attempting to resolve your problem. During the second step of the appeal process, you write a letter to the head of the department in which the course is taught asking for a meeting with that person and your instructor. If you are not satisfied with the results of this hearing or if your instructor is the department chair, you may appeal to the dean of the department in which the course was taught. If you are firmly convinced that you are in the right, your final appeal is made to the head of academic affairs at your institution.

It is possible to influence instructors favorably. You can do it by treating them as you want them to treat you.

Online Behavior

In today's online environments, instructors and students often interact through e-mail, online chats, and posts to discussions in course management systems. Some courses are **hybrids,** that is, a combination of face-to-face and online content. Some are fully online. Even instructors in face-to-face classes use the course management system to e-mail students, post content, and make other class assignments.

Even if an instructor never meets a student face-to-face, that instructor can form impressions—good or bad—from interactions with them. Communication today (e.g., text messages, e-mail) is often informal. But the kinds of casual comments between friends (Cn u help me? 'S up?) are not appropriate when contacting online faculty. Faculty expect you to use correct spelling and grammar in your e-mails and other work.

Failure to check into online classes regularly is just as problematic as failure to show up for onsite classes. Course management systems have tools that allow faculty to "see" how many times you access the course and what aspects of the course you have—or have not—used.

hybrids
Courses that are a combination of face-to-face and online content.

More than in onsite classes, instructors expect you to read course materials, follow directions, and promptly contact them when you have questions. Pleas for extra time to complete work due to procrastination on your part will not be granted.

Finally, online courses often have group work in which students interact virtually to create a response or project. Shirking your group work often results in negative impressions by peers as well as the instructor.

 activity

Classroom Behavior: What Are They Saying?

Next time you are in a face-to-face class, spend some time observing the students around you, but look at them from your instructor's viewpoint. What do you think the students are communicating through their body language and nonverbal behavior? Which students do you think would be enjoyable to teach if you were the instructor? Why? Which ones would be more difficult to teach? Why? What do you want your instructor's perspective of you to be? How can you achieve that goal?

Communication and Conflict Resolution

Interactions with others characterize human life. You communicate daily with others at home, in workplaces, and, now, in college. Some of these interactions are face-to-face. Others are in writing both online and on paper. Learning to communicate more effectively and to handle any problems that arise are skills that you will use throughout life.

Communication Skills

Communication involves understanding and being understood. Communication can be verbal or nonverbal. Thus, face-to-face communication involves how something is said (gestures, facial expressions, body language) as well as what is said. Communication can also be spoken or written. Conversations, lectures, discussions, text chapters, e-mails, Web pages all involve communication.

Communication depends on context. What and how you communicate informally to a close friend probably differs from what and how you communicate with a stranger. What and how you communicate with your peers should differ from what and how you communicate with college faculty and staff. For instance, the kind of shorthand used in text messages (*cn u c me 2day?*) is not appropriate for corresponding with college faculty and staff.

Communication also depends on an almost infinite number of factors within the speaker/writer and listener/reader. Emotions, interests, relationships, skills, and background are just some of the factors. These can affect what is said or written as well as how it is understood. For instance, a student who has had a bad day (unexpected bill in the mail, missed bus, forgot assignment) might react more strongly to a professor's comments. Or, a student with numerous responsibilities (family, work, academic) may be less patient with a group member who fails to show up for meetings. A student who has been taught to agree with authority figures may not know how to respond to an advisor's questions about career choices. Awareness of the dimensions of communication as well as the communication strengths and weaknesses in yourself and others is the first step in communication success.

Luckily, communication skills are learned. Good communication skills pay off in benefits for all kinds of relationships—personal, academic, and career. The following tips and suggestions help improve communication skills.

Developing Effective Communication Skills

1. **Think before speaking or writing.** Choose your words carefully. Consider how they will be heard or read.

2. **Listen actively.** Consider the viewpoint of the speaker or writer. In face-to-face communication, pay attention to how and what information is communicated. In writing, pay attention to the words the writer uses.

3. **Ask questions.** In face-to-face communications, ask the speaker for more information or explanations.

4. **Use *I* rather than *you*.** Use of *you* (e.g., *you* aren't being clear) can sound accusatory. Using *I* takes the pressure off others (*I* don't understand what you mean).

5. **Observe and learn from communication interactions between other people.** Become a student of communication. Look for interactions that model the kinds of communications you want for yourself. Similarly, pay attention to interactions that don't go well so you can learn what to avoid in communication.

6. **Take a speech course.** No matter who you are or what career you choose to pursue, you will be communicating with others. A speech course gives you the skills you need for a variety of communications situations.

Conflict Resolution

As you interact with others on your campus, conflicts may arise. Psychologists list several reasons why problems occur between people. First, defensiveness or excuses for inappropriate behavior instead of accepting responsibility for it often cause conflict. Second, always complaining and never complimenting build friction. Third, making countercharges for every charge instead of seeing that some accusations might be valid causes disunity. Last, being stubborn, uncompromising, belligerent, and rude quickly dooms any relationship.

Conflict resolution occurs in one of three ways. One, you give the person with whom you have conflict the gift of agreement. To do so, you make a conscious choice to give in. This gift needs to be offered with a willing spirit, free of complaint, or it is not a gift at all. Second, you and your opponent compromise. This does not make one of you the winner and the other the loser. Rather, the goal is to reach an outcome that is fair for both of you. Finally, you and your adversary need to see differences between you as positives, not negatives. Learning to accept people who are unlike you might be the greatest lesson you learn in college.

Techniques for Resolving Conflicts

1. **Can we talk?** Ask if the two of you can talk. Then ask permission to discuss a specific problem. For example, say, "Something's been worrying me, and I'd like to discuss it with you. Do you have a minute so we could talk?" If the other person indicates that this is not a good time, then ask when you can talk.

2. **Practice, practice, practice.** Think about what you want to say. Role-play both yourself and the other person. This way you can anticipate points of disagreement and be prepared for them.

3. **Choose your battles.** Determine if the situation is really a conflict situation worthy of the effort. If you belabor small points, you lose the value of large ones.

4. **Fault lines.** Don't assess blame. Neither of you is likely to think the fault lies with you. Remember that since conflict causes problems for both of you, both of you must work on its solution.

5. **Open communication.** Avoid questions with *Yes* or *No* responses. That is, ask *How do you feel about this?* not *Do you like this?*

6. **Give and take.** Give information to the other person. Don't judge or interpret the other person's behavior. Then, give the other person a chance to speak. Really listen to what he or she is saying.

7. **Avoid airing your dirty laundry.** This is a problem between you and the other person. Don't discuss it with or in front of others.

8. **Winners never quit.** Once the subject has been broached (the hardest part), keep the discussion going until a mutual agreement has been reached.

9. **Stick like glue.** When an agreement has been reached, honor it. The only way to build trust is to respect the commitments and decisions the two of you make.

10. **Leave the scene.** Suppose you and another person have a huge argument in a group meeting. To resolve it, you might need to leave the scene of the conflict. Going to lunch, meeting outside the classroom, and so on help alleviate stress and encourages positive results.

11. **If at first . . .** If your initial efforts fail, try another approach. For instance, try e-mail or leaving a voice mail if face-to-face efforts fail.

Winning at Conflict

activity 6

Apply the 5C process to a conflict challenge you recently faced. The conflict could be one that occurred on campus, at work, in a store, or with friends or family. What *Choices* did you have in the situation? What were the *Consequences* of each choice? What did you *Choose* to do? How did you *Check out* the results of your choice?

chapter review

Respond to the following on a separate sheet of paper or in your notebook.

1. Identify the three campus offices or resources you feel every entering student should know. Why did you choose these offices?

2. Which campus offices or resources have you found to be most helpful to you? Are these the same as those listed in your answer to question 1? Why or why not?

3. Identify two groups on your campus that you are eligible to join. Use the 5C process to decide which of the two groups you should join. What is the *Challenge?* What are your *Choices?* What do you think are the *Consequences* of each choice? Which would you *Choose* to join? How could you *Check out* the results of your choice?

4. How is interacting with faculty the same as or different from interacting with your boss at work, your family, or your friends?

5. Consider the suggestions for interacting with faculty in class. Create a list of suggestions to help you make a good impression on classmates.

6. Have you ever been in conflict with someone? How would the information about conflict resolution have helped or hindered you in the outcome of this situation?

did you decide?

Did you accomplish what you wanted to in this chapter? Check the items below that apply to you.

Review the *You Decide* questions that you identified at the beginning of the chapter, but look at them from a new direction. If you didn't check an item below, review that module until you feel you can confidently apply the strategies to your own situation. However, the best ideas are worthless unless they are put into effect. Decide what information you found helpful in the chapter and how you plan to use it. Record your comments after the statements below.

☐ **2.1** I can use catalog and website content to help me understand the language of my campus community.

_____

_____

☐ **2.2** I know where to find offices, resources, and services I need on campus.

_____

_____

☐ **2.3** I recognize the diverse groups that exist on my campus.

_____

_____

☐ **2.4** I know what organizations are on my campus and the advantages of joining them.

_____

_____

☐ **2.5** I can use ideas from this book to talk comfortably with my instructors.

_____

_____

☐ **2.6** I know ways to communicate with others and resolve any problems with them.

_____

_____

perspectives

Communication skills (listening, speaking, and writing) are keys for college, and life, success. As a college student, you have numerous opportunities to observe and learn these skills both in and out of classes. The following article, "The Maxed-Out Tech Student's Guide to Mastering Communication Skills" by Patrick Amaral, explains how you can use your college experiences to improve communication skills.

Think about and answer the questions that follow.

1. What communication skills can you gain from observing your faculty and peers?

2. In addition to what you learn from the content of a lecture, what can you learn from the ways in which information is presented?

3. How can you use your ability to ask questions in class or contribute to class discussions as the foundation for other verbal communication skills?

4. How can your notetaking skills contribute to your writing skills?

5. How does an in-depth conversation contribute to communication skills?

6. Think of a communication skill that you want to develop. Describe how the 5C decision-making process applies.

   A. What is the **C**hallenge, the communication skill you want to develop?

   B. What key **C**hoices for developing the skill are open to you?

   C. What would be the major **C**onsequence(s) of each choice?

   D. What do you plan to **C**hoose?

   E. How might you **C**heck the outcome of the decision?

You've already heard about the importance of communication skills—that catch-all phrase that encompasses everything from speaking to a crowd, writing memos, working in teams, conducting meetings, talking on the phone, conversing over a business lunch, introducing your boss to a business associate and most importantly, listening. So we won't go there. Rather, a more pertinent question is: How do you gain these communication skills when your curriculum allows one, maybe two, electives per semester and you have little time?

One of the best ways to build communication skills is to use them. Simply take advantage of any opportunity to practice communicating, especially outside of your discipline's setting. Taking part in some painless, perhaps even enjoyable, activities will build communication skills.

THE NO-PAIN WAY TO BUILD COMMUNICATION SKILLS   Read newspapers and magazines to learn how to have well-informed conversations. Staying current on the latest news and topics of general interest gives you the ability to converse intelligently with others.

Go to a movie or play with someone and then discuss it to learn how to persuade people to your point of view. Debating the merits and content of a movie or play with others allows you to explore some of the more abstract aspects of a topic. Without realizing it, you are learning about persuasive speaking.

Start or join a book club to learn how to connect your thoughts and opinions to someone else's ideas. What's good about this suggestion is that (1) you pick the book; and (2) you decide what you want to discuss. Regardless of the books or subjects, you practice connecting your thoughts and opinions to someone else's work.

Volunteer for campus or community organizations to learn how to empathize with your audience. The more variety of people you have contact with, the better your communication skills become. If you are tutoring a fifth grader, you have to learn to communicate complex ideas in a simple way. If you are working in a homeless shelter, you must empathize with the homeless. Such situations make you a better communicator because you master the art of understanding the people you want to reach.

Attend presentations by speakers, musicians, artists or authors, etc., to identify what good public speaking is. You don't have to be familiar with the topic in order to listen to what they are saying and how they are saying it. Figure out why they are effective communicators.

Challenge yourself to attend a presentation on a topic you know nothing about. Attend a debate to learn how to present material effectively and persuasively. As you listen, question why debaters present their arguments in a certain order. Look at how they get their points across and use inflection. Ask yourself what makes a good debate?

Talk to people in industry to learn how to organize your thoughts. By speaking with people in industry, you find out how they use language, how they organize their thoughts, and how they communicate information about fields they know well.

Read, read, read to learn basic speaking and writing skills. It doesn't matter what you read: novels, magazines, newspapers, reports, technical papers. The more you read, the more you know, and the more effectively you will speak and write.

Give presentations in class to practice public speaking. Take advantage of every opportunity to give oral presentations in class, any class. This is a great exercise, and you will never get fired from college if your presentation isn't perfect.

Join student organizations to learn how to interact effectively with others. Officers of clubs and organizations are responsible for scheduling, planning and conducting meetings, filing reports, submitting requests and interacting with people in various functions. Team members must communicate with each other to achieve the team's goals. Whatever your role, you are building communication skills.

Contribute articles to school or department publications to learn concise writing. One great way to master how to communicate is to write about something you believe in and make it comply with guidelines set by an editor. You also learn to accept criticism by having your document edited.

Get to know people outside of your major to observe how they communicate their ideas to you. Knowing a diverse group of people exposes you to new experiences and ways of thinking. Just talking with people who have different interests and backgrounds broadens your ability to communicate. Listening to others allows you to better understand different points of view.

Attend classes to take advantage of all the information out there about how to communicate. Take as many courses as you can. There is a wealth of knowledge that they offer. But don't rely solely on the classes. Communicating is something you can do every day. Socialize to learn how to listen, organize your thoughts, respect others' opinions and present your ideas. This may sound a little too obvious, but think back to the last time you had a substantial conversation with someone and talked about a topic that was really important to both of you. Having an in-depth conversation forces you to listen, organize your thoughts, respect the other person's opinion, and present your ideas clearly.

reflecting
on decisions

Now that you've gotten the big picture about your college community, what insights have you gained about the way your interactions within the college community might affect your academic progress and the outcomes of your life?

GET **ACTIVE**

Many campuses and campus organizations include service as a vital part of their mission. Joining an organization that does so allows you to become a citizen of your campus and community at one time—what a great time management win! You learn about these groups by visiting your campus office of Student Services. There organizations often list their charters or mission statements. You can also find out about them by announcements on your campus website, newspaper, or bulletin boards. Even if you don't want to join the organization, you can generally still participate in service activities such as a race/walk to raise funds for cancer research, food or clothing drive, or campus recycling initiative. Use the 5Cs—Define the **C**hallenge; Identify the **C**hoices; Predict the **C**onsequences; **C**hoose an option; **C**heck your outcome—to determine which organization you would choose to join to meet your service goals.

◄ CHOOSING TO SERVE

R EVIEW

Skim the notes you made throughout the chapter. How does the content fit together? What information is still unclear? Were your learning goals met? Can you answer the review questions and define terms?

◄ CHOOSING TO BE AN ACTIVE LEARNER

CHAPTER **THREE**

Deciding to Know Yourself

Your personality affects your decisions. What aspect(s) of your personality contributed to your decision to enroll in community college?

YOU DECIDE

To **wonder** means to think or have curiosity about. Things and ideas you wonder about often mask a need for a decision. Check the items below that apply to you.

In terms of my talents and skills, I've been wondering . . .

- ☐ 3.1 Which skills are among my best and which would I like to improve?
- ☐ 3.2 How do my values affect the choices I make?
- ☐ 3.3 How do my study surroundings affect the quantity or quality of what I learn?
- ☐ 3.4 What's the best way for me to learn?
- ☐ 3.5 What are my preferences for learning information?
- ☐ 3.6 What kinds of intelligences do I have?
- ☐ 3.7 How does my instructor's teaching style affect my learning preferences?

Each of these decision points corresponds to the numbered modules that follow. Turn to the module for immediate help.

CHOOSING TO BE AN ACTIVE LEARNER

SURVEY

Before reading this chapter, prepare for learning. Purposefully skim the title, introduction, headings, and graphics. As you survey, decide what information you already know and what information is new to you.

QUESTION

Change each section's heading into a question. This forms your learning goal for reading.

READ

Read the section without marking. Reread and mark key information that answers your question.

RECITE

Stop after each section and make sure you understood the content. Organize or summarize content and make notes.

Studying yourself is sometimes not as clear as you'd like it to be.

Few people start a journey without knowing if they have what it takes to get there. Instead, they make sure their transportation is reliable. They look at a map or Mapquest for the best route. They make sure they have enough cash to take them where they want to go.

As a college student, you, too, are on a journey. You are on your way to a college education. You, too, must see if you have what you need to make the trip. The first step is to become aware of what you do and do not know. Your first subject is yourself. This chapter provides you with ways to learn more about yourself. It also includes tips for using the results to your advantage in learning situations.

Some college students spend years learning everything from accounting to zoology. But they often fail to study one of the most interesting and revealing subjects of all—themselves. As a result, they often find themselves puzzled by the choices they make and unhappy with the consequences of those choices on their lives. The 5C process (Define the **C**hallenge; Identify **C**hoices; Predict **C**onsequences; **C**hoose an option; **C**heck your outcome) helps you avoid this problem.

You are a key part of any decision that affects you. So you need to analyze yourself to understand clearly your role in the situations you face. You are the product of your personality and experience. The way you approach life, your attitude, comes from the interaction of your aptitudes, abilities, interests, values, and learning style.

For instance, are you more comfortable in structured or casual situations? Would you rather learn by seeing, hearing, or doing? Do you focus more on details or on the "big picture" of a task? You may know that you have particular talents, interests, and abilities. Maybe you also know you believe in certain things—your values. You probably also have preferences for your learning environment, the way you best acquire information, and the way you process information most effectively. These together make up your **learning style.**

learning style
The mix of attributes that describe the ways that you best acquire and use information.

While you can learn in ways and situations that do not match your style, knowing your style preferences helps you make informed decisions about the learning options. For instance, being aware of your style lets you decide if online classes are better for you than face-to-face classes. Your decision to include your learning style into your study process is not a shortcut to learning. It is an asset in maximizing how you think, learn, and remember. Finally, your learning style affects your responses to your instructor's teaching style.

Aptitudes and Abilities

Has someone ever said that you had a talent or knack for doing something? Such natural or inborn traits and talents are called **aptitudes.** They reflect your potential. Some aptitudes are evident from an early age. For instance, children who play music by ear, draw well, win at sports, or solve math problems easily often do so because of aptitude. Your aptitude for doing something well may correspond to your having an interest in doing it. Other aptitudes are hidden. While you have an interest in a subject, you do not realize that you have the talent for that subject. For example, you might be interested in how cars work but don't realize that you could easily become your own mechanic. Learning about new aptitudes and interests is an integral part of being in college. As you experience new people and new situations, both will develop naturally.

Most likely, you have already recognized and developed noticeable aptitudes. That leaves the hidden ones for you to explore. Taking an aptitude test helps you do so. General aptitude tests estimate verbal, numerical, spatial, and some coordination skills. More specialized aptitudes, such as music and art, are not assessed by general aptitude tests. The advising, placement, or career center at your college (see Chapter 2) probably gives aptitude tests at little or no cost. Such tests help you find new possibilities for your consideration.

Abilities are what you can do. They are the results of aptitude combined with experience. Abilities are not constant. They increase with practice and decrease with disuse. And having ability does not equal success. Motivation and persistence also play a role (see Chapter 5).

Unlike aptitude, which is an estimated quality, ability can be measured by performance on formal and informal evaluation tools. Formal tests measure generalized areas of ability such as analytical intelligence or verbal skills. In contrast, informal assessments often help you identify specific abilities and individual strengths and weaknesses. For instance, each test you take in a class is a kind of subject-specific assessment of your ability to understand and use the information in the course.

Both aptitudes and abilities factor into the decisions you make whether you are at home, at school, or on the job. One way to increase your specific abilities is to analyze your preparation strategies as well as your score after each test. Consider what went well and explore what went wrong. Note the new skills you developed and the ones that still need work.

aptitudes
Inborn traits or talents.

abilities
Capabilities that result from aptitude combined with experience.

What Are Your Aptitudes?

Read through the following aptitudes, definitions, and examples.

Aptitude	Definition	Examples
Verbal or Nonverbal Communications	Communicating ideas, emotions, or information through spoken or unspoken language	Public speaking Writing essays, poems, plays Performing before an audience Teaching others Using Facebook or Twitter
Verbal Comprehension	Understanding verbal or nonverbal communications	Emphatic or sympathetic listening Selling Competing in debate Using Facebook or Twitter
Logical Understanding	Applying reason or logic	Solving mysteries Completing word or jigsaw puzzles Conducting scientific experiments Writing a computer program
Artistic Talent	Using artistic, musical or dramatic talents	Drawing Writing poems or plays Playing a musical instrument Singing Taking photographs Arranging displays
Mechanical Skills	Understanding relationships between parts of machines and/or how things are made and work	Putting a computer back together Repairing an automobile Reading blueprints Building models
Numerical Skills	Working with numbers	Working math problems Bookkeeping/working with spreadsheets Reading number graphs
Clerical Skills	Completing basic office work	Word Processing Filing records Controlling inventory Sending and receiving e-mail
Spatial Understanding	Understanding how parts of things fit together or multidimensional understanding	Completing a jigsaw puzzle Putting together models Reading blueprints
Physical Dexterity	Moving with bodily strength, coordination, and agility	Lifting weights Moving furniture Dancing
Organizational Talents	Planning, implementing and evaluating actions for yourself or others	Planning a party Organizing a trip Creating and editing simple databases
Intellectual Abilities	Original thinking, seeking knowledge, thinking ahead, and developing concepts	Reading books Studying Creating a new recipe Developing a business plan

1. Write a paragraph each about four experiences in your life you particularly enjoyed.

2. Reread your descriptions of each experience, and decide which of the list of aptitudes shown in the chart above best represents each experience.

3. Create a three-column chart of your own. List the aptitudes you identified in question 2 in the first column. In the second column, list the interests and experiences you have had that support your choice of aptitudes. In the third column, list the aptitudes you'd like to develop or improve.

4. Use the 5C process to identify how your aptitudes and abilities can guide your decisions about coursework and college experiences. First, state one of your aptitudes or abilities you wish to improve as a *Challenge* that requires a choice. For instance your statement might be "I want to perform before an audience." Next, identify your *Choices*—the courses or activities at your institution that might provide you with that experience. This might include joining the campus choir, auditioning for a play, or taking a class in dance. Your interests, aptitudes, and abilities naturally affect the choices you make. Consider how you might develop a further interest or acquire a new skill before you make a choice. What are the *Consequences* for each option? That is, if you implement that option, what would be the benefits of it? Which option would you *Choose?* How might you *Check* the outcome of your choice?

How do my values affect the choices I make?

Values

values
Personal beliefs and standards expressed in the topics and activities that are important to you.

Values are personal beliefs and standards that are reflected in your experiences. Whether you are consciously aware of them or not, you have a core set of personal values. When you look at the lives of people, you see the values that guide them. Perhaps you know someone who volunteers at a hospital. You may know someone who spends free time at art museums. Perhaps you know someone who is active in their church, synagogue or mosque. What each of these people does is directly related to what they value—service to others, art, or religion. The same is true of you.

You get some of your values from your family and friends. Your thoughts and reactions to situations and people form other values. Events and people you learn about through television, literature, and other media also shape them. Below you will find a list of common values. The importance you place on each one determines its value to you. There may be other aspects of life you value more.

One way to identify your values is to explore why you sit where you do now— that is, why are you in college? Recognizing the real reason or reasons why you're in school forms the first step in understanding your values because it helps show how and why you made one very important choice—to enroll in college.

Research suggests that students attend college for different reasons. The reasons, however, can be divided into three groups. First, some people attend college to reach self-fulfillment. They expect college to help them become the best, most learned persons that they can be. Second, some people come to college to get the education they need for the career they hope to have someday. While often uncertain about the specifics of that career choice, they know that they want to work as a professional and they see college as the road to that destination. Third, some people are avoiders. They attend college not to accomplish self-fulfillment or career goals but to satisfy the wishes of parents or peers or to avoid or delay making other important life decisions. Each of these reasons reflects differences in values.

Whatever your values, be assured that knowing your values strengthens everything concerned with them. Knowing your values and committing to them is an important step in achieving success and well-being.

What's Important? What's Not?

What are your values? Circle the top 10 terms in the list below that describe your values. Rank the ones you circled in order from most important (#1) to least important (#10). Think carefully about these values. Then think of a personal challenge and use the 5C (Define the **C**hallenge; Identify the **C**hoices; Predict the **C**onsequences; **C**hoose an option; **C**heck your outcome) approach to make a decision regarding the challenge reflecting your values. You may use one of the following questions to help you identify a challenge:

- Do my activities/school/job/career plans reflect my most important values?

- Are my values being met?

- What can I do to meet my values?

- I just feel that now that I know my values, so what? What action steps should I take?

- How might my values affect career choice?

achievement	agreement	ambition
authority	beauty	belonging
career/professional success	comfort	communication
competition	courage	creativity/innovation
equality	excellence	excitement/challenge/adventure
fame/prestige	family	financial stability/wealth
freedom/independence	friendship/companionship	happiness/personal satisfaction
health	helping	honesty/truth/integrity
honor	knowledge	leisure activity/play/fun
logic/wisdom	love	mental/intellectual development
neatness/orderliness	passion	peace/conflict resolution/harmony
physical development	power	responsibility
security	self-esteem	self-control
self-respect	social life	social recognition/respect of others
spiritual development	tradition	trust
truth	wisdom	

How do my study surroundings affect the quantity or quality of what I learn?

environmental preferences
Physical surroundings that are most comfortable for you.

Environmental Preferences

Where you learn—your **environmental preferences**—can be just as important as what you learn and how you learn it. For instance, you might prefer to study seated at a desk or spread out on the floor. You might like the room to be cool or warm. You might prefer to read in a well-lit room or in a darker room with light focused only on the page.

Accommodating these preferences adds to your learning efficiency and effectiveness. You probably can't always control where your classes are located. But you often can control some aspects of your classroom environment and most aspects of your learning environment. For instance, you might choose to study in a quiet library instead of in a noisy coffee shop. You might decide to take an online course rather than a face-to-face class.

Some people have to study where they can hear themselves think. Others prefer sound to help them study.

Checking Environmental Preferences

PART 1A: Your Preferences

Directions: Check the conditions you prefer in each section.

LIGHTING

_____**1.** I often turn on extra lamps for reading.

_____**2.** People sometimes tell me I'm reading in the dark.

_____**3.** I prefer to sit by windows at home, at work or in class.

_____**4.** I prefer to sit in the back or corner of a classroom or work area.

_____**5.** I often choose seats directly below overhead lights.

_____**6.** I find I sometimes shade my eyes while reading or solving math problems.

_____**7.** Low light makes me sleepy.

STRUCTURE

_____**1.** I prefer to stand and move around when studying or working.

_____**2.** I prefer to study seated on the floor rather than at a desk.

_____**3.** I find it more difficult to concentrate in lectures than in lab courses.

_____**4.** I find I fidget after sitting for a short length of time.

_____**5.** I find myself tapping my foot or knee after sitting for a short length of time.

SOUND

_____**1.** I prefer to study or work in silence.

_____**2.** When I really concentrate, I don't hear a thing.

_____**3.** I find myself easily distracted by noises in class, even when I am interested in the topic under discussion.

_____**4.** Background noises—conversation, soft music, TV—don't affect my ability to work or study.

_____**5.** Sometimes I wish I could tell my classmates or co-workers to be quiet.

_____**6.** I often hum to myself or tap while working.

_____**7.** I prefer podcasts and lectures to reading.

VISUAL

_____**1.** I am often distracted by classroom movement, even when I'm interested in the topic under discussion.

_____**2.** When I study, I have notes, papers, books, and other materials spread around me.

_____**3.** I find busy environments—crowded stores, cluttered desks, messy rooms—confusing.

_____**4.** I prefer highly colored, bold, and busy patterns.

_____**5.** I am very organized; when I study, I only have the bare essentials of what I need at hand.

_____**6.** I enjoy courses in which the lecturer is theatrical and moves freely around the classroom.

PART 1B: *Scoring and Analysis*

LIGHTING

If you checked the odd-numbered items, you probably prefer to study or work in strong light. If you checked the even-numbered items, you probably prefer to learn or work in more subdued light. Look for ways to adjust the lighting in your environment.

STRUCTURE

If you checked any three of the five statements, you probably prefer less structure and more mobility in your learning or work environment. Although you probably can't change your classroom environments, you can structure your study environment so that you can move around and feel less confined.

SOUND

If you checked the odd-numbered statements, you probably prefer to learn or work in quiet or silent surroundings. If you checked the even-numbered statements, you learn better with some background noise.

VISUAL

You withstand a high degree of visual stimulation if you checked the even-numbered statements in this category. If you checked the odd-numbered statements, you may be more easily distracted by what you see.

PART 2: Really Preferences or Just Habits?

Review what you checked in each category. Consider if what you checked is truly a preference or just a habit. For instance, do you actually learn better when seated in the back of a classroom or is that just where you usually sit? For this 5C (Define the **C**hallenge; Identify the **C**hoices; Predict the **C**onsequences; **C**hoose an option; **C**heck your outcome) application, use one of the environmental preference categories (stucture, sound, visual) as your challenge. For example, your challenge might be "In terms of structure, what kind of study environment is best for me?" Generate choices for both structured and unstructured environments (e.g., studying at a desk in the library versus standing/walking, seated on the floor, or in another less traditional environment). What do you think might be the consequences of each choice for you? What is the best evironment for you to choose? How can you check the outcome of this choice to determine if it is really the best or just a habit?

Sensory Preferences

Sensory preferences involve the way or ways in which you like to acquire information. If you are a visual learner, you like to aquire information through what you see. This includes pictures and written words. If you like to acquire information through what you hear, you are an auditory learner. This includes all kinds of sounds from spoken words to musical rhythms. If you are a tactile/kinesthetic learner, you learn through touch and physical experiences. This includes hands-on activities and other ways to learn by doing.

Once you know your sensory preferences, you can use them to maximize your performance. For example, suppose you have a list of items to remember. If auditory learning is your preference, you could create a song to help you recall the list. If visual learning is what you prefer, you might draw pictures of the items. If you are tactile/kinesthetic learner, you might make flash cards and then sort them into stacks, arranging the cards in order of importance to a particular topic or in order of how well you know the information. While you may show a preference for one type of learning or another, you may actually learn best if you combine two or more learning preferences. For example, you could use flash cards that have pictures you drew that you sort into stacks.

Some people find that bright colors and bold patterns help them think.

Making the Most of Your Sensory Preferences

Visual Learners . . .	Auditory Learners . . .	Tactile/Kinesthetic learners . . .
Sit near the front of a class to minimize visual distractions	Listen to podcasts of lectures	Use hands-on activities such as labs and models
Create flash cards and games	Take part in class discussions and ask questions in class	Think of real-life applications
Use supplemental handouts and text illustrations	Restate what you learn in your own words	Role-play concepts
Take notes while listening	Sit in the front of the class to avoid distractions	Take notes as you listen or read
Underline information		Use computers
Use different colors to highlight ideas in text or online	Get ebooks or use software that reads information on your computer aloud	Make and use learning games
Create graphic or symbolic arrangements of information on paper or online	Read notes and text aloud	Rewrite class notes
	Participate in tutorials or tutor others	Practice writing responses to exam questions
Use pictures, diagrams and other visuals		Teach others

Identifying Your Sensory Preferences

Directions: Rate your preference for each item using the following scale:
Almost always = 4 points, Often = 3 points, Occasionally = 2 points, Rarely = 1 point

Visual Modality

_____ I remember information better if I see it.

_____ When someone asks me how to spell a word, I have to see it spelled several different ways to know which one is correct.

_____ Looking at a person helps keep me focused on what s/he says.

_____ I need a quiet place to get my work done.

_____ When I take a test, I can see the textbook page in my head.

_____ I need to read directions for myself, not just hear them verbally.

_____ Music or background noise distracts me.

_____ I don't always get the meaning of a joke.

_____ I doodle and draw pictures on the margins of my notebook pages.

_____ I have trouble following lectures.

_____ I react very strongly to colors.

_____ I remember faces more easily than names.

_____ I learn best by watching someone else before trying something myself.

_____ When preparing for a test, I often use flash cards and study guides.

_____ The one thing I need in life is TV and videos.

_____ **Total**

Auditory Modality

_____ My papers and notebooks always seem messy.

_____ When someone asks me how to spell a word, I can easily identify the correct auditory spelling or verbally say how the word is spelled.

_____ When I read, I use my index finger to track my place on the line.

_____ I do not follow written directions well.

_____ If I hear something, I will remember it.

_____ Writing has always been difficult for me.

_____ I often misread words from the text (i.e., _them_ for _then_).

_____ When I do math, I say the numbers and steps to myself.

_____ I would rather listen and learn than read and learn.

_____ I'm not very good at interpreting an individual's body language.

_____ Pages with small print or poor quality copies are hard for me to read.

_____ My eyes tire quickly, even though my vision checkup is always fine.

_____ I remember names more easily than faces.

_____ I learn best from lectures and verbal directions.

_____ When studying for a test, I often use tapes or go to study groups.

_____ The one thing I need in life is music.

_____ Although I don't always contribute, I like in-class discussions.

_____ When I have to read, I read softly to myself.

_____ **Total**

Tactile/Kinesthetic Modality

_____ I start a project before reading the directions.

_____ When someone asks me how to spell a word, I have to see it spelled several different ways to know which one is correct.

_____ I hate to sit still for long periods of time.

_____ I prefer to learn by doing.

_____ I can handle multiple tasks.

_____ I use the trial-and-error approach to problem solving.

_____ I like to read my textbook while riding an exercise bike.

_____ I take frequent study breaks.

_____ I have a hard time giving step-by-step instructions to others.

_____ I enjoy sports and excel at several different types of sports.

_____ I use my hands when describing things.

_____ I have to rewrite or type my class notes to reinforce the material.

_____ I often "play" with small objects such as paper clips or pencils.

_____ When studying for a test, I often reorganize my notes or create maps.

_____ The one thing I need in life is sports.

_____ I like to make things to help me study.

_____ **Total**

Scoring: Total the score for each section. The highest of the three scores indicates the most efficient method of information intake. The second highest score indicates the modality that boosts the primary strength.

GROUP APPLICATION: Compare your results with those of other students in the class. What kinds of instructional and learning activities meet the need of visual learners? Auditory learners? Tactile/kinethetic learners? What kinds of study skills will meet the needs of each of these kinds of learners? What work situations would be best for each of these types of learners?

Processing Preferences

Once you get information, your brain processes it to incorporate it into your own thinking. Like all learners, you probably have a preference for either global or logical thinking. Global thinkers focus more on the "big picture" rather than details. They tend to be creative and visual. They are good at drawing conclusions and dealing with emotions. Logical thinkers are, by definition, more rational. They focus on details rather than main ideas. Logical thinkers approach information more systematically. They prefer to make decisions based on facts rather than emotion. The following table gives additional traits for logical and global processing.

What happens if you have an instructor whose thinking or teaching style differs from yours? For example, suppose you prefer structure such as outlines, intermediate deadlines, and detailed instructions, and your instructor likes to free-associate information? You will need to carefully note these free associations and then later create more organized notes for yourself either individually or in a study group, and by meeting with the instructor. Or, if you are a hands-on learner whose instructor only provides print information, you will need to create your own flash cards and look for activities on the Web to support the concepts you are learning.

Logical and Global Processing Traits

Logical	Global
Language (speech and writing)	Pattern recognition
Recall of names	Recall of faces
Recall of words in a song	Recall of a song's melody
Planned	Spontaneous
Math	Synthesis
Time	Holistic overview
Rhythm	Visual information
Systematic	Random
Sequencing	Spatial order
Analysis	Feelings
Linearity	Intuitiveness
Details	Creativity
Orderliness	Imagination
Abstraction	Multitasking
Factual or realistic applications	Nonverbal information
Objective test formats	Metaphoric thinking
	Improvisation
	Subjective test formats

Analyzing Your Preferences for Global or Logical Thinking

Directions: Circle the choice you prefer in each question.

1. How do you prefer making decisions? a. intuitively b. logically

2. Is it easier for you to remember people's names or faces? a. names b. faces

3. How do you schedule activities? a. plan activities in advance b. do things spontaneously

4. In social situations, which do you prefer to be? a. the listener b. the speaker

5. What do notice most when listening to a speaker? a. what the speaker says b. the speaker's body language

6. Do you consider yourself to be a goal-oriented person? a. yes b. no

7. How would you describe your main study area? a. messy b. neat and well organized

8. Are you usually aware of what time it is and how much time has passed? a. yes b. no

9. How would you describe your writing style? a. let ideas flow freely b. plan the sequence of ideas in advance

10. What do you remember about music? a. words b. tunes

11. Which do you prefer doing? a. watching a movie b. talking to others

12. Do you frequently move your furniture around in your home? a. yes b. no

13. Are you a good memorizer? a. yes b. no

14. When you doodle, what do you make? a. shapes b. words

15. Clasp your hands together. Which thumb is on top? a. left b. right

16. Which subject do you prefer? a. algebra b. geometry

17. How do you usually plan your day? a. list what you need to accomplish b. just let things happen

18. Are you good at expressing your feelings? a. yes b. no

19. What are you more likely to do in an argument with someone else? a. listen and consider the point of view of the other person b. insist that you are right

20. At the beginning of winter, are you likely to find change in last year's coat pocket? a. yes b. no

SCORING: Check or circle your answers below.

GLOBAL	1A	2B	3B	4A	5B	6B	7A	8B	9A	10B
LOGICAL	1B	2A	3A	4B	5A	6A	7B	8A	9B	10A

GLOBAL	11A	12B	13B	14A	15A	16B	17B	18A	19A	20A
LOGICAL	11B	12A	13A	14B	15B	16A	17A	18B	19B	20B

Total your answers: Total # Global _____ Total # Logical _____

GROUP APPLICATION: Share your totals for each type of processing with your group. What similarities and differences do you discover among your group's scores? Divide a piece of paper into four quadrants for recording your responses. In the top left quadrant, create a chart that describes how five of the logical processing traits in the list in Module 3.5 could be converted into strategies for learning. In the top right quadrant, identify how five of the global traits in that list could be converted into strategies for learning. In the bottom left quadrant, identify three ways in which a person who lacks skills in logical traits could develop those skills. In the right quadrant, identify three ways in which a person who lacks skills in global traits could develop those skills. Why is it important for a person to develop both logical and global traits in college? in the workplace?

What kinds of intelligences do I have?

Your Multiple Intelligences

Intelligence was once defined as the ability for thinking. People thought you were born with it. Standardized tests measured it. The result of this test was your IQ (intelligence quotient) score. Supposedly, the score determined if you were smart or not. But guess what? Like many standardized tests, the IQ tests were not always accurate.

Harvard researcher Howard Gardner defined intelligence differently. Intelligence, to him, was an ability to create a valuable product or offer an important service. Gardner said intelligence consisted of a set of skills that helped you solve different kinds of life problems, whether those were personal, social, work, or educational. And, he said, the intelligences could be developed and strengthened.

Gardner identified eight basic types of intelligences, which he called *multiple intelligences*. The table on the following page lists and defines these eight types. The table also shows preferences of and ways to develop each one.

The Eight Different Intelligences

Type	Definition	Preferences	Ways to Develop
Verbal-linguistic	Language and thoughts in terms of meaning and sound of words	Stories, jokes, arguments, poetry, reading, speaking	Listening to guest speakers, doing word puzzles, learning vocabulary, writing fiction and nonfiction
Logical-mathematical	Abstractions, numbers or reasoning	Solving math problems, sorting information, offering advice, computer programming, inventing	Finding patterns, using a calculator, finding examples, solving logic puzzles, classifying and organizing information
Spatial	Visualization and use of pictures and space	Seeing things in relationship to others things; parallel parking, design or decoration of personal spaces, packing items	Jigsaw puzzles, artwork, concept mapping, color coding, rearranging items in a room or space, examining similarities and differences
Bodily-kinesthetic	Control of physical movements and skill in handling objects	Acting, dancing, sports, hands-on activities	Stretching, charades, sign language, working with arts and crafts, individual and group sports
Musical	Use of rhythm, pitch, and timbre	Play or write music, create rhythm games or songs, dance	Playing instruments, having environmental music in the background, putting information to a rhythm, creating rhymes to remember information
Interpersonal	Understanding and responding appropriately to emotions, motivations, and goals of others	Small groups, peer learning, service learning	Cooperative groups, creating teams, sharing responses, clarifying emotions and motivations
Intrapersonal	Understanding and responding appropriately to one's own emotions, motivations, and goals	Individual work and achievement, journal writing, self-discovery	Provision of time for reflection, keeping a journal, reading published journals or diaries, self-assessments, identifies attitude, personality traits and learning styles
Naturalist	Recognition, categorization, and use of plants, animals and other objects in nature	Field trips, science experiments, observing how natural objects are similar and different	Lab courses, working in pairs on experiments, writing a journal about science experiments, reading about different scientists

Analyzing Your Intelligences

Directions: Circle the items you prefer in each box. Then rank your preferences with #1 being your strongest preference.

Box A Rank _____	Box B Rank _____	Box C Rank _____	Box D Rank _____
I like to read.	Math is one of my strengths.	I need to use visuals in order to learn new things.	I can tell when instruments play out of tune.
I like to write reports.	I like to solve logic problems and mysteries.	I have a good imagination.	I like to browse around music stores.
Names, places, dates, and details are easy to recall.	I like computers.	I like to look at videos.	I drum and tap on almost everything.
I prefer using a word processor to handwriting.	I can usually figure out how something works.	Mazes are fun.	I often listen to music while I study or work.
I use tape recorders to save/replay information.	I like to explore new things.	People say I am artistic.	I am highly aware of environmental sounds.
I can tell good stories or jokes.	I like to analyze things.	I can read maps and charts easily.	I listen to rhythm of a song more than the words.
I really like social studies subjects.	I enjoy puzzles and riddles.	I like to look at photographs.	I like to sing.
I like to browse in bookstores or libraries.	I like to sort and classify things.	I can design and give a media presentation.	Recalling melodies is easy for me.
I like to read books and magazines.	Science is interesting.	I like looking around at museums.	I can play one or more musical instruments.
Giving a speech isn't a problem for me.	I enjoy conducting experiments.	I like to daydream.	I enjoy live music.
I can write stories.	I like forms of instructional technology.	I can look at a 2-dimensional drawing and create it in 3-dimensions.	I can match pitches.

Box E Rank _____	Box F Rank _____	Box G Rank _____	Box H Rank _____
I like to touch things.	People say I'm a born leader.	People say I have confidence in myself.	I like being outdoors more than being indoors.
Sports personalities fascinate me.	I enjoy discussions.	I don't like group projects and study groups.	I do things to protect the environment.
People say I talk with my hands.	I like study groups.	I know what my strengths and abilities are.	People say I have a green thumb.
I have good fine motor coordination.	I am a good peacemaker.	I know how to get help to attain the goals I want to achieve.	I like animals.
I am good at sports.	I can organize other people.	I like cumulative writing projects.	I like to order things in hierarchies.
I enjoy watching sports events.	I am a "people person."	I like to sit quietly and think.	Ecological issues are important to me.

Box E Rank _____	Box F Rank _____	Box G Rank _____	Box H Rank _____
I can do arts and crafts.	I like to interview others.	I like pursuing my personal interests and hobbies.	I have plants in my house.
I like hands-on learning.	I can debate issues easily.	I prefer independent research projects.	I own at least one pet.
I have a difficult time keeping still.	I solve problems by talking though them.	I set goals for myself and achieve them.	Animal behavior interests me.
I like to communicate through movement or dance.	People think I am a good listener.		I like to camp and hike
I like to move around (sit, stand, walk, etc.).	I am a good communicator.		I know the names of different kinds of plants.

KEY

Box A = Verbal/Linguistic

Box B = Mathematical/Logical

Box C = Visual/Spatial

Box D = Musical/Rhythmic

Box E = Bodily/Kinesthetic

Box F = Interpersonal/Directed toward others

Box G = Intrapersonal/Directed toward self

Box H = Naturalist

List your intelligences in order from #1 to #8.

1. _____

2. _____

3. _____

4. _____

5. _____

6. _____

7. _____

8. _____

GROUP APPLICATION: Divide into groups based on your #1 rankings (e.g., everyone that ranked Verbal as #1 in a group, etc.). Give an example of something you do that exemplifies your strongest intelligence. Discuss how the results of this intelligence preference have more, or less, effect on success in college. If the effect is negative, discuss how you can minimize the effect. Compare your current majors and career interests. Discuss how specific intelligences might lead to decisions about majors and careers.

How does my instructor's teaching style affect my learning preferences?

Your Instructor's Style

No matter what course you take, instructors vary in the ways in which they structure their classes. Even instructors of the same topic structure their courses differently. Some instructors rely on verbal information. They just talk or lead a discussion among class members. The information in such classes is given only in spoken form. Other instructors provide visual reinforcement of what they say (for example, outlines, written lecture guides, overhead transparencies, or electronic presentations). Still others give demonstrations or lab activities that supply virtual or actual experiences.

Online courses also reflect an instructor's style. Some online courses are very structured with consistent features in each week's units, regularly scheduled deadlines, and easily usable navigation. Others, like the thinking of the faculty that create them, are more free-flowing. Many online courses depend more on written information to transmit directions and content. Others include interesting graphics, links to videos and websites, interactive games and flash cards, PowerPoint presentations enhanced with audio, files that can be downloaded and played on iPods or MP3 players, or content that can be accessed via cell phones.

College faculty differ from high school teachers in several ways. High school teachers must have a minimum of a four-year undergraduate degree. The degree is generally in some area of education. Their coursework specifically prepared them to teach. College faculty must generally have an advanced degree—either a master's or doctorate—to teach. Their degrees focus on specific subjects (such as history, math, or psychology). Their coursework provided them with additional information about the subject rather than ways to teach it. Many college campuses provide faculty development workshops to help instructors learn new teaching techniques; but it is often up to each faculty member to attend these and put the content into effect in their own classrooms. As a result, many instructors teach as they were taught or as they feel comfortable.

As a result, you may find some course styles—both in face-to-face and online classes—meet your needs better than others. You will also find that you will be able to adapt to some styles better than others. Whatever the case, learning remains your responsibility. Luckily, you can rethink information and structure it in ways that suit you.

What's Your Instructor's Teaching Style?

Select an instructor you feel has a teaching style that is the most different from your learning style.

Use the following inventory to identify your instructor's teaching style in terms of modality and thinking preferences.

PART 1: Sensory Prefernces

Uses lecture or podcasts as primary means of delivering information	Uses text as primary means of delivering information	Uses labs, demonstrations, or activities as primary means of delivering information
Uses large group discussion	Provides outlines and written study guides	Includes service learning
Provides verbal instructions or podcasts for assignments	Provides written instructions and examples for assignments	Demonstrates how assignments should be completed or provides a video clip to show how the assignment should be completed
Uses guest speakers or tells stories	Shows videos as lecture launchers	Uses problem or case-based learning
Subjective, essay exams	Objective, multiple-choice exams	Performance exams

Total the number of boxes you checked in each row. The following key helps you identify an instructor's sensory preferences: Column 1, auditory; Column 2, visual; Column 3, tactile-kinesthetic.

PART 2: Thinking Preferences

Student-centered classrooms	Subject-centered classrooms
Grades on a curve or more subjectively	Set grading system (e.g., grading rubrics)
Invites creativity in completing assignments; assignments may seem unclear	Clear, structured assignments
Focus on broad issues and application of ideas	Focus on details and memorization of specific knowledge
Flexible schedules for information and completing of assignments	Specified schedules and firm deadlines for coverage of information and assignments
General syllabus with broad topics assigned to nonspecific time frames	Organized syllabus with content identified for specific dates
In face-to-face classes, moveable desks arranged loosely in rows, small groupings; in online classes, includes icebreakers, activities and discussions to foster group interactions	Moveable desks placed in straight rows and columns; provides little opportunity for peer-to-peer interactions
No attendance requirement as long as students complete the work	Attendance requirement with assigned seats
Students can sit where they wish	Assigned seating

Total the number of boxes you checked in each row. The following key helps you identify an instructor's preferred modality: Column 1, global; Column 2, logical.

GROUP APPLICATION: Divide into pairs—one logical- and one global-processing student to each pair. Once you have identified your instructor's style, discuss ways you can make allowances for the differences between your learning style and the instructor's teaching style.

chapter review

Respond to the following on a separate sheet of paper or in your notebook.

1. What is the difference between aptitudes and abilities?
2. Other than aptitude, what affects the development of abilities?
3. How can course exams help you identify strengths and weaknesses in ability?
4. Choose one of the values you circled in Activity 2. How do you use that value in making decisions about your home life? School? Work?
5. List and define the types of intelligences a person can have. Which of your intelligences were you aware of? Which surprised you? What will you do to develop your intelligences?
6. What differences have you noted between college faculty and high school teachers or bosses on the job? Do you prefer to learn from college faculty or high school teachers or bosses on the job? Why?
7. Who ultimately controls learning—the instructor or the student? Explain.
8. Consider your learning style and preferences. How do they affect (a) the small decisions you make (for example, to miss a class or not) and (b) the big decisions you make (that is, selecting a major, for example)? Be specific.
9. Compare intelligences and aptitudes. What are the commonalities? Why do they exist?

did you decide?

Did you accomplish what you wanted to in this chapter? Check the items below that apply to you.

Review the *You Decide* questions that you identified at the beginning of the chapter, but look at them from a new direction. If you didn't check an item below, review that module until you feel you can confidently apply the strategies to your own situation. However, the best ideas are worthless unless they are put into effect. Use the 5Cs to help you decide what information you found most helpful in the chapter and how you plan to use it. Record your comments after the statements below.

☐ 3.1. I know which skills are among my best and which I would like to improve.

_____

_____

☐ 3.2. I see how my values affect the choices I make.

_____

_____

☐ 3.3. I can alter my study surroundings to improve the quantity and quality of what I learn.

_____

_____

☐ 3.4. I recognize my own best way to learn.

_____

_____

☐ 3.5. I can organize my study to best use my own preferences for learning information.

_____

_____

☐ 3.6. I know what kinds of intelligences I have.

_____

_____

☐ 3.7. I understand how my instructor's teaching style affects my learning preferences and can adapt to it.

_____

_____

perspectives

In the following article, "Olson Looks for Career in Education," journalist Morgan Muhlenbruch describes one student's interests and talents as well as his major.

Think about and answer these question:

1. Given Olson's experiences, how would you describe him? Why?
2. What do you think are Olson's interests?
3. Given Olson's background and interests, do you predict that he would enjoy being a teacher? Why or why not?
4. Describe how the 5C decision-making process applies to Olson.

   A. What was Olson's **C**hallenge in terms of choosing a major?

   B. What key **C**hoices do you think were open to him?

   C. What do you think are the major **C**onsequence(s) of each choice?

   D. What did Olson **C**hoose?

   E. How can he **C**heck the outcome of his decision?

Hit by a car.
Fell off a 30-foot waterfall.
Run over by a tractor.

Mychal Olson, an education major at NIACC, has done just that. Invincible? You tell me.

He has somehow survived several crazy stunts, giving him a status somewhere near Evil Knievel. Now he says he is settling down to become a teacher and survive in a classroom in the future.

Olson possesses many talents. In high school, he participated in football, basketball, track, band, dance team and drama/theater.

Olson said he debated about being a teacher while he was in high school, so he sat down and had a heart to heart conversation with one of his favorite teachers, Schlumbomb.

Olson said Schlumbomb told him that he should just go for it in the field of education. Olson is currently enrolled in classes to help him pursue his dream. He said Introduction to Teaching, taught by NIACC instructor Kacy Larson, is currently his favorite class. In the course, students learn about various factors that will affect them as teachers, such as the location of the school within the community or the organization and administration of schools. In Introduction to Teaching, many in-class group assignments are given, and many discussions are held.

"He is engaging [during discussions]," classmate Hannah Lupkes said. "When he speaks, you just want to hear more."

Another class that Olson said he is enrolled in is a field experience and seminar course. Olson said he will get to go into a classroom of his choice for 22 hours and observe a teacher. For this course, Olson goes to Waverly-Shell Rock High School to observe another favorite teacher, Mrs. Hanfelt. Olson said he is excited about becoming a teacher, which is why he enjoys these courses.

"It's the first step," Olson said. "I love it."

"Mychal has a great sense of humor that [future] students will really enjoy in the classroom," Larson said. "He also has the ability to think critically about topics being discussed."

Once Olson graduates from NIACC, he said he plans to transfer to UNI, so he can continue his education and further pursue his dreams. Eventually, Olson said he wants to be an English teacher at a small high school in Iowa. Despite the fact that he has traveled to all of the contiguous 48 states, he said his heart is stuck in Iowa.

"I feel best when I'm helping others feel at their best," Olson said. "The best way to do that is to teach."

reflecting on decisions

Now that you've gotten the big picture about your assets, what have you learned about your aptitudes, abilities, interests, values or preferences that can help you make decisions more effectively?

SERVICE LEARNING

Learn and Serve America's National Clearinghouse defines service learning as "combining service objectives with learning objectives with the intent that the activity changes both the recipient and the provider of the service. This is accomplished by combining service tasks with structured opportunities that link the task to self-reflection, self-discovery, and the acquisition and comprehension of values, skills, and knowledge content." Rather than an unrelated volunteer experience, service learning serves to extend thinking about the content of a course. For instance, students in a freshman composition course might volunteer at community agencies and then write descriptive papers about their experiences or a letter to someone at the agency to persuade them to change something at the site. Students also reflect on the meaning of their service in terms of how the service impacted the recipients and the community as a whole, affected themselves, and resulted in clearer understanding of course content. Check to see which courses on your campus include service learning and think about taking one. You'll gain new insights about yourself, others, your course, and the world. Use the 5Cs—Define the **C**hallenge; Identify the **C**hoices; Predict the **C**onsequences; **C**hoose an option; **C**heck your outcome—to determine if a course that has a service learning component is one you'd like to take.

◀ **CHOOSING TO SERVE**

REVIEW

Skim the notes you made throughout the chapter. How does the content fit together? What information is still unclear? Were your learning goals met? Can you answer the review questions and define terms?

◀ **CHOOSING TO BE AN ACTIVE LEARNER**

CHAPTER **FOUR**

Choosing Goals for College and Life

Goal setting includes facing the past . . . and anticipating the future. How do you think the goals you've decided to pursue will affect your future?

YOU DECIDE

To *wonder* means to think or have curiosity about. Things and ideas you wonder about often mask a need for a decision. Check the items below that apply to you.

In terms of setting goals, I've been wondering . . .

☐ 4.1 What are my goals?

☐ 4.2 Do I have a realistic plan for achieving my goals?

☐ 4.3 What contributes to my success or failure?

☐ 4.4 Am I working toward my goals?

☐ 4.5 How does GPA contribute to the achievement of my goals?

Each of these decision points corresponds to the numbered modules that follow. Turn to the module for immediate help.

Most people would not purchase a cell phone without knowing the coverage details that come with it. They'd want to know what areas of the country the plan covers. They'd want to know how many text messages come free with it each month. They'd want to know if Internet usage was part of the plan. Oddly enough, few people put the same kind of thought into their daily lives. This chapter gives you the tools to help you make decisions about and plan your life course.

CHOOSING TO BE AN ACTIVE LEARNER

SURVEY

Before reading this chapter, prepare for learning. Purposefully skim the title, introduction, headings, and graphics. As you survey, decide what information you already know and what information is new to you.

QUESTION

Change each section's heading into a question. This forms your learning goal for reading.

READ

Read the section without marking. Reread and mark key information that answers your question.

RECITE

Stop after each section and make sure you understood the content. Organize or summarize content and make notes.

What are my goals?

Identifying Goals

Short-term goals can lead to long-term happiness.

short-term goals
Goals that can be achieved in a relatively short amount of time.

mid-range goals
Goals that serve as a checkpoint on the way to achieving long-term goals.

long-range goals
Goals that take a long time, even a lifetime, to accomplish.

Goals form the compass by which you organize and manage your life. Just as a compass shows direction, your goals shape the path you take. The decisions you make either take you closer—or farther—from the goals you set. One way goals vary is in the length of time it takes to achieve them.

You set **short-term goals** all the time. By their very definition, short-term goals don't relate to any specific length of time. They can be met in a day, week, month, year, etc. Their length depends on the context in which the goal is set. Short-term goals could include developing a new skill, gaining work experience, or getting married.

Each goal you set in life should contribute to the achievement of larger goals. Your current goals are probably short-term goals. Current goals might include ending the semester with a 3.5 grade average, running for office in a campus group, volunteering time at a neighborhood school, or becoming more fit.

Mid-range goals are short-term goals with a longer payout. They act as checkpoints for success, as you complete them within the next three to five years. Mid-range goals might include completing a degree, having a successful career, buying a house, raising a family, or owning a business. By reaching a mid-range goal, you know that you are closer to your anticipated outcome. They ultimately lead to your lifetime goals.

Lifetime or **long-range goals** are those ambitions you hope to attain in life. Few worthy goals are achieved overnight. Most require years of effort. Goals like happiness, health, and success will take a lifetime. You will work on them until you die.

Goals affect all aspects of your life. *Personal goals* are those that relate only to you. They focus on you as a person. For instance, getting more exercise is a personal goal. As a community college student, it's easy to forget personal goals. You can become so fixated on your responsibilities to your family, friends, and work that you forget yourself. That's a mistake. Flight attendants include the following in their preflight instructions—in case of emergency, put your oxygen mask on before helping anyone else. At first, that seems kind of self-centered. But if you can't keep yourself healthy and productive, how can you help others? Take time to set and meet some personal goals.

Social goals are those goals that focus on you and your relationships with others. Wanting to spend time with friends and family is a social goal. Similar to personal goals, social goals can get lost while you are in school. Work and school pressures can force you to ignore relationships. Not a good idea. Find a way to involve family and friends in your new school community. Perhaps they would be interested in attending campus activities and events with you.

An academic goal relates to you as a college student. An academic goal might be to make certain grades. This is probably one of your goals, whether you were an "A" or "C" student in the past. In other words, having been successful in high school doesn't guarantee that college will be a breeze. Having had past academic difficulties doesn't mean college is going to blow you away. In college and beyond, you'll find that your academic history is just that: history. Although it may—or may not—have prepared you for college-level work, you're here. What you do now is what counts. If you had a successful academic history, congratulations, but don't rely on past efforts. Set some high academic goals and get started. If your academic history was less than perfect, set goals to use the resources you need for a second chance at academic success.

Write Your Goals

Brainstorm as many academic, career, or personal goals as you can in the chart below.

PERSONAL GOALS	ACADEMIC GOALS	CAREER GOALS

Do I have a realistic plan for achieving my goals?

Setting S.M.A.R.T.E.R. Goals

S.M.A.R.T.E.R.

Acronym for the necessary parts of a goal: Specific, Measurable, Achievable, Relevant, Time-Sensitive, Evident, and Recorded.

Reaching goals depends on the decisions and choices you make along the way. You need a plan with goals that are **S.M.A.R.T.E.R.** This acronym stands for the necessary parts of a goal: **S**pecific, **M**easurable, **A**chievable, **R**elevant, **T**ime-Sensitive, **E**vident, and **R**ecorded. S.M.A.R.T.E.R. changes a goal from a general idea to one that is action-oriented.

For instance, perhaps your goal is to finish school while you work. A S.M.A.R.T.E.R. goal would be to complete an AA degree in business in three years with a 3.0 GPA. It's *specific* because you have a clear idea of what you want to achieve. It's *measurable* in two ways: the degree itself and the GPA you want to have when you graduate. Your choice to complete a two-year degree in three years makes it *achievable*. This gives you time to study and work. It is *relevant* to your particular situation and your long-range goal of success. It is also *time-sensitive* because it includes a deadline for completion. If your goal is written (*recorded*) and put somewhere (e.g., a bathroom mirror, refrigerator) that you will see often (*evident*), you won't forget what you were trying to achieve.

Additionally, goals should be stated in positive form—what you want to achieve, rather than what you want to avoid. For instance, one of your goals might be to complete your degree. Stated positively, your goal is to stay in college until you graduate. Stated negatively, the goal is to avoid dropping out of college before completing a degree. The positive one is more inspiring.

No matter what goals you set, each involves gaining knowledge and using strategies. For instance, to enroll in college, you had to learn new terms (e.g., transcript, registrar, catalog) and new skills (e.g., how to apply for admission; locate campus resources). Part of your responsibility in achieving your goals is to decide exactly what you need to know and what you need to do. Unfortunately, that's not always clear early in the process. Sometimes you have only a vague sense of what you want. It's only after you learn more and try different things that you refine and continue—or discontinue—a goal.

The 5C approach—Define the **C**hallenge; Identify **C**hoices; Predict **C**onsequences; **C**hoose an option; **C**heck your outcome—can be particularly useful in goal setting. For instance, as you learn more about your college's resources and services, you'll be more able to identify choices available to you and the consequences of each choice. As you narrow your options and make a choice, you use your new knowledge and skills to determine if the choice was right for you. Then you either pursue the goal or make the decision to go in a different direction.

Backward planning involves setting goals by starting with an end goal in mind and working backward. This is a method of goal setting that helps you deal with the unknowns that might cause you to give up on your plan. The interim goals have an organic connection to the end that helps you visualize it. The idea is to start with your end goal and then work backward by setting milestones you need to reach along the way. A backward plan doesn't look much different from any other set of goals. The difference is in the way you think about your goal. To create a backward plan, you think from a new perspective.

backward planning
Setting goals by starting with an end goal and working backward.

The Backward Planning Process

1. Write down your final S.M.A.R.T.E.R. goal. What do you want to achieve, and by what date?

2. Ask yourself what milestone immediately precedes your goal. What do you have to do, and by when, so that you're in a position to reach your final objective?

3. Continue to work backward. What do you need to do to make sure each previous goal is reached?

4. Continue this process until you identify the very first milestone that you need to complete.

Visualization is a tool you can use to work through goal setting as you consider and keep or eliminate options. Some people think visualization is the same as daydreaming, but it is quite different. To visualize, you actively picture yourself working through the steps until your goal is realized. Keep in mind that visualization is not a substitute for the actions required to achieve the goal. For instance, perhaps your goal is to make an A on your next math test. Without the practice and study required to learn the math, visualizing an A on your returned paper is not likely to achieve the goal. Instead, as you study, you visualize yourself successfully recalling formulas and using them to solve problems. You visualize yourself taking the test with competence and confidence.

visualization
Creating mental visual images of achieving a goal.

S.M.A.R.T.E.R.: Parts of a Goal

- Specific: Is the goal clearly described?

- Measurable: Is your goal quantifiable?

- Achievable: Is the goal possible given your current resources?

- Relevant: Does the goal contribute to the achievement of a larger goal?

- Time-Sensitive: Does the goal have a deadline for completion?

- Evident: Is your goal in a place where you will see it often?

- Recorded: Did you put your goal in writing?

What's Your Plan?

Complete Figure 4.1. Write your birth date to the right of point A. Write today's date to the right of point X. You don't have to put a date for the Z point. Go back and examine your answers to Activity 1. Now write what you hope to *do,* the qualities and experiences you hope to *have,* the things you want to *be,* and the things or services you want to *give* by the end of your life. Consider what you need to do in order to accomplish the goals you set at the Z point. Identify at least three mid-range goals that will take you closer to the achievement of your lifetime goals. Now identify at least three short-term goals that will take you closer to the achievement of your mid-range goals. What can you do today to take you closer to your short-term, mid-range, and lifetime goals? Make sure all of your goals are S.M.A.R.T.E.R.

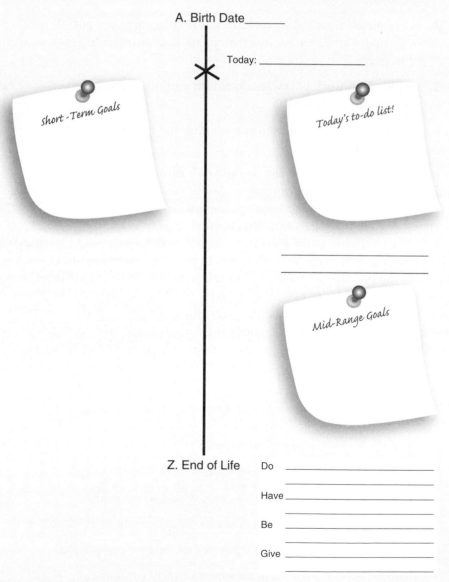

A. Birth Date_____

Today: _____

Short-Term Goals

Today's to-do list!

_____
_____

Mid-Range Goals

Z. End of Life

Do _____
_____

Have _____

Be _____
_____

Give _____
_____

Figure 4.1 Your Life Plan.

GROUP APPLICATION: Compare your timeline with others in your class. Then discuss these questions together: What can you learn from the way they identify and specify goals? What do you think they can learn from you? What did you like about completing this activity? What was difficult for you? What challenges or obstacles might keep you from obtaining a goal? How could you overcome those?

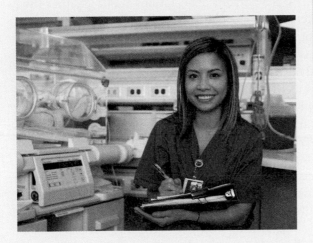

TIPS FOR MAKING YOUR GOALS REALITY

1. **Make a plan.** Research shows it's essential to think ahead about what you'll do and when, says John C. Norcross, PhD, a psychologist at the University of Scranton. Consider what you want to accomplish, what you need to do to meet your goal, and what could stop you from reaching it.

2. **Be realistic.** Remember the saying "Rome wasn't built in a day." Don't set goals that are unachievable.

3. **Be positive.** Consider other goals you've met. Talk with others who have similar goals as yours and get advice for succeeding.

4. **Believe in yourself.** The belief that you will succeed keeps you trying when the going gets tough. Start with quick, short-term goals first and then moving on to bigger ones.

5. **Have a support system.** Having people who care about you helps in good times and bad. Plus their concern can be a big motivator.

6. **Keep your goal in mind.** Think about why you want to meet this goal and the rewards you'll receive for doing so.

7. **Keep a record of your success.** Knowing what you've already accomplished toward your goal helps you stay motivated.

8. **Change your perspective.** Changing viewpoints can change your interpretation. Observing yourself as a third person—looking at yourself from an outside observer's perspective—can help accentuate the changes you've made, says Thomas Gilovich, professor of psychology at Cornell.

9. **Reward yourself.** Set short-term goals and reward yourself when you meet them. This encourages you to set and meet other goals.

10. **Keep trying.** If you falter, pick yourself back up. Remember that mistakes are learning opportunities.

What contributes to my success or failure?

Locus of Control

locus of control
A person's expectations about who or what causes events to occur.

Who or what do you see as responsible for your failures or achievements? In the 1950s, psychologist Julian Rotter suggested that behavior can be explained by whether a person has an internal or external **locus of control.** Locus means "place" in Latin. Locus of control is a person's expectations about whether their behavior is controlled by external or internal factors. People with an internal locus of control are more optimistic. They attribute their decisions to themselves. They take personal responsibility for the outcomes—good or bad. As a result, they feel confident and have high self-esteem.

People with an external locus of control tend to be more negative. They see events that happen as the result of luck, destiny, or other people and outside influences. They don't take credit for the successes they achieve. Their perceived lack of success and control often creates feelings of low self-esteem.

How does your locus of control affect you? The control you perceive you have over your life affects your decisions. If your locus of control is strongly external, then you may feel that you have little control over your life. As a result, you may not see how seeking out resources and finding solutions can ever help. And you won't recognize that studying—or lack of studying—might affect test performance and grades. Rather, you'll continue to view life as something that happens to you rather than something that you make happen. You may think "Why bother? It doesn't matter what I do anyway." You'll tend to see success as something that results from chance or from the intervention of others. You'll also tend to see failure as something that results from nothing you do or are responsible for. If, however, your locus of control is internal, then you see yourself as having the personal power for making decisions that affect the outcome of your life. Thus, you'll see success—and failure—as outcomes that you affect and control.

What if your locus of control is external, and you want it to be more internal? Changing your locus of control is much easier said than done. In fact, some people spend years trying to do so.

Awareness is the first step in altering your locus of control. A second step might be keeping a written record of your successes and failures. The record should answer the following questions: (1) If the result was successful, who or what deserves the credit? (2) If the result was not successful, who or what deserves the blame? (3) How would someone else view this success or failure? (4) If someone else had the same success or failure, how would you view it? (5) If the result was successful, what did you do that affected the success? (6) If the result was not successful, what could you realistically have done to avoid the failure?

In addition to reviewing your own decisions and sources of control, talk to others about how they make decisions and view the results. For instance, after an exam, talk to other students about what they did to prepare for the test and how that affected their grades. Specifically, see if you can find out how successful students justify their grades. Do they think they were just lucky? Do they think the instructor just gives them good grades? Do they think their high school or other academic background prepared them for the course? Do they think they studied hard to get the grades they got?

Being aware that *you* are in control of your future is an important step in getting the future you want. Once you recognize that *you* are the creator of your fate, you become more conscious of the decisions you make and how they'll affect your future.

Who Controls Your Grades?

PART 1: Locus of Control

Directions: Answer Y if you agree with the statement and N if you do not.

_____ **1.** My grades reflect the amount of effort I put into classes.

_____ **2.** I came to college because someone told me it would be a good idea.

_____ **3.** I decided for myself what I would have as a career.

_____ **4.** Some people are good in math, but some people will never understand it.

_____ **5.** I look for easy classes.

_____ **6.** Some instructors either like or dislike me and there's not much I can do about it.

_____ **7.** There are some subjects in which I will never make good grades.

_____ **8.** Some students get by easy in college classes.

_____ **9.** There's nothing I can do to change the way I study.

_____ **10.** I am in control of my life.

_____ **11.** School is more important than partying.

_____ **12.** Friends, family, and work are all more important than getting good grades.

_____ **13.** I study almost every day.

_____ **14.** It's not important to go to class all the time.

_____ **15.** I am and will be successful.

_____ **16.** I am a good writer.

_____ **17.** I hate being late and missing deadlines.

_____ **18.** I am here to take the courses I'm told to take—the courses I want to take have nothing to do with it.

_____ **19.** I like to think through a situation and make decisions for myself.

_____ **20.** I get distracted easily.

_____ **21.** I can always find something to do rather than study.

_____ **22.** It depresses me to know there is no way I can get done all I know I should be doing.

_____ **23.** If things can go wrong, they will.

_____ **24.** I cannot decide what to do with my life.

_____ **25.** I can change the world, even if it is a small change.

_____ **26.** Friends, family, and work have interfered with my study needs.

_____ **27.** I may get my degree but there are more important things in my life.

_____ **28.** Once I make a plan, I stick to it.

Scoring: Circle the answers that match your own answers. Add up the number of matches.

1. N   2. Y   3. N   4. Y   5. Y   6. Y   7. Y   8. Y   9. Y   10. N   11. N   12. Y   13. N   14. Y   15. N
16. N   17. Y   18. N   19. Y   20. Y   21. Y   22. Y   23. Y   24. Y   25. N   26. Y   27. Y   28. N

Total = _____

Interpretation of score:

If your score is between 0 and 13, your locus of control is INTERNAL.
If your score is between 14 and 28, your locus of control is EXTERNAL.

PART 2:   Whose Goals Are They?

Take another look at the goals you set in Activity 1. Then think of the source of these goals: Does the goal come from you or is it something someone else wants from you? Which goals are easier for you to achieve—lifetime, mid-range, short-term, or current goals? How does the source of the goals affect their importance and ease in achieving?

PART 3:   Use the 5Cs

Use the 5C approach to identify one area in your life where your locus of control is external and identify a method for moving that locus of control to within you.

Myths and Realities of Achieving Goals

Am I working toward my goals?

According to Nike, you "just do it" and your goals are achieved . . . unless of course, you're just not doing much of anything. The answer may lie in what you *think* is true—and what *is* true—about achieving the goals you set.

For instance, some people think that there's a right time to work on goals and, in some respects, that may be true. Time, money, resources, and responsibilities affect what you can and can't do. But in other respects, delaying a goal for an arbitrary date is a myth that works against you. You've already decided that the time is right for you to pursue your college goals. What other goals need your attention today?

Maybe you think you should work on only one goal at a time. Then, when you achieve it, you can move on to the next goal. But the reality of life is that it is more about balance than about single-mindedness. College may be your newest goal but don't forget to maintain goals that involve your health, family, friends, work, and so on.

Although you may think that maintaining your status quo is not an acceptable goal, that's a myth. As a new college student, you're literally juggling a number of roles—student, friend, parent, employee, volunteer, and so on. You're also juggling many responsibilities—household, work, study, financial, and health. You really don't have to set new and higher goals in every area of life. Balance in your life is a goal within itself, even if it means maintenance rather than progress.

As a new college student, you—and others—may have certain expectations. You may think that you have to be a "perfect" student with an A+ in every class. You may feel pressure from family members to be perfect. But your reason for attending college (e.g., a 2-year degree, transfer to a 4-year program, certifications, personal fulfillment) affects the kinds of grades you make, and perfection is rarely necessary. For instance, if you want to transfer into a 4-year program that is competitive, you need to focus more on good grades than if you are attending college to complete a certification program. If your goal is to become certified, then your completion of coursework may be more important than perfect grades.

Some people think that setting and achieving goals is too much work. That's also a myth. Certainly, most things worth doing require effort. That's a reality. Goals are no different. But goals should also be something that you *want* to do. Personal goals do require effort, but you should enjoy pursuing them. Why? Because achieving goals aren't just occasional milestones in your life—they *are* your life.

It may seem that when you achieve a goal, you should acknowledge it modestly, if at all. This is completely untrue. While you don't need to brag about achieving your goals, you should definitely acknowledge what you did to achieve them. For instance, your goal might be to make an A in a particular class. And at the end of the term, you achieve that goal. When a friend congratulates you on your success, you respond, "It was no big deal." Rather, what you want to appreciate and savor is the new knowledge and strategies you used to make that A— regular class attendance, active participation in class, and efforts on tests and projects that resulted in the grade you wanted. The reality is that you need to celebrate your successes.

Finally, you may think that you should remain committed to your goal no matter what. The truth is you can change your mind and abandon a goal that is no longer important to you. For instance, maybe you're attending college because you want to become a nurse. But you've already realized that you don't like science and the sight of blood makes you faint. If so, then you need to re-evaluate that goal and work on a different one.

activity 4

Achieving *S.M.A.R.T.E.R.* Academic Goals

Complete the following on a separate sheet of paper.

1. List the courses you are taking, the grades you wish to make, and the biggest challenge you face in each course.

2. What study habits do you need to improve to overcome these obstacles and reach your academic goals?

3. Create a chart that identifies a S.M.A.R.T.E.R. goal for each course you are taking.

Course	Specific	Measureable	Attainable	Realistic	Timely	Evident	Recorded

4. Identify five people who can help you reach your goals.

Grade Point Average

How does GPA contribute to the achievement of my goals?

The main goal in attending college is to get an education. The learning you acquire will remain with you the rest of your life. While it may then seem hypocritical to emphasize grades, grades are how the college system measures learning. Your GPA (grade point average) is also a way that employers judge how hard you worked and how much you learned in college. What then is GPA and how is it calculated?

Traditional grading systems consist of the letter grades A, B, C, D, and F. Other marks include NC (no credit), P (pass), W (withdraw), W-grade (withdraw with a grade), and I (incomplete). NC, P, W, and I grades are not used to compute GPA. Policies about W-grades vary. Some colleges use the W-grade in computing GPA while others do not. Check your college's rules to be sure.

Computation of GPA is a ratio of **quality points,** or the numerical value assigned to each letter grade from A to F, earned to course hours attempted. Quality points use the following scale: A = 4, B = 3, C = 2, D = 1, and F = 0. Because courses vary in credit hours, you cannot always assume that the average of an A, a B, and a C equals a 3.0 GPA. (See Table 4.1.)

All colleges set requirements for obtaining a degree. One of the most important requirements is that you maintain a minimum grade point average (GPA). A college usually places students on academic probation whenever their grade point average is 10 or more quality points below a 2.0 or C average. If you are ever placed on probation, you stay there until your grade point average reaches 2.0 or higher.

> **quality points**
> Numerical value assigned to each letter grade from A to F when given as the final grade in a course; used to calculate grade point average.

Table 4.1 GPA Computation

Course	Grade	Credit Hours	×	Point Equivalent	=	Total Quality Points
English 101	C	3		(C) 2		6
Math 104	D	4		(D) 1		4
Speech 130	B	3		(B) 3		9
Music 106	A	1		(A) 4		4
Biology 103	W	3				0
TOTALS		**11**				**23**

23 QUALITY POINTS/SEMESTER HOURS ATTEMPTED = **23/11** = **2.09** GPA

At the end of the first and each succeeding term, the school requires that you make a 2.0. If you do not, you may stay on probation for a period of time before being academically suspended. The first **suspension** is usually for one regular term (summers often don't count). A second suspension often spans an entire calendar year. Suspensions for colleges other than the one you are currently attending often count in computing this formula. Any additional suspensions will also be for a whole year.

Clearly, you can't take coursework from the suspending college during the time you are suspended. And coursework you take from another school during your suspension most likely will not count toward your degree at your present college. Most colleges will not even admit students who are currently suspended from another school. Once your suspension ends, you must reapply for admission to your institution. Readmission is not guaranteed.

GPA can also affect your eligibility for grants or loans. Federal programs specify what GPA is needed and how many credits must be passed in order to be considered as satisfactory academic progress. College scholarships also have specific GPA requirements to apply for or keep them. Once you've lost a scholarship, it is usually lost forever, no matter how high your GPA climbs.

Once you let your GPA drop, it takes more time than you might imagine to improve it. If it can be done at all and how long it will take depend on your current GPA, your future grades, and the number of credit hours you have left. For instance, perhaps your goal is to transfer to a 4-year college to complete a degree. You now have 45 hours with a GPA of 2.0. You need 83 hours to graduate (including the 15 you are taking this term) and wish to graduate with a 3.3 GPA. To reach your goal, you'll need to maintain a 4.0 for each remaining term you are in school.

If you are considering transferring to a different school, you need to understand that the school may have GPA requirements of its own. It's a good idea for you to know those now before you move very far along your academic plan. These guidelines can usually be found online or by contacting the school and asking they be sent to you. (See Figure 4.2)

Figure 4.2 GPA Scale.

Determining Effects of GPA on Your Future

Grades affect your future. But what grades do you need for the future you want? You may not know exactly what you want to do in the future; but what you want to do may depend on the grades you get. For instance, you may want to transfer to a 4-year school; to do so you will need to be in good standing (2.0 GPA) at your future university. But some programs within the 4-year school may require a higher GPA. First, you need to know what you have now. Then, you need to know what you will need to have in the future.

PART 1: The GPA You Want

1. Identify the number of quality points your institution gives for an A, B, C, D, or F. Then determine how your institution treats W and W-grade.

2. List the courses you are currently taking, the number of credits each course is worth, and the grade you currently have in each course. Then compute the grade point average these grades would give you.

3. List the courses you are currently taking, the number of credits each course is worth, and the grade you wish to make in each course. Then compute the grade point average.

PART 2: Calculating GPA

Raising a GPA is harder than maintaining a GPA. Go to the *GPA Calculator* on this textbook's website (or visit http://appl015.lsu.edu/slas/cas.nsf/$Content/Study+Strategies+Helpful+Links/$FILE/gpa.htm). *Now answer the following:*

1. You have 30 hours of credit and a 2.5 GPA. What GPA do you need if you want to have a 3.5 GPA at 60 hours of credit?

2. You have 45 hours of credit with a 2.8 GPA. You need a 3.2 GPA to transfer to the college you want. Will you be able to do so with 60 hours of credit? Why or why not?

3. You had a good time in your first semester of college but your GPA is now a 1.5 for the 15 hours you took. You want to finish your AA degree (60 hours) with a 3.0. What grades do you need?

What have you learned about your future GPA needs? How will you use that information to set academic goals for this term?

chapter review

Respond to the following on a separate sheet of paper or in your notebook.

1. What's the difference between identifying and specifying goals?

2. Why do you think goals should be stated in positive, rather than negative, form?

3. Which tip for making goals into realities was most surprising to you? Why? Which tip do you think is easiest for you to accomplish? Why?

Which tip do you think is most difficult for you to apply to your life? Why?

4. Did Activity 2 experiences cause you to view your life experiences differently? If so, how?

5. Based on your academic history, what would you predict your chances for success at college would be? Do you think those predictions will be accurate? Why or why not?

6. Identify what you perceive to be your current level of basic, technical, and other skills and your current GPA? How might these affect your ability to achieve—or fail to achieve—your goals?

7. What is backward goal setting?

8. Do you think your locus of control is internal or external? If it is external, what can you do to alter it?

9. List myths of goal setting. Identify the realities of each.

10. Explain how GPA is computed.

Did you accomplish what you wanted to in this chapter? Check the items below that apply to you.

Review the *You Decide* questions that you identified at the beginning of the chapter, but look at them from a new direction. If you didn't check an item below, review that module until you feel you can confidently apply the strategies to your own situation. However, the best ideas are worthless unless they are put into effect. Use the 5Cs to help you decide what information you found most helpful in the chapter and how you plan to use it. Record your comments after the statements below.

☐ 4.1 I know what my goals are.

_____

_____

☐ 4.2 I have a realistic plan for achieving my goals.

_____

_____

☐ 4.3 I can identify what contributes to my success or failure.

_____

_____

☐ 4.4 I am working toward my goals.

_____

_____

☐ 4.5 I understand how GPA contributes to the achievement of my goals.

_____

_____

perspectives

How can your community college experience help you achieve your goals? In the following passage, Philip Berry describes how he used his community college experiences as a launching pad for his goals.

Think about and answer the questions that follow.

1. Berry discusses how he used community college as a stepping stone to a 4-year degree. What is your reason for attending?

2. Explain the phrase "short-term pain for long-term gain." How does this relate to your goal setting? Provide some examples from your own life.

3. Explain the saying, "When life gives you lemons, make lemonade." How did Berry accomplish this? How can or have you?

4. What do you see as the main idea of the last three paragraphs?

5. Berry has two graduate degrees. Identify each one, and explain how you think this combination might contribute to Berry's success in his current position at Colgate-Palmolive.

6. Working nights while going to college was a decision Berry describes in the passage. Explain how he might have used the 5C process to make this choice.

   A. What was Berry's **C**hallenge?

   B. What key **C**hoices might have been open to Berry?

   C. What would have been the major **C**onsequence(s) of each choice?

   D. What do you think made Berry **C**hoose to work at night?

   E. In what way(s) might Berry have **C**hecked the outcome of the decision?

Since graduating from BMCC (Borough of Manhattan Community College) in 1971, Philip Berry has become vice president of global workplace initiatives at Colgate-Palmolive; he is one of the "100 Most Powerful Minority Leaders in New York City," according to Crain's New York Business *magazine, and vice chairperson of the CUNY (City University of New York) Board of Trustees.*

"BMCC had an excellent marketing curriculum and a good reputation," he said. "I got a very sound foundation in that area, and they also gave me perspectives on the whole business world—not just marketing, but accounting, economics and finance." While there, Berry took courses that would be a foundation for his goals in life, from his move to CUNY's Queens College for his Bachelor's degree, to his career when school was over. "That was how I used BMCC," said Berry, who went on to get his Master's from Columbia University's School of Social Work, and an M.B.A. from Xavier University. "It was a great launching pad for me. It really helped me to transition."

But he didn't have it easy, as is the story for most BMCC students. To pay for his education, Berry worked 11 p.m. to 7 a.m., then came to classes at 8 a.m. "It was difficult, but that was what I needed to do to pay for my education. I always kept in mind that this was only for a short period of time," he said. "That kind of context helps you feel a lot more comfortable about what you're doing. It helps you to understand that this is short-term pain for long-term gain."

Berry said those leaving BMCC this spring should always maintain focus—whether it's while searching for a job, when settled into one, or even as a student elsewhere. "Stay focused on what it is you want to do, and be able to define that very clearly," he said. "Understand what your strengths are, and your development needs, and set some goals for yourself, and then a mission for yourself, so that you can understand exactly how to realize those goals and objectives within an organization. You have to be very strategic, and you have to be willing to work hard."

One way of doing this successfully is to keep a three-year plan, Berry said. "Your one-year horizon should be in the context of a three-year plan," he said. "I have had a rolling three-year plan in my mind ever since I was at BMCC, and I update it every three years."

Finally, Berry said that while remaining focused, graduates should remain flexible as well. "All of the jobs and opportunities don't happen to be in New York City," he said. "When you look at BMCC, it's an extremely diverse college. You have students from all kinds of other countries, and they uproot themselves from their country and they come here to the United States looking for opportunity. People here ought to have that same degree of flexibility to go wherever they have to in order to get the job or opportunity. "As old adage goes, he said: "When life gives you lemons, make lemonade."

reflecting on decisions

Now that you've learned about setting goals, what can you do this week that will contribute to the achievement of one of your future goals?

MAKE A DIFFERENCE **DAY**

Make A Difference Day is a national day with the goal of helping others. Created by *USA Weekend* Magazine and supported by its 600 carrier newspapers, Make A Difference Day is an annual event that takes place on the fourth Saturday of every October. In addition to the good done on this day, some projects done on Make A Difference Day are selected for honors, headlines and charitable donations. For example, Paul Newman and the Newman's Own Foundation provide $10,000 donations to the charities of each of 10 national honorees. These honorees, plus others, are highlighted in an April edition of *USA Weekend* Magazine. Projects can be big or small and done in conjunction with another group or alone. Use the 5Cs—Define the **C**hallenge; Identify the **C**hoices; Predict the **C**onsequences; **C**hoose an option; **C**heck your outcome—to identify a project that you could do to make a difference.

◀ **CHOOSING TO SERVE**

R E V I E W

Skim the notes you made throughout the chapter. How does the content fit together? What information is still unclear? Were your learning goals met? Can you answer the review questions and define terms?

◀ **CHOOSING TO BE AN ACTIVE LEARNER**

CHAPTER **FIVE**

Decisions for Managing Time

Time management is life management. Explain how the way you manage your time reflects the way you manage your life.

YOU DECIDE

To *wonder* means to think or have curiosity about. Things and ideas you wonder about often mask a need for a decision. Check the items below that apply to you.

In terms of time management, I've been wondering . . .

- ☐ 5.1 Do I ever put assignments off until the last minute?
- ☐ 5.2 How does what I have to accomplish this term affect my weekly schedule?
- ☐ 5.3 Am I able to get my more important tasks done each day?
- ☐ 5.4 How does what I think affect my time management?
- ☐ 5.5 How can I avoid feeling overextended?
- ☐ 5.6 What online time management tools can help me organize?
- ☐ 5.7 How does commuting to campus affect me as a student?

Each of these decision points corresponds to the numbered modules that follow. Turn to the module for immediate help.

CHOOSING TO BE AN ACTIVE LEARNER

SURVEY

Before reading this chapter, prepare for learning. Purposefully skim the title, introduction, headings, and graphics. As you survey, decide what information you already know and what information is new to you.

QUESTION

Change each section's heading into a question. This forms your learning goal for reading.

READ

Read the section without marking. Reread and mark key information that answers your question.

RECITE

Stop after each section and make sure you understood the content. Organize or summarize content and make notes.

Congratulations! You have just received $86,400 from a rich aunt! Unfortunately, your aunt is a little bit odd. To get the $86,400, you must agree to the following:

1. You must spend all of the money in the next 24 hours.
2. Stores will be closed part of this time. But that's not a problem. You'll need to get some sleep.
3. You must attend all your classes today. Your professor accepts no excuses, and your rich aunt believes in education.
4. If you wish, your family and friends, as well as the other people you meet today, can help you spend the $86,400.

Take just a moment and decide what you will choose to buy. Jot your choices in the space below.

With my $86,400, I choose . . .

Now imagine that someone stole some of your $86,400 or that you carelessly lost part of it. How would you feel? What items on your list would you have to give up?

Having $86,400 would, indeed, be wonderful. But unless you really do have a rich aunt, that's unlikely to happen today. What you do have, however, is 86,400 seconds each day to spend as you choose. What you do and how you spend your time can take you closer—or farther—from the goals you set.

Time management problems often come from an inability to organize time and from ineffective self-talk. Like other challenges you face, you can change your behaviors based on the decisions you make. This chapter gives you tools to help manage time more effectively and shows you how to use 5C process (Define the **C**hallenge; Identify **C**hoices; Predict **C**onsequences; **C**hoose an option; **C**heck your outcome) to achieve your goals.

Overcoming Procrastination

Do I ever put assignments off until the last minute?

People put things off and fail to complete goals for many reasons. One of the most common misconceptions about **procrastination** is that it results from laziness. Another is that people just don't care enough about the work to do it. Generally, if you've had enough drive and ambition to get into a college, laziness is not your problem. Lack of **closure,** unfinished business, and **burnout** are far more common reasons for procrastination.

Closure results when you divide a task into manageable goals, list them, and check them off as you complete them. Closure helps you avoid procrastination. For instance, suppose your history professor assigns three chapters of reading. If your goal is to read all three chapters, you may feel overwhelmed. This feeling will most likely cause you to put the assignment off.

A more effective way to complete the assignment involves dividing the assignment into smaller goals. Think of each chapter as a separate goal. You could even subdivide the chapters into sections. You experience success by completing each section or chapter. Even if you fail to complete all three chapters in one sitting, your progress results in feelings of success.

Without closure, changing tasks too often wastes time. Each time you switch, you lose momentum. You may be unable to change gears fast enough or find yourself out of the studying mood. In addition, when you return to the first task, you lose time. This happens because you have to review where you were and what steps remain. Often you solve this problem by determining how much time you have to work. If the time available is short (that is, an hour or less), focus on one task. Alternate tasks when you have more time. Completing one task or a large portion of a task contributes to the feeling of closure.

Sometimes, when working on a long-term assignment (e.g., writing a paper, completing a project), other unrelated tasks (e.g., a more pressing assignment, going to work, carpool) often take priority. If this occurs, take time to write a few notes before moving to the new task. The clarity of your thinking or the status of your progress may seem fresh at the time. It's always possible, though, that you'll forget what you were doing after a while. Your notes could include the goal of the task, where you are toward its completion, and a list of questions or next steps. You need to store materials and notes for the project together either in hard copy or electronic form. This provides important organization when you return to your work.

procrastination
Delaying or putting off assignments or other activities.

closure
The positive feeling that occurs when you complete a task.

burnout
Physical or emotional exhaustion.

tips

TIPS FOR AVOIDING PROCRASTINATION

- Focus on how completion of tasks or assignments leads to achievement of goals.
- Divide work into small, manageable chunks.
- Set deadlines and share them with others. You're more likely to finish if you know someone may ask about your commitment.
- After you complete one task, plan the next one. This helps you achieve closure and saves time when you prepare to begin again.
- Reward yourself for completing a task, especially one that is difficult or unpleasant.
- Never stop when the going gets tough. Stopping then makes it more likely you will have a hard time starting again.
- If you get stuck, don't be afraid to ask for help. Friends, family, and faculty are available resources.
- Establish a routine. Having a set study time makes it harder for you to procrastinate.
- Create a study environment. Like having a routine, having a place to study makes it more likely that you *will* study when you get there.
- Let technology work for, not against, you. Make conscious choices about how and when you will use technology to lighten, instead of add to, your workload.

Burnout also contributes to procrastination. It often results when you work without breaks. Burnout is odd in that its causes are the same as its symptoms. Fatigue, boredom, and stress are both signs and causes of burnout. Tough course loads and cramming add to burnout. Balancing work, family, and academic schedules can overburden you. And while it may be fun, an overloaded social or family calendar often results in burnout. Burnout commonly occurs around exam times such as midterms and finals, in December as the result of the long, unbroken stretch between Labor Day and Thanksgiving holidays, and at the end of the academic year.

Balancing break time and worktime helps you avoid burnout. Thus, you need to plan for breaks as well as study time. A break does not have to be recreational to be effective. It simply might be a change from one task to another, such as switching from working math problems to responding to an online discussion question. Although you sometimes lose momentum by switching tasks, doing so is better than burning out. Another way to avoid burnout is to leave flexibility in your schedule. If you schedule commitments too tightly, you won't complete your goals and achieve closure. This defeats you psychologically because you fail to do what you planned. This defeat may lead you to procrastinate the next time a commitment appears.

Not long ago, technology was hailed as a time-saver. Computers would shorten work days. Instead of going to the library, you could find what you needed online. But in many cases, technology extends, rather than shortens, worktime. Instead of only getting mail once a day, e-mail arrives continuously. Instead of getting news once a day in the newspaper or on television, news is updated 24/7. Rather than working on a paper only when the library is open, online research can continue all night. As a new college student, you're probably adding a new layer of technology to what you already use. Students are advised to check college e-mail accounts and online coursework daily. Pay attention to when and how long you use technology as well as how you use it. Although you may feel productive, you may be using technology to keep you from doing other tasks.

Procrastination can also be affected by your learning style. For instance, if you have global preferences, you may be a spontaneous multitasker. You might look at the big picture more than the details. But too many spontaneous choices and too many tasks may overwhelm you. You may be putting off tasks because you don't have enough time or energy. You may forget about the details. This will appear as procrastination even if you consciously don't realize it is.

Why Do You Procrastinate?

Think of the last time you procrastinated on a task. What do you think contributed to your procrastination? Then identify your next major assignment. Use the 5C process (Define the **C**hallenge; Identify **C**hoices; Predict **C**onsequences; **C**hoose an option; **C**heck your outcome) and what you have learned about closure, unfinished business, technology overuse, burnout, and learning style to create a schedule, in the space below, for completing this assignment while avoiding your usual procrastination problems.

How does what I have to accomplish this term affect my weekly schedule?

Managing Your Term and Week

Most people think of time as being divided into parts—days, weeks, months, terms, or years. The concept of *day* or *week* is just a way of dividing what really occurs in a continuous form. Managing a term involves relating the time available and information you need to learn into one big picture. This helps you prioritize and plan more effectively in order to get your work done and achieve your goals.

Many students organize time by carrying small planners or by using the calendars on their cell phones. They record everything they need to do; but they

A weekly calendar helps you recognize and set priorities.

can only look at one week or month of the planner's calendar at a time or they can only see the activities for a specific day on their cell phones. So, in looking at the current week, they might see few assignments due and no tests scheduled. They breathe a sigh of relief and relax . . . until the next week when they turn the page or get an event alarm on their cell phones. They find that three major tests and an important paper are due in the next few days. This forces them into a frantic, cramming mode. You want to avoid this.

A term calendar lets you see a whole term's requirements at one time. This helps you become proactive in planning ahead during weeks with few assignments, rather than reactive by panicking at the last minute. Of course, the best time to create a term planner is at the beginning of a term. But it's never too late to organize for the rest of the term. The twelve tips we gave you for your first week in college (take a look at them again in Chapter 1) provide you with the steps you need. Just start with the current month and continue through the end of the term.

Looking at your term calendar, you may feel overwhelmed by the number and difficulty of the tasks before you. Luckily, not all assignments are due at the same time. You can get work done bit by bit, week by week. A weekly schedule helps you identify fixed commitments and free time. Reviewing your term calendar activities on a weekly basis helps you begin to set **priorities** and schedule them into your weekly plan.

priorities
The people or items that you feel are most important to you.

Steps in Planning Your Week

1. **List fixed commitments first.** These include classes, meals, work, family responsibilities, sleep, travel time to class, and so on. Allow a realistic amount of time for each activity. For instance, commuting times differ by time of day, amount of traffic, and route taken. You may spend more time getting to campus at rush hour than at other times of the day.

2. **Plan to review.** Just as you tend to forget the name of someone you meet only once, you tend to forget information you see or hear only once. Set aside a few minutes before each class to review your notes. You can often do this in the time you have between getting to class and waiting for it to start. This review jogs your memory. Then preview that day's topic to begin building a memory. Leave a few minutes following each class to review, correct, and add to your notes. This provides an additional review and helps you fill in any gaps in understanding you might have while lecture information is still fresh in your mind. If you are taking online classes, you can start your online session in much the same way. Complete a quick review of what you last learned. Preview that session's content. When the session ends, take a few moments to review what you did and learned.

3. **Estimate your time needs.** By the third or fourth week in the term, you probably can estimate how long it takes to do certain tasks without interruption. For instance, you may be able to read a chapter in an hour. You may be able to work 10 math problems in a half-hour. Be aware, however, that work and/or family commitments affect your ability to schedule as much study time as your course load may require.

4. **Identify and maximize your use of remaining free time.** As you schedule time to study, complete projects, or refine skills, look for ways to group activities. For example, if you have to buy supplies for a project, try to use that time to get other items you need rather than making two trips.

5. **Plan ahead.** Schedule completion dates prior to the due date to allow for unexpected delays.

6. **Schedule recreational breaks.** This helps you avoid burnout.

activity 2
Making a Weekly Schedule

Use your term calendar to develop a weekly plan for next week using the Steps in Planning Your Week list in module 5.2.

GROUP APPLICATION: Bring your weekly plan to class and compare it with those of other students. How do your priorities and commitments differ from theirs?

Daily To-Do Lists

Am I able to get my more important tasks done each day?

Once you set your weekly priorities, you need to create a daily to-do list—an agenda of items to complete that day. While many people make such lists, few people use them well. The secret lies in prioritizing your activities. Without setting priorities, most people tend to do those items that are most fun or finished most quickly. The dreadful or difficult tasks—those you really need to complete—get left until later. Sometimes later never arrives because you don't get around to getting started. Prioritizing your list and scheduling a specific time (from blocks of free time on your weekly schedule) to work on each item help you make decisions get the work done.

To create a to-do list, you list (1) that day's commitments transferred from your weekly calendar and (2) any items left over from the previous day. You add other items as you think of them. Your next step is to rank the items in the order of their importance. Next, you look for free blocks of time in your day and schedule tasks for specific times.

Chances are you may not complete your to-do list by the end of the day. But if you ranked your commitments, you will have finished the most important items. Keep in mind that what is a priority today may not be a priority tomorrow. Buying gas for the car today may be a top priority if the gauge has been on empty for three days. Buying gas for the car when you still have a half-tank left is less important.

What's the best way to set learning priorities? You might think you should save the best for last. But in time management, you need to use the best time you have available to work on your most important, most difficult, or least interesting courses. These require your greatest concentration and effort. You'll always have enough energy to do easy or interesting tasks later. Most people—even night owls—tend to think more clearly during daylight hours. Specifically, more efficient mental processing (such as solving difficult problems or synthesizing ideas for a paper) and short-term memory learning (for example, memorizing a speech) occur in morning hours. If you work, consider scheduling study time before work or during lunch. If you have family responsibilities, consider getting up earlier than the rest of the family and studying while they are occupied during the day.

On the other hand, you often can get the best results from long-term memory activities (such as learning concepts) and tasks requiring physical activity (for example, lab classes and course projects) during afternoon hours. Unless you work or have other afternoon commitments, it's a good idea to protect those time periods (from friends, activities, technology, or yourself) and use them for the academic or technical activities. It also helps to save the last hours of the day for routine, physical and/or recreational activities.

You also need to think about how you use waiting time. At the beginning of this chapter, you learned that you have 86,400 seconds each day. One way to cut down on wasted time is to rearrange your schedule so that you do things at off times. If you can commute at a later time, you'll miss the early-morning rush hour. If you can eat an early or late lunch, your wait in line or for service will be shortened. If you can go to the post office or bank in the middle of the morning or afternoon, you'll miss the people who take care of business before work or at lunch. You can use a laptop's built-in microphone to create your own MP3 study files and play those as you exercise or drive. If you review flash cards as you wait or listen to podcasts of lectures as you commute, you'll have more time to do the things you want or need to do.

You need to design your to-do lists to foster feelings of closure and achievement. For instance, as you divide a lengthy project (e.g., a research paper) into manageable tasks (e.g., select a topic, do the research, write rough draft, etc.), you estimate how long you need to complete each step. You schedule these intermediate points on your term planner and weekly schedule (select topic Wednesday, research topic Thursday, complete rough draft Sunday). Then, you add these as appropriate to your daily to-do list. These interim deadlines ensure that you will finish without rushing at the last minute. Checking them off your daily to-do list gives you a feeling of progress toward your goal.

If you create your weekly schedule at the end of the previous week and tomorrow's daily to-do list at the end of the day, you will find that you manage time more effectively. At the end of the week or day, what you still have to do is

Table 5.1 To-Do Lists or Not-To-Do Lists?

Common Reasons People Don't Use To-Do Lists	The Reality
Takes too much time to make the list.	It's only the first list that takes time. Once you start, you remove things from the list that are completed. You add new items.
Can't find the list when I need it.	Keep your list in same place. If you use a computer, consider keeping a list as a digital document. Then, you can copy and e-mail it to yourself for reference at school.
I don't need it. I can keep track of everything.	College life adds a new layer of complexity to what you're doing. Your brain has a limited memory capacity. Keep what you need to do on a list and save your memory for other, more important information.
I'm not sure what to put on the list.	Start with information on your weekly calendar. Add other priorities. As you develop your list-making skills, you'll get a better idea of what you need to include.
Lists are too confining.	A list is just a starting point. Changing priorities can change the list.
When I look at everything on the list, I just get discouraged.	Don't put everything on your daily to do list . . . just those things that need to be—and can be—done that day. If you have too many items, you need to rethink your priorities and commitments.
I made a list, but never looked at it.	Place your list in a place where you will see it (e.g., refrigerator door, kitchen table, mirror).

fresh in your mind. If you wait until the start of the next week or day, you'll have to re-create where you were on each project or assignment. If your list is already prepared, you'll be ready to go.

You might feel confined by having a list of tasks, but that's not the point. While you want to stick to your schedule, you also need to remain flexible. Your time management plan is designed to help you structure your time and achieve your goals. Its purpose is not to bind you to an inflexible schedule. If you get started on a project and want to work on it longer than you planned rather than moving to another task, you can choose to do so without guilt. Even if you decide you need a break rather than work more math, you can choose to do so. The key is knowing you are making choices and that you will return to your schedule.

Finally, you should regularly review and revise your time management procedures. You want to know where your time management problems start and end. If you're not happy with your progress, you need to analyze how you spend your time and what keeps you from spending your time effectively. From time to time, you should ask yourself, "Is what I'm doing now the best use of my time? If not, why not?" Or, at the end of the day, you need to compare your scheduled to-do list with what you actually did. What or who altered your schedule and why?

Making a To-Do List

activity 3

Create a prioritized to-do list for tomorrow. Follow it. At the end of the day, review your to-do list. Evaluate its effectiveness and accuracy. What better ways can you plan and manage your time? Create a prioritized to-do list for the next day. Use the space below to draft your to-do list.

How does what I think affect my time management?

Choices about Self-Talk

self-talk
The internal communication that you have with yourself; can be positive or negative; affects time management and self-confidence.

child
The part of you that wants to have *fun* and have it *now*.

critic
Role that suggests that you are unworthy or incapable.

adult
One of the three inner dialogue voices, the part of you that thinks analytically and solves problems rationally.

Do you talk to yourself? Of course you do. You constantly carry on a mental conversation with yourself. This mental conversation—your thoughts—or **self-talk**—directs and shapes your behavior. Some self-talk is informational. It might consist of mental rehearsal of what you are learning (e.g., a math formula) or an ongoing commentary about your daily life (e.g., it looks like rain). But other kinds of self-talk can affect your use of time. Worrying, procrastination, overcommitment, unfinished business, lack of self-discipline, and indecision often result in self-sabotage occurring from your **child** (the part of you that wants to have *fun* and have it *now*) or **critic** (voice that suggests that you are unworthy or incapable) roles and their self-talk. Both negatively affect your ability to achieve your goals.

Recognizing these roles and the kind of self-talk each uses are the first steps to controlling them and regaining your ability to think in the role of the **adult** (the part of you that thinks analytically and solves problems rationally). The role in which you function affects the way you work and the way in which you perceive problems.

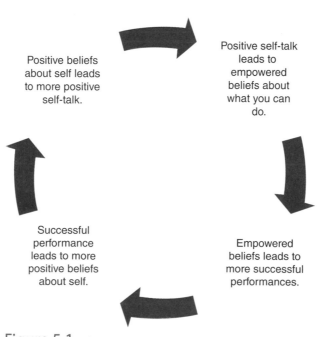

Figure 5.1 The Positive Self-Talk Cycle.

Who Says What: Self-Talk of the Child, Critic, and Adult Roles

CHILD COMMENTS

I'm too hungry/tired/thirsty to work on this now.

I don't feel well.

I don't want to do this.

I wish I hadn't taken this course.

This is boring.

I think I'll skip this next class. The professor is dull.

I don't see how this assignment will help me when I graduate.

CRITIC COMMENTS

This is too much for me to do. I feel so overwhelmed.

I don't know where to start on a project like this.

I should be able to handle a job, family responsibilities, and going to school full-time.

This is too hard for me. Everyone said I wouldn't make it.

I studied last time and I failed. No matter how hard I try, I'll fail again.

Everyone in my family is bad at math.

I've always been an A student. What's the matter with me?

Maybe I am just not cut out for college.

ADULT COMMENTS

This is difficult, but I have a plan.

I didn't do well on the last test, but I know what to do now.

I can do this, one step at a time.

Other people have learned this, and I can too.

This isn't very interesting, but I know I still need to do it.

These problems are hard, but I've learned hard things before.

Child Behaviors

The child is the fun-loving part of you that lives in the present without worrying about the future. When the child within you gains control, you avoid those tasks that seem dull, boring, or too difficult. Talking with friends, partying, and other leisure activities prevent the child from ever getting to work.

The child often responds to logic and rewards. If you find that you fail to start some activities because they're boring or unappealing, remind yourself that every career and job involves some tasks that just aren't fun. Learning to cope with such tasks in college will benefit you on future jobs. But you may find that the future is so far in the distance that you just can't see the benefit. In that case, create a reward system (e.g., a short break to do something fun for small tasks; larger rewards for more complex tasks).

▶ Critic Comments

The role of the critic causes you to doubt your abilities, goals, and self. The critic predicts failure at every turn. It says that a task is too hard for you or that you don't have the right background or skills to get the job done. With such encouragement, why even try?

Worry is the critic's chief activity. By definition, worry has no productive outcome. Thus, instead of studying, the critic worries about studying. Instead of logically and calmly taking a test for which you have prepared, the critic insists that you're not ready and you're doomed to fail. When worry causes you to avoid a task or freeze from fear, you find it hard to do the task well. This results in poor performance that supports the critic's claim. When you find yourself worrying, ask, "Am I worrying or am I solving?" It's OK to have worries, but you need to recognize them for what they are and move on to a solution. The 5C process helps you do so.

Worrying also results in overcommitment that stems from a desire for approval. If you don't agree to go places with your friends, the critic worries that you may not be invited again. If you don't agree to do everything anyone asks you to do (e.g., at school, work or home), you fear people might think you can't cope. The critic suggests that you should be able to do more and more, if only you managed your time well. But the truth is that overcommitment results in a list of tasks that all the superheroes in the world couldn't complete on a good day. If that's the case, why should you be able to do so?

You can control overcommitment by the way you use your calendar. When someone asks you to do something, your first response should be, "Let me check my calendar." As you do so, you think, "Is this something I really want to do or have time to do?" As you analyze your other commitments, you also should also ask yourself, "Would agreeing take me closer to my goals?" If the answer to your questions is yes, then add it to your list. If not, graciously refuse. If you feel guilty or pressured, remember that your "no" allows someone else to say "yes."

Perfectionism is a by-product of the critic and worry as well. The critic says that if you are to do something, it must be done perfectly. You must be the perfect friend, student, roommate, relative, worker, and on and on. Like overcommitment, it's hard to do everything and do it perfectly every time.

Perfectionism leads to procrastination and burnout. If you get a late start, you can logically say that a low grade resulted from a lack of time rather than to what the critic says was a lack of ability. Or, you may find yourself overcome with indecision. If you can't decide, you can't get started. If you can't get started, you can't be expected to meet the critic's standards of perfection. As a result, you fall behind and don't finish the job. You can avoid perfectionism by deciding what must be done well and what does not need to be completed to those standards. For instance, writing a paper needs to be done well. Handwriting on your notes does not.

The critic is a difficult role to control because it strongly influences your thoughts and behavior. The self-talk it generates often has been internalized as a belief system. Thus, when you refute the critic's worries through logic, your heart often fails to go along. The solution is to replace those worries with other thoughts.

What's the difference? You really can't *not* think about something once you identify what that concept is. For example, if you try to *not* think about elephants, it's too late; you've already thought about them. Instead, you replace the thought. So, don't think "I'm not going to worry that I will get nervous and forget all I know." Instead, think, "I know this. I will do the best I can. I will be calm and careful. I'll take it a question at a time."

Replacing thoughts sounds deceptively easy. But if you have a strong critic voice within you, controlling it will be one of the most difficult—and rewarding—goals you achieve.

Adult Actions

The adult in you provides the voice of reason and logic. The adult knows that some tasks are no fun but must be finished anyway. The adult then musters the internal motivation to begin dull and distasteful tasks and see them through. To do so, the adult must outtalk the critic, stop worrying, and start solving.

The 5C process is particularly applicable to study problems. When it's time to study, the adult in you identifies the challenge and thinks about your choices. "What do I have to learn? What would be the best way to learn this?" Then you consider the consequences in terms of which study methods best match the materials you have to learn and the amount of time you have available. Once you make a choice of study methods, you begin studying. From time to time, you stop and check the outcome of your choice: how well your study process is working.

As an adult, you can also use procrastination to an advantage. Suppose you have a problem and decide to postpone its solution. What seems to be simple procrastination is actually a good choice. The difference is in why you procrastinated. For instance, you may be wondering if you should drop a course after the first month of class. You've regularly attended class. Your grades are good. However, your financial status shows that you need to increase your work hours. Logically, you decide you cannot do well in the course and work more hours. What looks like procrastination (e.g., taking the class next term) is actually a logical decision based on the reality of the situation.

How to Motivate Yourself to Get Things Done

1. You can do almost anything for 10 minutes, and you can choose to work on a task for only that amount of time. At the end of the time, you may find that the task was not as dreadful as you thought. You can choose to work for another 10 minutes. Or, you can quit and schedule another 10 minutes for another day or study session.

2. Forming or joining a study group motivates you because if you know others are depending on you to prepare and meet, you may be psychologically more inclined to do so. (See Chapter 8 for more on study groups.)

3. Varying your tasks and active study prevents the child in you from getting bored and losing interest.

4. Use visualizations to your advantage. When you sense yourself losing focus, stop and visualize the content of the information you're studying. How could you picture or sketch an algebra problem? How would you visualize the process of mitosis? Can you sense the imagery in a poem?

5. Monitor your concentration. Select a short time period (e.g., 30 minutes) and write a check mark each time you become distracted. The goal of the game is to decrease the number of check marks within the specified time period (and increase your attention span).

activity 4

What Are You Saying to Yourself?

1. Identify a time management situation that causes you problems. What child statements do you make to yourself that perpetuate the problem? What critic statements?

2. Draw a line down the center of the sheet of paper. In the left column, list all of the child and critic self-talk statements you have used in this particular time management situation. In the right-hand column, list examples of adult self-talk you can substitute in that situation.

3. Create a circle graph that shows your amounts of self-talk for critic, child, and adult roles.

4. Create a second circle graph to show how you would prefer to allocate your self-talk among child, critic, and adult roles.

5. Use the 5C process to analyze and resolve your situation so that the two graphs are more alike. What **C**hallenge do you face? What **C**hoices are available? What are the **C**onsequences of each choice? What do you think you will **C**hoose to do? How could you **C**heck the outcome, or the results, of your choices?

GROUP APPLICATION: Compare answers with others in your class. What similarities and differences did you notice? What do you think caused those similarities and differences?

Achieving Balance

You're doing it all: full-time student, part-time employee, team player in intramural sports, scholarship student, Web designer for a campus organization, and member of the debate team. How do you do it all?

You're doing it all, too: full-time student, full-time parent, part-time employee, member of the National Guard, scholarship student, Spanish Club treasurer, and member of a student government committee. How do you manage everything?

So, how are you doing? Most students feel overwhelmed by the number of roles they hold. The truth is, you may not be able to do it all and do it well. At some point, you must reassess your priorities. Your goal is to achieve balance, not lose your balance!

Unrealistic expectations may add to your situation. Perhaps you plan to complete your associate's degree and transfer to a four-year college. Your goal is to finish your coursework in four years and graduate with a 4.0 average. If you are a traditional freshman student who begins college at age 17 or 18, this means that you will finish at age 21 or 22. And then what? You get to work for the rest of your life! If you work until you're 65, this means you will work for the next 43 or 44 years. It may be better to take an extra semester and do well in your classes.

If you are a nontraditional student, you may feel compelled to complete your courses quickly in order to make up for lost time in your next career. You may feel that you need to take the maximum number of hours. Perhaps you see the suggested course loads in your college catalog as written in stone. For instance, suppose you are working toward an associate's degree in nursing. The catalog suggests that you take 17–18 course hours each term. But catalog suggestions are merely that—suggestions. Students who are financially independent and who have no responsibilities beyond academic ones might consider such heavy course loads. In truth, few students take more than 15 hours per semester. That's because there is more to getting an education than just taking courses. You owe it to yourself to take full advantage of the college experience.

Adding college to an already busy life can be overwhelming.

Keep in mind, too, that some academic goals (for instance, transferring to a four-year college, admission to programs with limited enrollments, and so on) require a show of academic excellence. If you schedule too many classes, you cannot make the grades you need to accomplish your longer-term goals. While grades are important, many employers prefer to see a prospective employee that can handle a variety of tasks in addition to academic pursuits.

Values also play a key role in achieving balance. If what you do as a student conflicts with what you believe is important in life, you will not feel fulfilled no matter how well you do academically. For instance, you might value academic achievement and family. But doing well as a full-time student takes too much time from your role as a parent. Taking fewer courses at a time might take you longer to graduate but allow you to both raise a family and complete a degree in a way that is a better fit with your values. Or perhaps you like to be involved in campus or civic organizations. You value what you learn as a result but find that your grades are suffering. Again you could choose to take fewer classes in order to serve in organizations and make the grades you want. In both cases, your choice might take you another year or so to complete your degree. If you are a traditionally aged student, an extra year means you still get to work for the next 40 or so years instead of the next 41 or 42 years. Seen from that perspective, the trade-off is worth achieving the balance you want. If you are a nontraditionally aged student, the trade-off is a decision you will need to make with your life goals in mind.

Thus, whatever your academic goals, view them in terms of your life goals (see Chapter 4) and values (see Chapter 2). Choose to take the time you need to get the experiences and education that will take you closer to the goals you set while maintaining the life you want to lead.

activity 5 — How Am I Doing with Time Management?

For each of the following statements, put an X by the one word (agree, disagree, unsure) that best describes you general experience and actions.

	Agree	Disagree	Unsure
1. I have difficulty thinking about the future and setting long-range goals.			
2. My long-range goals are too far in the future to predict a time frame for completion.			
3. I file things for future reference but often forget to refer to them later on.			
4. I grab odd, spare bits of time in order to chip away at relatively complex tasks.			
5. I handle a glut of information by categorizing things and then going back to deal with them when I have a chance.			
6. I put decisions and problems on "hold" until I have a block of time to give to them.			
7. My intentions—my plans and goals—are my own business. I rarely announce them to others.			
8. I know where I want to be in 5 years; deciding how to get there is the hard part.			
9. I do what I have to do at the time; it's confusing to think about tomorrow or next week.			
10. Making daily or weekly lists makes me feel overwhelmed.			
11. I'm too busy to plan each week's schedule.			
12. I always have to alter my schedule, so I often don't bother to create one.			
13. Making a "to-do" list is a waste of time.			
14. Writing a "to-do" list down is a waste of paper; I keep a "to-do" list in my head.			
15. I can make a list, but I find it difficult to decide in what order to do things.			

	Agree	Disagree	Unsure
16. When I have many tasks to complete, I plunge into any one in order to get started.			
17. I like to work my way into difficult or boring tasks by doing the easier ones first.			
18. I don't think about my peak energy time; I have to perform well all of the time.			
19. Things often take longer than I plan, so I seem to be in a perpetual state of "catch-up."			
20. I tend to procrastinate since I work better under pressure.			
21. I make plans and set aside time for projects but don't usually use that time as planned; other things seem to get in the way.			
22. I usually run to answer the telephone when it rings.			
23. Most major household/office responsibilities seem to fall on my shoulders.			
24. Piles of paper in my house/office are getting out of control.			
25. I usually say "yes" when I'm asked to be on a committee, bake a cake, do some optional overtime, etc.			
26. Others don't do things as I like them done, so I do them myself.			
27. I often solve other people's problems.			
28. Each time I start something, I seem to be interrupted by family, friends, co-workers.			
29. People and situations to whom I am responsible (small children, spouse, elderly parents, work) really do make demands on my time.			
30. I seem to add to instead of eliminate activities.			
31. I will not lower my standards just to save a bit of time.			
TOTALS OF EACH COLUMN			

RESULTS

Look at the totals in the "Agree" columns. Agreement with more than 4 for questions 1–8 indicates problems in Area 1: goals or setting them. Agreement with more than 6 for questions 9–20 indicates problems in Area 2: prioritizing or short-term goals. Agreement with more than 6 for questions 21–31 indicates problems in Area 3: controlling your environment.

Use the 5C process and your results above to respond to the following:

1. Based on your results, what area is most problematic for you? Within that area, how do you define the most important **C**hallenge?

2. What **C**hoices do you have for managing time and achieving balance?

3. Identify **C**onsequences by describing what would logically happen as the result of each option.

4. What will you **C**hoose to do to meet this challenge?

5. Identify how you will **C**heck the outcome of your choice.

GROUP APPLICATION: Share individual answers with your group. What similarities and differences do you discover among your group's answers? What factors might contribute to these similarities?

What online time management tools can help me organize?

Using Online Time Management Tools

Are you online more than you're offline? Do you have a cell phone? Do you have problems keeping up with your to-do list? Online and cell phone time management tools may be the solutions you need. (To find these and others, see the text website for links or search for the name of the tool online.)

Google Calendar is a free online shareable calendar service. Using Google Calendar, you can add events, share with friends and family (or keep things to yourself), and search across the Web for public calendars, including television and sports events as well other scheduled events. You can share your calendar with family and friends and view theirs as well. Google Calendar is available in a number of languages. It allows you to view a day, a 4-day period, a week, or a month at a time. One special feature lets you get reminders on your cell phone.

Although you can easily create paper and pencil to-do lists, there are several websites such as Ta Da and Orchestrate that allow you to create electronic to-do lists. Toodledo is a to-do list creator that also includes tools to analyze your dates, priorities, and time estimates to create a schedule that helps you get everything done on time. If you tend to procrastinate or forget, try HassleMe which nags you via e-mail or BitBomb which sends reminder text messages to your cell phone.

Work often expands to fill the time you have. For instance, if you have a whole day to write a one-page paper, that's probably how long it will take. But if you only have an hour and a half in which to write it, you'll be more focused and complete it in the time you have. One way to monitor your time is to install a digital timer on your computer desktop. Set a time for reasonable completion of a task to help you complete it. You can download free shareware for digital clocks and timers at Brothersoft.

activity **6**

Online Time Management Tools

Choose one of the time management tools and create a week's calendar, showing academic, personal, and work-related events as well as a to-do list for one day.

GROUP APPLICATION: Compare tools with others in your class in terms of ease of use and features.

Coping with Commuting

How does commuting to campus affect me as a student?

In the 1930s, the *rat race* was a jazz dance. Then the business world changed it to mean *struggling to stay ahead of the competition*. Today, *rat race* refers to any undertaking in which you feel that time moves faster than you do. If you've ever seen a hamster playing on an exercise wheel, you understand the term. If you commute, you live it.

As a commuter, you face unique problems: courses that meet at inconvenient times; schedule conflicts that cause you to miss the learning experiences that enrich academic life; traffic jams and constant search for the elusive "good" parking space; or mass transit schedules that don't match your needs. As a commuting student, you are part of a group often called suitcase students. With no room or office to serve as a base, you often find that the materials you need are at home, in your car, or at your job. Traveling back and forth limits your contact with both your family and people on campus. Creative planning is the secret to being a successful commuter student.

Solving scheduling problems involves effective time management. Each minute you stay on campus needs to be stretched to two. You can stretch time through careful organization and planning.

The biggest problem that commuters face is often limited involvement in campus life. You can avoid feeling separated from others on campus by consciously trying to make yourself a part of campus life. Reading the campus newspaper, talking with others before and after class, and exchanging phone numbers and e-mail addresses with classmates help decrease your feelings of alienation. You can look for or add campus friends to your social networking site. Campus activities organizers plan events that meet the interests—and schedules—for the students they serve. You may find breakfast meetings, lunch study groups, or afternoon club meetings. You will probably find that many cultural events—concerts, plays, art exhibits, science demonstrations and so on—will interest family members and give you a chance to participate in campus life. If not, be sure to reserve family time on weekends or evenings. And don't forget to build some time in for exercise and relaxation—even just by parking a bit farther away from the classroom building so that you get in a brisk walk before class.

Commuters have opportunities to study or meet other students in transit.

▶ Choosing to Get the Most from Your Commute

As a commuter, you get to choose how you spend the time while you commute. You can choose for that to be "your" time and listen to music or just relax. But if you'd rather spend "your" time doing something else, you need to choose to use that time more productively.

Commuting Time

- If you drive to campus, find other commuters and car pool. If you and your fellow commuters are in the same classes, you can discuss course content in the car. On days you don't drive, you can study. As a driver, although some technologies (e.g., books on tape, audio notes) can be used, you should never text message or use technology in a way that distracts you from driving.

- Listen to notes or review questions. Obtain lecture podcasts or create your own. Commuting time then becomes study time.

- If you use public transportation, use commuting time as study time. You can read course materials, make note cards, listen to review tapes and podcasts, or review for exams.

- If you are not driving, you can return cell calls or text messages. This will free time.

Time on Campus

- To avoid misplacing important materials, get organized and be prepared. Organize your backpack each night so that you are ready for the next day. Keep a box in your car that contains your textbooks, notebooks, and other supplies.

- Most students have some time between classes. Use that time to study while the information is still fresh from lectures.

- Think of your time on campus like worktime. Plan to study as much as you can in the library or another quiet place before you leave campus. This gives you uninterrupted study time and allows your home time to be home time.

Study Time

- If an emergency prevents you from going to a class, use your neighborhood library, notes from other students, information from the Web, lecture podcasts, and course websites to supplement what you missed.

- Be flexible. Leave time in your schedule for unplanned events, and schedule extra time between appointments or activities in case of traffic or other emergencies. If an emergency arises, you will still have time to study or do other things.

What Took You So Long?

activity 7

If you commute, describe what you do to make the most of your commuting time. If you are not a commuter, create a list of three activities that commuters could safely do to maximize their time.

1. _____

2. _____

3. _____

chapter review

Respond to the following on a separate sheet of paper or in your notebook.

1. What is procrastination? Do you procrastinate? Try to identify some of the reasons you procrastinate. If not, explain how you avoid procrastination.

2. Observe the kinds of self-talk you employ in the courses in which you are enrolled. How would you categorize these according to the three modes of self-talk?

3. What do you see as your greatest obstacles to making and/or using a term calendar? Why?

4. What do you see as your greatest obstacles to constructing, maintaining, and/or following a weekly calendar and to-do list? Why?

5. How do you prioritize family vs. work vs. school? List your priorities in terms of each.

6. Which of the online time management tools most appeals to you? Why?

did you decide?

Did you accomplish what you wanted to in this chapter? Check the items below that apply to you.

Review the *You Decide* questions that you identified at the beginning of the chapter, but look at them from a new direction. If you didn't check an item below, review that module until you feel you can confidently apply the strategies to your own situation. However, the best ideas are worthless unless they are put into effect. Use the 5Cs to help you decide what information you found most helpful in the chapter and how you plan to use it. Record your comments after the statements below.

☐ 5.1 I know to what extent I put assignments off until the last minute.

_____

☐ 5.2 I recognize that what I have to accomplish this term affects my weekly schedule.

_____

☐ 5.3 I am able to get my more important tasks done each day.

_____

☐ 5.4 I know how my thinking affects my time management.

_____

☐ 5.5 I can devise strategies to avoid feeling overextended.

_____

☐ 5.6 I know some online time management tools that might help me organize.

_____

☐ 5.7 I am able to put my commuting time to campus to good use.

_____

perspectives

Another aspect of time that you manage is *timing,* knowing when it is the right time to do something. It is something you take advantage of as in being aware of *the right time to speak or act.* In the following excerpt from an editorial written by President Obama, you'll read why he thinks now is the right time to increase support for community colleges.

Respond to the following after reading the passage:

1. How can changes in community colleges impact the economy?
2. If jobs requiring no college experience were to grow at a rate of 10 percent, what would be the rate of growth of jobs requiring an associate's degree?
3. How many graduates does President Obama want to complete community colleges by 2020?
4. What is one of the goals of reallocation of funding for community colleges?
5. What effect does this article have on you?
6. President Obama states, "It's time to reform our community colleges so that they provide Americans of all ages a chance to learn the skills and knowledge necessary to compete for the jobs of the future." What change would you like to see at your community college? Describe how the 5C process could be used to make a decision about the change.

   A. What is the **C**hallenge you want to face?
   B. What key **C**hoices might be available at your community college?
   C. What would be the major **C**onsequence(s) of each choice?
   D. What should your community college **C**hoose?
   E. How might your community college **C**heck the outcome of the decision?

Now is the time to build a firmer, stronger foundation for growth that not only will withstand future economic storms but that helps us thrive and compete in a global economy. To build that foundation, we must lower the health-care costs that are driving us into debt, create the jobs of the future within our borders, give our workers the skills and training they need to compete for those jobs, and make the tough choices necessary to bring down our deficit in the long run. . . .

And this week, I'll be talking about how we give our workers the skills they need to compete for these jobs of the future. In an economy where jobs requiring at least an associate's degree are projected to grow twice as fast as jobs requiring no college experience, it's never been more essential to continue education and training after high school. That's why we've set a goal of leading the world in college degrees by 2020. Part of this goal will be met by helping

Americans better afford a college education. But part of it will also be strengthening our network of community colleges.

We believe it's time to reform our community colleges so that they provide Americans of all ages a chance to learn the skills and knowledge necessary to compete for the jobs of the future. Our community colleges can serve as 21st-century job training centers, working with local businesses to help workers learn the skills they need to fill the jobs of the future. We can reallocate funding to help them modernize their facilities, increase the quality of online courses and ultimately meet the goal of graduating 5 million more Americans from community colleges by 2020.

Providing all Americans with the skills they need to compete is a pillar of a stronger economic foundation, and, like health care or energy, we cannot wait to make the necessary changes. We must continue to clean up the wreckage of this recession, but it is time to rebuild something better in its place. It won't be easy, and there will continue to be those who argue that we have to put off hard decisions that we have already deferred for far too long. But earlier generations of Americans didn't build this great country by fearing the future and shrinking our dreams. This generation has to show that same courage and determination. I believe we will.

reflecting on decisions

Based on what you learned about time management in this chapter, what insights have you gained about the way your decisions about time affect the outcomes of your life?

CURING ILLNESS WITH **COMPUTER DOWNTIME**

How would you like to help cure an incurable disease in your spare time? If you have a computer, you can . . .

To understand how you can help cure illness with your computer's downtime, you need to know about distributed computing. Distributed computing uses different computers in different places to perform an application that is connected to a network. Professor Vijay Pande of Stanford University came up with the idea of distributed computing in 1991. That's when he needed calculations that would take about a million days on a fast computer. So he thought that if he and his students wanted to get the work done in 10 days, they needed access to 100,000 processors. Using distributed computing, they ran pieces of the simulation through networked computers to speed up the results. It worked!

Their current project, folding@home, has the goal of studying proteins. Before proteins work in the body, they assemble themselves, or "fold." When proteins misfold, there can be serious consequences such as Alzheimer's, ALS, Parkinson's disease, and cancer. The folding@home project asks people throughout the world to run software during the downtime of their home computers. It's safe and takes no more of your time than downloading a program. Ready to help find a cure? Visit **http://folding.stanford.edu.**

◀ **CHOOSING TO SERVE**

REVIEW

Skim the notes you made throughout the chapter. How does the content fit together? What information is still unclear? Were your learning goals met? Can you answer the review questions and define terms?

◀ **CHOOSING TO BE AN ACTIVE LEARNER**

CHAPTER **SIX**

Choices for Succeeding in Class and Online Courses

One of the most important skills in life is listening, not simply hearing. Respond to the following: How do you decide what's important to listen for in lectures?

YOU DECIDE

To *wonder* means to think or have curiosity about. Things and ideas you wonder about often mask a need for a decision. Check the items below that apply to you.

In terms of my listening and notetaking, I've been wondering . . .

☐ 6.1 What can I do to be a better listener?

☐ 6.2 What should I listen for in different classes?

☐ 6.3 Am I a good notetaker?

☐ 6.4 What should I do with notes after I take them?

☐ 6.5 What technologies can be used for notetaking?

Each of these decision points corresponds to the numbered modules that follow. Turn to the module for immediate help.

CHOOSING TO BE AN ACTIVE LEARNER

SURVEY

Before reading this chapter, prepare for learning. Purposefully skim the title, introduction, headings, and graphics. As you survey, decide what information you already know and what information is new to you.

QUESTION

Change each section's heading into a question. This forms your learning goal for reading.

READ

Read the section without marking. Reread and mark key information that answers your question.

RECITE

Stop after each section and make sure you understood the content. Organize or summarize content and make notes.

Have you ever sat in class and thought, "Boring! I'm never going to need to know this." When you feel this way, it's easy to lose interest and even easier to tune out. But what if someone paid you to sit in class and *really* listen and take notes with enthusiasm? What is the minimum amount you would take for the job? $100 an hour? $50 an hour? $25 an hour? $10 an hour? Minimum wage? For most students, there is a dollar amount that would guarantee their interest. Some students say they would take the job for $10 an hour or less.

Right now, college is at least one of your jobs. The classroom is one of your worksites. This job, like most others, is work—and by definition, work isn't always fun. In college, you work for yourself and your future. As an adult, you know that you are more motivated in situations in which you are in control. That works well in college because you control how you approach the job of being a student.

But, honestly, will you need the lecture information again? Yes . . . and no. In many courses you are, indeed, learning specific skills—how to write well, ways to use computers, what to do in a medical emergency—that you will apply directly on the job. Still, in these and many other community college courses, *what* you learn is only part of the experience. Your college courses also teach you *how* to learn new information and think critically about it.

Learning, then, becomes *less* of a product that may or may not be useful and *more* of a process that can be applied to any situation. For instance, you might be in college to take courses for computer certification. However, once you com-

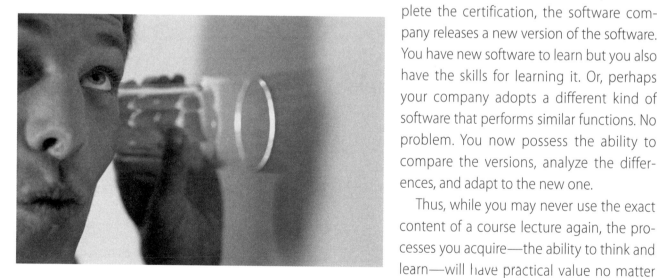

plete the certification, the software company releases a new version of the software. You have new software to learn but you also have the skills for learning it. Or, perhaps your company adopts a different kind of software that performs similar functions. No problem. You now possess the ability to compare the versions, analyze the differences, and adapt to the new one.

Thus, while you may never use the exact content of a course lecture again, the processes you acquire—the ability to think and learn—will have practical value no matter

active listener
A student who consciously controls the listening process through preplanned strategies.

what you do. They will be just as relevant to achieving your goals in the work world as they will to achieving your academic goals. This chapter provides you with four such processes: becoming an **active listener;** preparing for and participating in learning in class; developing a system for recording and reviewing information; and taking notes from online courses.

Choosing to Become an Active Listener in Class

Did you know that babies can hear before they're born? If it's something we've done since before birth, why aren't we better listeners? The answer is that hearing and listening are not the same. Hearing is passive. Listening is an active process you choose by what you do, and what you don't do, in class.

▶ What to Do in Class

As you've probably noticed, not all instructors would win points on *American Idol*. Few radiate star power. They are just regular people who are experts in their fields. Their job is to communicate information to you, not to entertain you. Your job is to acquire the content no matter how it is presented.

Consider this. What if someone forced you to stand outside in the cold, rain, or heat for several hours? Would you do it? How would you feel? What if you were waiting in line to get tickets to a ballgame or a concert? Would this change how you feel? Why? Motivation is the difference. You do lots of things that you don't necessarily like if you choose to do so. Interest in course information is a choice you make as you prepare for class.

Being prepared is a good way to make sitting through a lecture a more positive experience. Look again at the survey and question steps of the SQ3R process at the start of this chapter. You can apply this process to prepare you for what the instructor will be covering. Phrase the lecture topic to yourself as a question. It makes what's said in class relevant.

What you do in class also helps you focus on lecture content. First, bring your course materials to class so that, should your instructor refer to them, you'll have them. This includes your textbook, notebook, handouts, and perhaps even information from your class's online site.

Second, arrive on time. If you are late, you might miss introductory statements that set the tone for the rest of the lecture. Also being late could contribute to your feeling disorganized or panicked. These feelings could lessen your ability to listen attentively.

Sometimes a favorite instructor becomes a mentor.

mentors
Wise and trusted counselors or teachers who advise, instruct or train a student outside a regular classroom.

advisors
Persons who provide information and advice on a range of topics including college policies and course schedules.

Third, choose your seat strategically. When possible, sit near the front of the classroom. This is especially important if you have an attention disorder. If you sit in the middle or back, you can get distracted by people sitting between you and the instructor. If window views, hall noise, or friends distract you, sit away from them. If you are a visual or auditory learner (see Chapter 3), you need to sit where you can see or hear best. Choose your seat based on what's best for your focus and concentration.

Fourth, when you get to class, spend the time before an instructor begins, briefly reviewing your previous class notes to refresh memory and provide continuity. Because notes are taken in a class-by-class fashion, many students tend to think of their subject in a piece-by-piece manner. This review helps you avoid that.

Fifth, you need to be aware of the impression you make. Talking to friends, texting, playing on your laptop, or looking bored makes a lasting impression on instructors. It also shifts your focus away from content.

Last, respond to lecture material with body language, mental comments, and written notes. Your body language tells the instructor how well you understand the lecture. Mental comments—the thoughts you have about the lecture—should question what is said as well as what and how you think about it. As you listen, ask yourself, "What?" "So what?" and "Now what?" These help you identify "*What* is this about?" "*So what* does that mean to me?" and "*Now what* is coming next?" Written notes are your summary of the answers to these mental questions.

Class preparation and participation have another important benefit. Sometimes the same faculty member teaches more than one course that you need to take. The favorable impression you create will pay dividends in your continued coursework. The instructors in your field of study may become your **mentors** or faculty **advisors.** During your college career, mentors and advisors provide valuable insights about fields of study and careers. You will need some to write letters of recommendation when you finish your degree. Mentors also provide tips and leads on job opportunities after you leave school. A mentor's help can be so valuable that many students maintain professional contacts with their mentors after they leave the institution.

What Not to Do in Class

Speakers talk at a rate of about 125–150 words per minute but most people can listen at a rate of about 400–500 words per minute. What happens during the rest of the time? You have plenty of time to think about other things while you appear to be listening. This often results in either daydreaming or worry. To avoid this, you must make a decision to consciously avoid the two. After all, you can choose what you think. Most worries can't be resolved during class so you should put them aside until you can do something about them. One way to do so is to jot notes about the problems and put the notes away. This allows you to put them out of sight and out of mind until class ends.

A second way to get back on track is to ask yourself, "What is the best use of my time right now?" Chances are the things that distract you can't be resolved while you are in class. And you'll probably have to spend more time catching up on what you missed than the time you would be spending in class. So, in most cases, you will conclude that the best use of your time will be actively listening to the lecture.

Everything—from interesting window views to classroom noises—has the power to divert your attention. To refocus, you need to follow a couple of steps. First, be aware of what distracts you. If you can, move to another seat where the distractions are less evident. Second, sit as close to the speaker as possible. This helps you focus your attention.

Hunger, room temperature, fatigue and other physical concerns affect concentration. The best way to handle factors like these is to take care of these before class. Have a snack, take along a jacket, get rest, or go to the bathroom before you go to class.

Academic freedom in higher education means the freedom to teach or communicate ideas or facts even if unpopular or controversial, and this often may mean that instructors say things that contradict what you think and value. This might arouse such emotional responses in you that you stop listening as you mentally argue with the speaker. To resolve this situation is to become aware of your responses. Decide to continue listening and hear the person out. If necessary, jot down your arguments. This may release some pent-up feelings and energy. Keep in mind that sometimes an instructor says things just to create discussion or to make you think.

Tapping, doodling, clicking a pen, or other physical behaviors detract from your focus and can distract others. To avoid this, put your physical energies to work in notetaking and participating in class. Create drawings to help you recall lecture information.

Negative comments from your inner critic or child (see Chapter 5) such as "Who cares?" "I am never going to figure this out," "The instructor talks funny," "I should have never taken this class; it's too hard for me," "What shall I do after class?" and so forth affect concentration. To solve this problem, you decide to monitor and control your self-talk. Replace negative comments with more positive ones such as "I don't really care about this, but it must be important information so I'm going to be sure I understand it," "I don't get this, but I've figured out difficult things before," "The instructor has a different way of saying things, but what is said is more important than how it is said," "This is a hard class but I'll see the instructor to get help or join a study group," or "I'll think about what to do after class."

You, like many other students, might take your notebook computer with you to take notes. First, be sure that your instructor allows you to do so. Then be sure that you are using it to take notes rather than playing games, checking e-mail, surfing the net, and sending IMs. Not only is it a distraction to you, but most instructors can see what you're doing. Should you leave your computer at home? Not necessarily. Like many other distractions, awareness is the first step. Once you get to class, open only your word processor. Choose to leave all other applications unopened or unavailable.

Unlike high school, no bells ring to signal the start and end of class. Some students watch the clock and pack up early so they can be ready to race out the door at the end of class. Not only is this rude and distracting—it's ineffective. Instructors often provide summaries of key points, reminders of impending assignments, and other important content in the last few minutes of class.

academic freedom
Freedom to teach or communicate even ideas or facts that are unpopular or controversial.

You attend class at your instructor's discretion. If your behavior is not appropriate (e.g. you engage in side conversations, make or answer cell phone calls, act rudely), your instructor can dismiss you from class and/or drop you from the course.

A computer taken to class is best used for notetaking only.

activity 1

Becoming an Active Listener

Access http://www.mhhe.com/business/management/buildyourmanagementskills/updated_flash/topic13b/quiz.html

Complete the inventory there and read the suggestions for active listening. Use the 5C approach to identify and make a decision about your active learning skills. Summarize what you decided in the space below.

Listening in Different Learning Situations

What should I listen for in different classes?

As a college student you'll listen to lectures, complete lab experiments, and work in groups to solve problems . . . all in the same day. Just as one size doesn't fit all bodies, one listening strategy doesn't fit all classes. Listening in traditional lecture classes differs from listening in classes that deliver content through discussion or hands-on activities

Traditional Classes

Your academic success often depends on your ability to listen for the heart—or pattern—of lectures. Many students think that lecture information can be arranged in an infinite number of ways. But there are really only a few main patterns. It's just that lectures often flow from one pattern to another. Once you know which words signal each pattern, you can start to organize information more easily. Your instructor gives signals that point to other important information as well.

During class, record everything you think is relevant to the topic. When your lecturer tells a story, write the topic of the story and a few key details. If possible, record how you think the story related to the lecture. If the relationship is not immediately clear, leave some space and keep taking notes.

After class, look for the connection. Why would the lecturer have included that story? What was the point, in terms of the course content? Record your conclusions in the space you left during the notetaking phase. If you're still not sure, talk to other classmates about their conclusions. You might also ask the lecturer to discuss your notes with you outside of class. You can tell how well you have taken notes when you get your first test. Its content should help you pinpoint how, if at all, a lecturer's stories relate to your understanding of course content.

Many students use laptop computers to take notes. That's both a good and bad idea for several reasons. First, your classroom might be wireless. This works well if you need to connect to course materials that the instructor has placed online. Another plus to using a computer is that printed notes are easier to study. You'll never waste time trying to read your handwriting. Digital notes are also easier to manipulate. That is, you can move notes around to make studying materials easier. But this can work against you because the writing by hand you normally do in making flash cards or other study materials contributes to **tactile/kinesthetic** memory.

tactile/kinesthetic
Sense of touch.

Of course, the disadvantages of the laptop are integral to it. You'll need to keep your battery charged and find space for it on your desk or table in the classroom. And sometimes computers crash. If you use a notebook computer, e-mail notes to yourself or save them on a flashdrive as soon as class is over. For this same reason, don't forget to print a hard copy to study as soon as you have access to a printer.

❯ Nontraditional Class Formats

What if there isn't a lecture? Many instructors use discussions among students as their delivery format. Discussions generate ideas among class members. They help students debate pros and cons or explore solutions to problems.

Because a discussion seems like a kind of conversation, students often lay down their pencils/close their computers, sit back, and simply listen. But of course discussions are more like a business meeting. That means someone, namely you, needs to be taking minutes—a record of main points, lists of ideas, sequences of events, pros and cons and so on. Later, in a business meeting, the group as a whole reviews the notes for accuracy and completeness. They use the notes to remind themselves of meeting content and to look for trends or relationships that might not have been clear during the meeting. You need to review your notes for this same sort of information. You are both the notetaker who records ideas and the participant who reviews them.

Lab courses like nursing, computer-aided drafting, automotive technology, biology, or art provide you with hands-on activity. Practice, experimentation, observation, and practical application form the content. The first step in taking notes in a lab course is recording your starting point. This includes the materials you're using and your hypothesis or goals for the session. As you work, make occasional notes about your progress. When the class ends, record your final conclusions and thoughts. You can also revise your hypothesis or set goals for the next session while your work is fresh in your mind.

Table 6.1 Lecture Signals and Meanings

Signal	Meaning
Today's lecture covers . . . To sum up, in summary, as a review, in con-clusion (located at either the beginning or end of a discussion).	**Introductory/summary pattern:** briefly previews topics to be covered or highlights main points of the lecture.
First, second, third . . . First, next, and, then . . . Finally . . . Most/least important . . .	**List/sequence pattern:** lists points in a topical list or steps in a sequence.
Comparisons: Similarly Both As well as In like manner Likewise *Contrasts:* However On the other hand On the contrary But Instead of Although Nevertheless Yet	**Comparison/contrast pattern:** shows likenesses and differ-ences among concepts.
Therefore, thus, as a result, because, in turn, then, hence, for this reason, results in, cause(s), effect(s).	**Cause/effect or problem-solving pattern:** how or why things happen and their reasons; problems and solutions; premises and conclusions.
Instructor repeats information or speaks more slowly.	Such wait time is usually a cue for you to record information in your notes.
Instructor changes tone of voice, tempo of speech, or uses body language to emphasize information.	Variations of any kind in speech or body language generally mean that such information is important.
Instructor refers to information by page number or refers to information as a test item.	Generally means that the information is important to your understanding of course content and ability to perform well on a test.
Instructor writes on board, has notes on a Web page, or uses other visual aids.	The extra effort that goes into finding and using markers or using visual aids shows that the information they provide is important to your understanding and academic success.

activity 2

Analyzing Instructors

Identify two of your instructors who lecture frequently. Use the list below to analyze what they do by marking either A—Always; U—Usually; S—Sometimes; or N—Never. Then write a paragraph in which you compare the two instructors. Consider your behavior in each class. In which class do you perform better? Why?

	Instructor #1	Instructor #2
Review previous lecture materials before beginning the new lecture?		
State main ideas in introduction and summary of lecture?		
Provide an outline of the lecture?		
Provide "wait time" for writing notes?		
Speak clearly with appropriate volume?		
Answer questions without sarcasm?		
Stay on topic?		
Refrain from reading directly from the text?		
Emphasize main points?		
Use transition words?		
Give examples to illustrate difficult ideas?		
Write important words, dates, and so forth on board?		
Define important terms?		
Use audiovisual aids to reinforce ideas?		

Scoring: The more *A*s and *U*s your instructor has, the less you have to do as a listener. Note the items that you rated *S* or *N*. You may need to do what your instructor doesn't provide you.

The following table provides suggestions for coping with an instructor's lecture style.

If your instructor fails to . . .	Then you . . .
1. Explain the goals of the lecture.	Use your text and syllabus to set objectives.
2. Review previous lecture material before beginning a new lecture.	Set aside time before each class to review notes.
3. State main ideas in an introduction and summary of a lecture.	Write short summaries of the day's lecture immediately after class.
4. Provide an outline of the lecture.	Preview assigned readings beforehand.
5. Provide "wait time" for writing notes.	Politely ask instructor to repeat information or speak more slowly.
6. Speak clearly with appropriate volume.	Politely ask instructor to repeat information or speak more loudly, or move closer to the instructor.
7. Answer questions without sarcasm.	Refrain from taking comments personally.
8. Stay on topic.	Discover how anecdotes relate to the content or use them as a memory cue.

If your instructor fails to . . .	Then you . . .
9. Refrain from reading from the text.	Mark passages in the text as instructor reads and/or summarize or outline these in the text margin.
10. Emphasize main points.	Supplement lectures through text previews and reading.
11. Use transition words.	Supplement lectures through text previews and reading.
12. Give examples to explain difficult ideas.	Politely ask instructor for an example, discuss idea with other students and/or create an example for yourself.
13. Write important names, dates, ideas, etc.	Supplement notes with terms listed in text and highlight information contained in lecture and/or text.
14. Define important terms.	Use text glossary or definition.
15. Use audiovisual aids to reinforce ideas.	Relate information to what you know about the topic or create an example for yourself.

Am I a good notetaker?

Taking Good Lecture Notes

formal outline
Main points arranged vertically first using Roman numerals and indented capital letters, and then Arabic numerals and lowercase letters to sequence supporting ideas.

informal outline
Same idea as formal outline, but uses spacing as you like and special markings you choose (e.g., all capital letters, dashes, stars).

Notes differ from dictation. You can't and shouldn't record everything your instructor says. Lecture notes are just that—a way to help you note the major and minor points of a lecture. Ultimately, they will help you understand and remember new information.

You can take notes in many ways. Contrary to popular rumor, there is no one best form for notes. The format you prefer varies depending on the ways you learn best (see Chapter 3). It also depends on the subject and the instructor's lecture style.

Structured notes often suit learners whose brain dominance favors the logical side. In using a **formal outline** to take notes that arranges main points vertically using Roman numerals and indented capital letters, and then Arabic numerals and lowercase letters to sequence supporting ideas, the structure of your notes is highly organized. **Informal outlines** use the same structural format but in a more creative way, by using spacing as you like and special markings you choose (e.g., all capital letters, dashes, stars, etc.). But unless your instructor clearly cues new

Hydraulic Pr. Of Braking—Pascal's Law (1800s):
compression, motion, and force
Rules of Hydraulics
(1) prss (= pressure) constant in closed syst.
(2) prss. Determined by force on brake pedal
    and MC (= master cylinder)
(3) ← (smaller) MC, = → (higher) prss
(4) → (larger) MC, = ← (lower) prss
(5) lg output pistons > force than small dd

Figure 6.1 Automotive Technology Notes: Running Text Form with Abbreviations.

I. Hydraulic Principles of Braking
    A. Based on Pascal's Law (1800s)
    B. compression, motion, and force
II. Rules of Hydraulics
    A. Pressure is constant in a closed system.
    B. Brake system pressure determined by
        force applied
        1. to brake pedal
        2. to cross-section of master cylinder
    C. The smaller the master cylinder (input)
        piston, the higher the system pressure
        with a given amount of force.
    D. The larger the master cylinder (input)
        piston, the lower the system pressure
        with a given amount of force.
    E. Large output pistons have greater force
        than small ones.

Figure 6.2 Automotive Technology Notes: Formal Outline.

Hydraulic Principles of Braking
- Based on Pascal's Law (1800s)
- compression, motion, and force Rules of Hydraulics
- Pressure is constant in a closed system.
- Brake system pressure determined by force applied
  ~~ to brake pedal
  ~~ to cross-section of master cylinder
- The smaller the master cylinder (input) piston, the higher the system pressure with a given amount of pressure.
- The larger the master cylinder (input) piston, the lower the system pressure with a given amount of pressure.
- Large output pistons have greater force than small ones.

Figure 6.3 Automotive Technology Notes: Informal Outline.

RECALL NOTES

—3 factors of Pascal's Law
—What are the 5 Rules of Hydraulics?

Hydraulic Pr. of Braking—Pascal's Law (1800s): compression, motion, and force Rules of Hydraulics
(1) prss (= pressure) constant in closed syst.
(2) prss. determined by force on brake pedal and MC (= master cylinder)
(3) ← (smaller) MC, = → (higher) prss
(4) ← (larger) MC, = → (lower) prss
(5) lg output pistons. force than small

Figure 6.4 Automotive Technology Notes: Cornell Form.

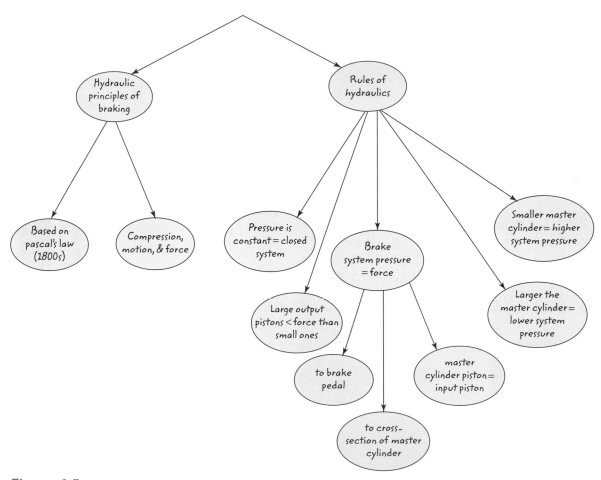

Figure 6.5 Automotive Technology Notes: Idea Map.

TIPS FOR EFFECTIVE NOTES

DATE IT. Date each day's notes. Writing the date helps if you need to compare notes with someone or identify missing notes.

GET ORGANIZED. If you handwrite notes, use the same legible notetaking system for each course (e.g., Cornell, outline, informal outline, paragraphs, idea map). As you take notes, use only one side of your paper and number pages as you go. You can use the back of pages to summarize, correct, or add information after class. It may sound like a given, but keep notes together. If you handwrite notes, use a single spiral notebook or ring binder for each subject, or two multisubject notebooks or loose-leaf binders, one for Monday-Wednesday-Friday classes and one for Tuesday-Thursday classes. Notebooks or binders with pockets are especially helpful for storing course handouts or other class materials. If you take notes on a computer, create folders for each class. Your notes can be in separate files by day or week or in a continuous file. Be sure to back up your files on a regular basis.

STICK TO IT. As you take notes, leave blank spaces to separate important groups of ideas. Abbreviate when possible. Develop a key for any symbols and abbreviations and record it in your notebook. Note words or references you don't understand. Do not try to figure them out at the time. Look them up later or ask about them in class. You need to be flexible. Adjust your listening and notetaking pace to the lecture.

GET THE POINT. Listen for transition words that signal main points. As you identify the main patterns of the lecture, try to group and label information for recall. If you can't do this as you take notes, you can do so in your after-class follow-through (see next section). Highlight important text information with a colored pen or marker or with the highlight feature on your word processing program.

main points, you are responsible for deciding how to organize your outline. Thus, to use these styles, you have to figure out which points are main ideas and which subpoints support main ideas. Previewing the chapter before class is one way to figure out which is which. Formal and informal outlines also work well with subjects that involve step-by-step processes such as math or science problem solving. Some instructors lecture in an outline fashion. They take the pressure off you by clearly identifying main ideas and giving details in an orderly way.

Cornell notes combine less structure and more structure. To take these notes, you divide a page into two sections by drawing a vertical line about one-third from the left side of the page. In the larger right section of the page, you take notes during class. Almost anything goes here as you get key ideas on the page in whatever way you wish. After class, you review what you wrote and write more organized notes in the smaller left column. This side will become your recall column for the details in the larger column. This combination makes it a good fit for different personal styles, subjects, and instructor approaches. It encourages you to analyze notes recorded in class so you can organize the left side of the page.

Global or visual learners tend to use more pictorial forms such as **idea mapping.** Maps help capture relationships among ideas. Thus, this style works well for topics such as literature, the arts, or social sciences. It can also be used when instructors provide common characteristics for each topic. For instance, an instructor lecturing on theories of psychology might always provide the theorist, key points, impact, and problems.

Cornell notes
Page divided vertically into two sections with right side about $\frac{2}{3}$ of the page for class notes and left column for recall tips you create afterward.

idea mapping
Graphical picture you make of main ideas and details.

Assessing the Effectiveness of Your Notes

Notes reflect course information that will likely show up on course exams. So they are crucial for you to study for exams. Thus, your notes need to be the best that they can be for each course you take. Notetaking effectiveness varies according to the format and content of each class. Thus, you should assess your notes for each course you take so you can improve your notetaking. Use the following form to rate your notes in each class you take. Record your score next to each course you listed. Are your assessment scores similar? Why or why not? What can you do to make your notes more effective? Use the 5Cs to determine which notetaking format works best for you. Then begin using that format in all of your classes immediately. At first, it may feel strange. But after time and with practice, it will become natural.

Notes Evaluation Criteria

Value points and descriptors of notetaking habits		
Format	**3**	**2**	**1**
Use of ink	I use pen consistently.	I use pen and pencil.	I use pencil.
Handwriting	Others can read my notes.	Only I can read my notes.	I can't read my notes.
Notebook	I use a loose-leaf binder.	I use a spiral notebook.	I don't use a notebook.
Use of page	I leave enough space for editing.	I leave some space for editing.	My notes cover the page.
Organization	**3**	**2**	**1**
Headings	I use new headings for each main idea.	I use headings inconsistently.	I don't use headings for changes in main ideas.
Subtopics	I group subtopics under headings.	I don't indent subtopics under headings.	My subtopics are not grouped.
Recall column	I use cue words and symbols to make practice questions.	I use cue words in a recall column.	I do not use a recall column.
Abbreviation	I abbreviate whenever possible.	I use some abbreviation.	I don't abbreviate.
Summaries	I summarize lectures in writing.	I write a list of summary lecture topics.	I don't summarize.
Meaning	**3**	**2**	**1**
Main points	I identify main points with symbols and underlining.	I list main points.	I don't list main points.
Supporting details	I show the relationships between main ideas and details.	My notes list details.	I don't list details.
Examples	I list examples under main.	I list some examples.	I don't record examples.
Restatement	I use my own words.	I use some of my own words.	I use none of my own words.

Source: Reprinted with permission of Norman A. Stahl and the International Reading Association.

Your Courses	Scores

What I should
do with notes
after I take
them?

After-Class
Follow-Through

Lecture notes and study notes are not always the same. Lecture notes are often little more than words you write during class or brief bits of information you gather from a lecture. They may—or may not—be good enough for study. Your after-class follow-through transforms them into a more powerful learning tool: study notes.

You don't create study notes by just recopying lecture notes more neatly because you can copy information without thinking about it. Instead, you need to reorganize and summarize information to find connections, draw conclusions, and analyze information. The resulting study notes comprise a complete source of information that includes everything you need to learn the information you need. To create a good set of study notes, you may need to add textbook details and your own analysis or comments.

Completed by hand or on a computer, you can use the same kinds of formats that you use for lecture notes. For instance, you can organize information using formal or informal outlines or visually using idea maps. You can write summaries in paragraph form. If you use Cornell notes, you can write key words and questions in the recall column.

It's easy to forget the connecting information that you didn't have time to write in your notes. As a result, your notes might fail to make sense when you use them to study before an exam. So *when* you make study notes and *how often* you review them are just as important as *what* you include in them.

Because most people tend to forget about half of lecture content very quickly, the most effective review occurs within an hour of the time you took your notes. A brief first review of 5 to 10 minutes is all you need to read over your notes and add missing details while they are still fresh in your mind. Review your notes again during a weekly review of all course notes. This helps you reconnect ideas and build understanding.

Why do you need to review so often? Last-minute processing doesn't give you enough time to absorb information fully. As a result, you may not get the same insights that you will after thinking about information over time. It's practice that makes permanent. At the least, you should update your notes as soon as possible after class or at least within a few hours of taking them.

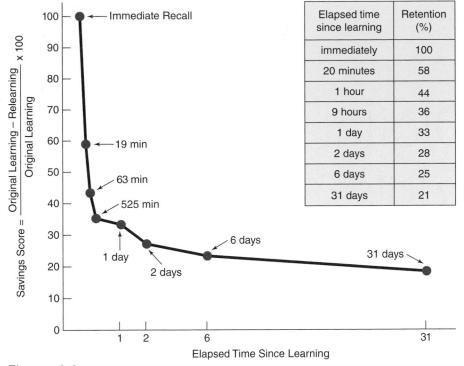

Elapsed time since learning	Retention (%)
immediately	100
20 minutes	58
1 hour	44
9 hours	36
1 day	33
2 days	28
6 days	25
31 days	21

Figure 6.6 The Curve of Forgetting.

Processing Your Notes

To complete this activity, you will need three days of lecture notes. Create a set of study notes using the format you prefer: formal or informal outline, idea map, paragraphs, or Cornell recall column. Write the information that came from your lecture notes in one color of ink or marker. Use a second color to show information that comes from the textbook or other course material. Use a third color for your own comments, reflections, and questions.

Digital Notetaking Tools

Whatever notetaking method you choose, you need to process the material actively as part of the after-class follow-through. If you use Microsoft Word, you can use the *track changes* tool to make notes and comments on the electronic copy. You can also write notes directly on your printed copies. Or, you can open Notepad, and use it to take notes. Additionally, you can use online notetaking tools such as *Google Notebook, MyNoteIT, Notefish, Yahoo Notes,* or *Notezz!* For instance, *A Note* is a free online notetaking program. When the program closes, it uploads and saves your notes. When you restart the program, the notes are downloaded. Because the notes are stored somewhere other than your computer, you can use your notes on different computers. Links are also provided at the text website www.mhhe.com/Atkinson.

In a way, your notes in an online class are much like the notes you create in a discussion course. Rather than noting the contributions of each person, your notes document and summarize the information contributed by each online source: readings, assignments, discussion boards, chats, and so on. Organizing these notes into bulleted lists of key terms or an outline of key points helps you process information more deeply.

Or, if you prefer using graphics to structure information, you may need to acquire a program like *Inspiration*, a program for creating idea maps. Should you find information complicated or puzzling, open the discussion board and post questions or comments. Once your notes are organized, the review process is the same that you use for face-to-face classes.

activity 5

Digital Sticky Notes

Wouldn't it be nice if you could put sticky notes on digital documents you find online? Actually, you can. Go online and search for *Web 2.0 digital sticky notes.* Choose one you find and try it out. Create a document with your name and the name of your college. Add a digital sticky note that provides three adjectives that describe your college.

GROUP APPLICATION: Compare the digital sticky note tool you used with others in your class in terms of ease of use and features. List the ones you like best.

chapter review

Respond to the following on a separate sheet of paper or in your notebook.

1. What is the difference between thinking of education as a product and thinking of it as a process?

2. List three ways to prepare for lectures.

3. This chapter listed ways to make a favorable impression through classroom behavior. List five ways to create an *unfavorable* impression that you've observed at your institution.

4. Based on your observations, what listening problem do you think is most common in your classes? Why?

5. Compare notetaking in lecture, discussion, online and lab courses.

6. Reexamine the suggestions for taking notes. Put a check mark by the suggestions you already use. Put an exclamation point by the suggestions that were new to you.

7. Imagine that the person who used to sit next to you in class hasn't come to class for three weeks. She left a message on your answering machine asking to borrow your notes. In a brief paragraph, explain how effective you judge your notes to be and provide an argument for why she should or should not get a copy of your notes.

8. What is the difference between lecture notes and study notes?

did you decide?

Did you accomplish what you wanted to in this chapter? Check the items below that apply to you.

Review the *You Decide* questions that you identified at the beginning of the chapter, but look at them from a new direction. If you didn't check an item below, review that module until you feel you can confidently apply the strategies to your own situations. However, the best ideas are worthless unless they are put into effect. Use the 5Cs to help you decide what information you found most helpful in the chapter and how you plan to use it. Record your comments after the statements below.

☐ 6.1   I know what I can do to be a better listener.

_____

☐ 6.2   I understand what I should listen for in different classes.

_____

☐ 6.3   I have some ideas for improving my notetaking.

_____

☐ 6.4   After I take them, I know how to use my notes for study purposes.

_____

☐ 6.5   I can use technologies for notetaking.

_____

perspectives

George Lucas, Academy Award–winning American film director, producer, screenwriter, and chairman of Lucasfilm, was named as a Distinguished Community College Alumnus in 2004. This article, "Changing Landscapes," by Evelyn L. Kent, discusses the role education has had and continues to play in his success.

Think about and answer the questions that follow:

1. In what way do you think Lucas has changed the landscape of what is possible?
2. In what ways does Lucas support education?
3. Identify three companies in the Lucas "empire."
4. What does the George Lucas Educational Foundation do?
5. What event caused Lucas to enroll in a junior college?
6. Lucas donates funds to many educational causes. Imagine that he is thinking about giving your community college some money and wants your help in deciding specifically what he should fund. How could you use the 5C process to help make that decision?

   A. What is a group, service, department, or individual that needs financial assistance on your campus? This is your **C**hallenge.
   B. What other **C**hoices are available for funding?
   C. What would be the major **C**onsequence(s) of each choice?
   D. Should Lucas **C**hoose to contribute his funds to your idea?
   E. How can you help Lucas **C**heck the outcome of this decision?

George Lucas has something in common with community colleges—they both change the landscape of what is possible.

The movie producer, director, and writer hardly needs an introduction. Since 1973 when *American Graffiti* was an enormous success, America has been familiar with Lucas. *Star Wars* moved that familiarity to intimacy in 1977.

In 1997, the *San Francisco Chronicle* wrote: "So many years, so much exposure, so many spin-offs, special-effects trends and continuous warp-speed hype have made it nearly impossible to look at 'Star Wars' as just a movie anymore. It remains an icon on the ever-changing pop culture landscape . . ."

Lucas readily admits that school was not a priority for him. "Frankly, I was not very engaged in my classes; in fact, as a boy, I liked to daydream and write stories," he writes in the resource book *Edutopia: Success Stories for Learning in the Digital Age.*

Regardless, after a near-fatal car accident, he began his venture into higher education at Modesto Junior College in California, where he earned an associate of arts degree in history in 1964.

He earned a bachelor's from the University of Southern California in 1966 and began making movies. His empire includes the visual effects company Industrial Light & Magic (formed during the making of *Star Wars*), THX, and Lucasfilm.

In 1992, the Board of Governors of the Academy of Motion Pictures Arts and Sciences bestowed the Irving G. Thalberg Memorial Award, which honors "creative producers whose bodies of work reflect a consistently high quality of motion picture production," on Lucas.

In addition, in 1999 he received the DigiGlobe Award for his ongoing contribution to culture and entertainment through the use of information technology.

The father of three adopted children, Lucas also is the founder and chairman of the board of the George Lucas Educational Foundation, which focuses on best practices and innovation in primary education. It focuses on project-based learning that stimulates children's passions and emphasizes well-prepared teachers to improve student learning.

On his website, www.glef.org, Lucas says, "Our Foundation documents and disseminates the most exciting classrooms where these innovations are taking place." The foundation does this through the creation and dissemination of media—from films, books, and newsletters, to CD-ROMs and DVDs.

He remains active in the Modesto-area community and nationally through his support of children's charities. In addition, Lucas and his sisters recently gave Modesto Junior College a cash gift to be used toward the construction of an arts center on campus.

reflecting
on decisions

Now that you've learned about listening and notetaking, what decisions about these processes will help you achieve your academic or career goals?

CREATING A
RECORD OF SERVICE

Taking notes about the service you do may not seem all that important. But a record of service serves two purposes. One, while you are in school, you can track how your service relates to your classes. It also helps you keep track of new experiences and skills you gain. Two, this record of service can be documentation for future employers. You can keep a record of your community service online. Networkforgood.org provides you with an online space to note your service. The benefit here is that you can return to your notes as often as you like and can access them from wherever you need to. To create your Record of Service, go to **http://www .networkforgood.org/Default.aspx,** click on *Volunteer* in the top tool bar, scroll down to *Volunteer Record of Service,* and follow the directions there.

◀ CHOOSING TO SERVE

R E V I E W

Skim the notes you made throughout the chapter. How does the content fit together? What information is still unclear? Were your learning goals met? Can you answer the review questions and define terms?

◀ CHOOSING TO BE AN ACTIVE LEARNER

CHAPTER **SEVEN**

Choosing to Read Actively

Much of what you learn comes from print either in texts or online. How do you decide what is important to learn from what you read?

YOU DECIDE

To *wonder* means to think or have curiosity about. Things and ideas you wonder about often mask a need for a decision. Check the items below that apply to you.
   In terms of course readings and homework, I've been wondering . . .

- [ ] 7.1 How do I get ready for learning?
- [ ] 7.2 What's the best way to highlight and mark key information in print materials?
- [ ] 7.3 How do I read and note information from nontraditional sources?
- [ ] 7.4 How do I take notes on online readings ?
- [ ] 7.5 What does it mean to think or read critically?

Each of these decision points corresponds to the numbered modules that follow. Turn to the module for immediate help.

CHOOSING TO BE AN ACTIVE LEARNER

SURVEY

Before reading this chapter, prepare for learning. Purposefully skim the title, introduction, headings, and graphics. As you survey, decide what information you already know and what information is new to you.

QUESTION

Change each section's heading into a question. This forms your learning goal for reading.

READ

Read the section without marking. Reread and mark key information that answers your question.

RECITE

Stop after each section and make sure you understood the content. Organize or summarize content and make notes.

Although college life involves more than academics, the real point of college is learning. Your willingness and ability to learn determine your grades and, ultimately, your success as a student. How you participate in class (see Chapter 6) is a part of what you need to do to succeed. The rest comes from reading and studying on your own. Your success depends on your decision to master the art of learning.

Of all the activities involved in higher education learning, reading assigned materials—both in texts and online—often poses the greatest challenge for students. Many students complain that they don't have enough time to read assignments. They find their textbooks boring. They protest that readings are too long. Still others say that they can't concentrate or recall what they read. When reading online, they get sidetracked by other, more interesting, websites. Some students aren't even sure if their reading skills are sufficient. They think, why even try?

The SQ3R study plan you're using in this text provides a way for you to approach print materials. As you know, the process requires you to examine chapter content before you begin reading and ask questions. When you read to answer questions, you read actively and learn how to self-monitor your understanding. These processes make information easier to recall when you begin the review process.

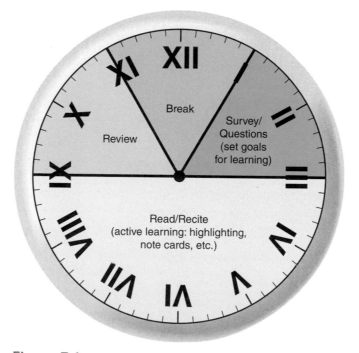

Figure 7.1 Learning as a Cyclical Process.

Preparing to Learn

You may think that the less you know, the more there will be to learn. And since there's more to learn, it will be easier to find new information to master. But learning doesn't work that way. In fact, the more you know about a subject, the more easily you make sense of new information about it. Why?

Learning is not a simple collection of information. What you learn makes more sense when you place it into the context of what you already know. When you learn, you add information to your understanding a little at a time. As new learning combines with your knowledge and experiences, it becomes greater than the sum of its parts. The main way you gain knowledge in college is by completing homework and reading all assigned texts.

Completing Assignments

A key aspect of classroom success is doing the work that's assigned to you. Completing all course assignments—working math and science problems, writing papers and paragraphs, practicing a new language—as well as reading assigned materials contributes to your mental fitness as a student. The assignments prepare *you* for the next step or steps in the learning process.

Assignments fall into two groups: those you submit for grades and those that are for your own use. Assignments for grades should be started early enough for you to get help if you need it. For instance, in writing a paper, you may need to ask your instructor questions or get help from the writing center. Although assignment grades in college courses often don't count as much as tests, they do affect your grade.

Surprisingly, you may find that you spend as much, if not more, time on work that you do not turn in as on work you do. Such extra assignments often give you practice in new skills or ask you to reflect on complex topics. Thus, as you complete them, it's important to note problems or information that is difficult or unclear and use this in asking questions in class, with a tutor, or in a study group.

Why do homework if you don't turn it in or get a grade? Your homework is for you. Indeed, by doing it, you are the one who benefits. Like exercise, it increases your fitness. You are readier for the next level of learning than you would be if you didn't do the homework.

Active Learning Options for Surveying and Setting Learning Goals

As you already know, surveying and questioning are the first two steps in the SQ3R process introduced in Chapter 1. This involves quickly examining a chapter's features to gain a sense of content and organization and to set your goals for learning. You've practiced this in Chapters 2 through 6. Now you'll refine those skills by learning about other options that make surveying and setting learning goals more active processes.

For instance, knowing an author's rationale for different features provides clues to what you should notice while surveying. This helps you survey more actively because you are examining why information is important as well as what the information is.

Although texts vary, authors use common features to direct your attention in different ways. For example, authors use pre-chapter features such as the title, introduction, objectives, outlines, or key terms to provide overviews of chapter content and set the stage for learning. They organize content through the use headings and subheading. They use typographical aids (e.g., boldface terms),

Table 7.1 Chapter Guides and Corresponding Sample Questions

Pre-chapter Guides	Purpose-Setting Questions
Title	What do I already know about this topic?
Introduction	What will be the main idea of the chapter? Is the introduction designed to be thought provoking or attention getting?
Prereading questions	What does the author consider to be important questions about the chapter?
Terms	What new words will be introduced in this chapter? What do I already know about their meanings?
Outline/map	How does the author organize ideas?
Learning outcomes	What does the author expect me to know or do by the end of the chapter?
Intra-chapter Guides	**Purpose-Setting Questions**
Headings/subheadings	How does the author indicate levels of importance among ideas?
Terms in context	How are new terms used?
Boxed information	What is the relationship between this information and the rest of the chapter? What is its purpose?
Different typefaces	What kind or kinds of information do different typefaces highlight?
Graphics	Why are these visual aids (e.g., maps, diagrams) included? What do they show and mean?
Marginal notes	How do the marginal notes relate to the text? Why were they included?
Post-chapter Guides	**Purpose-Setting Questions**
Summaries	What did the author consider to be the main point of the chapter?
Review questions	What information should I review or reconsider?
Terms	Did I find and understand the vocabulary specific to the chapter?
Suggested readings	Do I need additional background information? If so, which materials would be most useful for my purposes?

graphics and other features to highlight and clarify important concepts. Chapter summaries or review questions at the end of a chapter provide ways for authors to help you identify what you should be learning.

These features also provide more options for setting more specific learning goals in the *Question* step of SQ3R. Each feature points to a different kind of question about the content. See Table 7.1 for how to use chapter features to phrase helpful questions for your reading.

Analyzing information you're surveying in terms of your background knowledge is a second way to make the *Survey* and *Question* steps more active processes. For each key concept you see, you ask, "How well do I know this now?" You achieve this by rating concepts using a 0–3 scale. Rate completely new concepts as 0. Rate concepts you know a little about as 1. Rate ideas you generally understand as 2. Rate ideas you can confidently and correctly use in writing or speaking as 3. When you go to class or read the chapter, focus on increasing your understanding of items ranked as 0 or 1.

Some texts provide outlines as overviews of content. If yours doesn't, you can create your own using formal or informal styles (see Chapter 6 for examples). Creating chapter maps provides a way for you to get the "big picture" of course content by creating a visual map of a chapter's headings and subheadings. To do so, first turn a sheet of paper horizontally (landscape orientation). At the top of the page write the title. Write the first major heading in the top left corner. Place the next level headings under the major heading. Draw lines to show their relationship to the major heading. Place the next level headings, if any, below the second-level subheadings. Continue the process until you come to the next major heading. Repeat the process until you come to the end of the chapter. Review your map to see what topics are covered and in how much detail. The map also allows you to identify relationships among ideas.

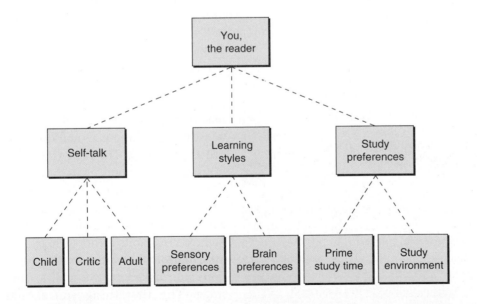

Figure 7.2 Example of a Chapter Map.

Surveying and Setting Learning Goals

activity 1

Use the next chapter of this textbook or a textbook in another course you are currently taking, and complete the survey and question steps of SQ3R to set goals for reading that chapter. List and rate the chapter's key terms using the 0–3 rating scale discussed in this module.

What's the best way to highlight and mark key information in print materials?

Reading Textbooks

Have you ever considered that watching someone read is sometimes like watching someone sleep? Except for the open book, what really looks different? This is a problem because reading should not be as passive an activity as it appears. It should be an active exercise in finding relevant and important information. Surveying and setting learning goals are the first two steps in the process. What exactly happens when you *Read*?

Take a look at what you've marked and written within this book in Chapters 1 through 6. What did you find? Lots of highlighted information? A few notes? Hardly anything at all? What about other texts? Many students feel uncomfortable writing or marking in their textbooks. Most public and private high schools forbid marking in texts because the texts must be used year after year. Even in college, some students still feel the need to follow such rules. Other students want to resell their texts and hope to get top dollar for "clean" books. Some schools even rent textbooks to help ease tight student budgets. Downloaded digital texts are also commonly used. But in whatever form, your texts are your tools for a course, the same as your pens, notebooks, and computer. If you never wrote in your notebooks or turned on your computer, they would all remain as good as new. But for what? You would get no value from them. The same is true of textbooks. To maximize your text as a tool, you need to use it fully. This means marking your text as you read it. The value you derive from learning far outweighs the cost.

So, how do you read and mark your chapters? First, try to read a whole section at a time. Stop and make a conscious effort to mark the information that answers the questions you asked in the goal-setting stage. The first thing you should mark should be major headings and subheadings. Although they seem obvious, many students skip over them when reading. Marking headings and subheadings focuses your attention on main ideas. Next, mark the key points that answer your questions or add important details. Key

Healthy Snacks
Snacks can add essential vitamins, minerals, and calories to diets.
The key to healthy snacking at any age is what you choose to eat.
Low-fat, high-fiber, nutrient-rich foods instead of snacks are better than foods with fat, calories and few nutrients. A snack that balances carbohydrate, fat, and protein satisfies hunger longer than food with just carbohydrates or sugars.
How do you get this balance? Choosing snacks from two or more food groups makes healthy snacks. Some snacks may be deceiving. For instance, fruit drinks, mixes, and punches are loaded with sugar. This sugar usually in the form of high-fructose corn syrup. They are more like soft drinks than fruit juice. Fruit rolls and bars are not fresh fruit. They are more like jams and jelly. Sugar is added to them. And, most of the nutrients in the fruit are lost when it cooked. Energy and protein bars can also fool you. They are like candy bars. They have sugar and fat. Even some kinds of microwave popcorn aren't good snacks because of added oil and salt. You can microwave your own popcorn and not add extras. When snacking, try alternatives that provide at least two food groups. Choose snacks that have 100–250 calories per serving.

Figure 7.3 Overmarked Text.

points and details are generally less than complete sentences but more than just a word or two. If you mark complete sentences, you're probably not being selective enough. If you mark only boldfaced or other terms, you are probably not getting enough information. You'll need more to fully understand the details that support the key points. Last, you should selectively mark graphics (photos and figures). Graphics have different purposes. Photos usually reinforce a key concept. The captions of graphics convey major ideas that would be useful for you to mark. Diagrams, charts, and other nonphoto graphics are included to provide additional details about a topic or to give you a visual perspective on important information. Visual learners prefer gathering information from graphs, charts, and pictures in much the same way verbal learners might prefer written information. Mark the key terms within them as you would in paragraphs.

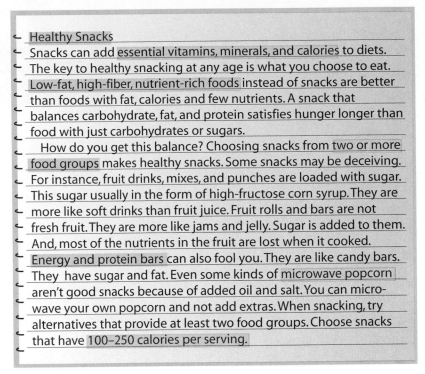

Healthy Snacks
Snacks can add essential vitamins, minerals, and calories to diets.
The key to healthy snacking at any age is what you choose to eat. Low-fat, high-fiber, nutrient-rich foods instead of snacks are better than foods with fat, calories and few nutrients. A snack that balances carbohydrate, fat, and protein satisfies hunger longer than food with just carbohydrates or sugars.

How do you get this balance? Choosing snacks from two or more food groups makes healthy snacks. Some snacks may be deceiving. For instance, fruit drinks, mixes, and punches are loaded with sugar. This sugar usually in the form of high-fructose corn syrup. They are more like soft drinks than fruit juice. Fruit rolls and bars are not fresh fruit. They are more like jams and jelly. Sugar is added to them. And, most of the nutrients in the fruit are lost when it cooked. Energy and protein bars can also fool you. They are like candy bars. They have sugar and fat. Even some kinds of microwave popcorn aren't good snacks because of added oil and salt. You can microwave your own popcorn and not add extras. When snacking, try alternatives that provide at least two food groups. Choose snacks that have 100–250 calories per serving.

Figure 7.4 Undermarked Text.

Learning occurs when you convert information you see or hear into your own understanding. Unfortunately, after time, marking can become almost automatic. You do it with little, if any, thought. Before you know it, an entire page is marked and you have no idea what it is about. **Labeling,** or making a note on the side of the page, is a way of taking notes as you read. It is an alternative to mindless marking. Labeling captures your thoughts as part of the *Recite* stage of the SQ3R process. This then creates a kind of index for study and Review in the last stage of the process. It lessens the need for rereading highlighted text each time you review.

To label text, you look at what you've read and marked. You summarize what you marked and write your summaries in your text, notebook or computer. These summaries are your labels. They organize what you read. They become review cues for use in preparing for a test.

What if you don't understand a section well enough to summarize and label it? First, check to be sure that you understand the key terms. Use your text's glossary or a dictionary to define words you don't know. Second, analyze the section by rereading it sentence by sentence. If you've been reading and studying for an extended time, a brief break before rereading may also help you regain focus. Third, determine if the problems you are having result from a lack of background knowledge. If so, refer to other, less-difficult treatments of the topic such as online dictionary or encyclopedia entries. You could also ask your instructor or campus librarian to recommend resources on the Internet or in your campus library. Once you understand the basics from the outside source, reread your text. If all your independent strategies fail, get help from your instructor, classmates or study group. These and other reading problems and solutions are all within your control—you decide what the problem is, and you find a solution. See Table 7.2 for some hints on how to find solutions to reading problems you may have.

labeling
A note that identifies important information, usually written on the side of a page.

What are healthy snacks?	Healthy Sancks
—low-fat, high-fiber, nutrient	Snacks can add essential vitamins, minerals, and calories to diets. The key to
(vit/min)-rich	healthy snacking at any age is what you choose to eat. Low-fat, high-fiber, nutrient-
—balanced in carbs, proteins,	rich foods instead of snacks are better than foods with fat, calories and few nutrients.
fats = hunger satisfied	A snack that balances carbohydrate, fat, and protein satisfies hunger longer than
	food with just carbohydrates or sugars.

Choose snacks from 2 or more groups

Deceptive snacks (hidden sugar, too much fats or salt)

How do you get this balance? Choosing snacks from two or more food groups makes healthy snacks. Some snacks may be deceiving. For instance, fruit drinks, mixes, and punches are loaded with sugar. This sugar usually in the form of high-fructose corn syrup. They are more like soft drinks than fruit juice. Fruit rolls and bars are not fresh fruit. They are more like jams and jelly. Sugar is added to them. And, most of the nutrients in the fruit are lost when it cooked. Energy and protein bars can also fool you. They are like candy bars. They have sugar and fat. Even some kinds of microwave popcorn aren't good snacks because of added oil and salt. You can microwave your own popcorn and not add extras. When snacking, try alternatives that provide at least two food groups. Choose snacks that have 100–250 calories per serving.

Figure 7.5 Labeled Notes.

Table 7.2 Reading Problems and Solutions

Lack of experience in asking questions	• Practice with index cards by putting a question on one side and the answer on the other. • Practice with a study partner. • Review types of questioning words.
Lack of concentration/too many distractions	• Study in a quiet place. • Study in short blocks of time over a longer period. • Use SQ3R. • Set learning goals.
Unfamiliar terms	• Use context (words surrounding the unknown word). • Use structural analysis (prefixes and suffixes). • Use the text's glossary. • Find the word in a dictionary or thesaurus.
Lack of understanding	• Reread or skim for main ideas. • Scan for specific information. • Verbalize confusing points. • Paraphrase, summarize, or outline main ideas. • Consult an alternate source. • Reset learning goals. • See your instructor or a tutor. • Form a study group.
Speed	• Adjust speed to purpose. • Take a speed-reading course. • Practice with a variety of materials. • Read recreationally.
Failure to identify text structure	• Examine transition words as you reread (similar to lecture transition words). • Outline or map the paragraph or passage. • Find and label the main idea of each paragraph.
Identify text patterns	• Outline or map details. • Summarize the main idea in your own words.

Marking, Organizing, and Labeling Content

1. Using the text you chose for Activity 1, mark the text to answer the learning goals you identified. Create text labels for the text you read in Activity 1.

2. Reexamine your goals. How much of the information do you recall? How and why does marking and labeling content affect memory?

3. Use the 5C process—Define the **C**hallenge; Identify **C**hoices; Predict **C**onsequences; **C**hoose an option; **C**heck your outcome—to decide if text labeling and marking is the process you should use to read textbooks.

GROUP APPLICATION: Discuss with your group your feelings about the time requirements for marking and labeling texts and the trade-off that comes with the time expenditure. Compare marked and labeled chapters to evaluate how your group feels each of you did with this activity.

How do I read and note information from nontraditional sources?

Course Readings in Nontraditional Text Formats

narrative text
Readings that tell a story; narrative text can be both fiction and nonfiction.

The use of SQ3R depends on the kinds of headings and subheadings found in subject-area textbooks. You need another way to read short stories, literature, and other forms of **narrative texts** that have no headings or subheadings. That's because not every course uses a textbook with traditional chapter formats. Some course texts consist of a collection of readings or essays.

Students often find such texts confusing because they contain a variety of writing styles and text types. However, authors usually organize the readings in some systematic way. Previewing helps you determine how the readings and the lecture will fit together. Collections of articles, portions of chapters from books, examples, study guides, or other nontraditional course readings serve three important purposes. If used in addition to a traditional text, some reinforce information in a text chapter. These may provide extra information about topics briefly discussed in the chapter. They might simplify complex concepts. Others, such as study guides, help you learn text information more easily. Such materials often present more current information. This information may provide new or conflicting points of view on the topic.

Tomlinson (1997) created a six-step process for taking notes from nontraditional text. It lets you progress from simple recall of details to a deeper understanding. Step 1 suggests that you give a code letter to each theme, character, and concept you need to trace throughout the text. In Step 2, you create a directory of your codes either in the front of your book or in your notebook. Consistent use of a code for particular concept simplifies the process. In Step 3, list the code letters in your notebook leaving space between the letters. In Step 4, you read your text and place the appropriate code letter beside relevant information. List the page number next to the code number you have already written in your notebook in Step 5. Step 6, the last one, suggests you keep a notebook page for each major theme, character, or concept and write a brief summary or make notes about key details. You should also note text page numbers for future reference. An example of this notetaking system is applied to *After the First Death* in Figure 7.6.

Code Directory Inside Front Cover

I–innocence

B–bravery

L–love

P–physical

I–intellectual

E–emotional

S–social

Code Directory Inside Back Cover

I   129, 144, 183
B   146, 211,
L   145,

Kate
P–68, 144
I–68, 69
E–68, 69, 99, 105, 123,
S–69, 129–130

Miro

. . .

Ben

. . .

Page 68 Coded

P   . . . She was blond, fair skinned, slender, no
        weight problems, had managed to avoid
P   adolescent acne. A healthy body with one
        exception: the weak bladder. . . . cheer-
P   leader, prom queen, captain of the girls'
        swimming team, budding actress in the
        Drama Club. . . . But there were other Kate
        Forresters, and she wondered about them
        sometimes. The Kate Forrester who awoke
E   suddenly at four in the morning and for no
        reason at all couldn't fall back to sleep. The
        Kate Forrester who couldn't stand the sight
        of blood. . . .

Page 69 Coded

She wanted to find somebody to love, to love
forever . . . That question brought up another   E
Kate Forrester disguise. Kate the manipulator
. . . Getting straight A's from Mr. Kelliher in   E
math and barely lifting a finger to do so but
knowing how to smile at him, feign interest . . .
She'd always been an excellent student in   I
math. She didn't know why she'd gone out of
her way to charm Mr. Kelliher. Just as she didn't
know why she used the same charm to win
the role of Emily in the Drama Club's presentation of *Our Town*. She knew she could play
the part, she was certain of the talent. . . . Gene
Sherman. Kate had been enthralled by him . . .   S
until they sat together during a lunch break

Figure 7.6   Example of Tomlinson Notetaking System.

Tomlinson Notetaking

activity 3

Visit the archive at *The Logos*, the student newspaper at North Iowa Area Community College (http://staff.niacc.edu/logos/vol33/current/archive.html) and choose a date. Examine the articles found and select one that you find interesting. Download and print this article. Use the notetaking system designed by Tomlinson and discussed in this section to mark and label what you think is important.

GROUP APPLICATION: In small groups, discuss the differences and similarities in marking and labeling nontraditional text and textbooks.

How do I take notes from online readings?

Online Reading Techniques and Tools

The goal in any kind of academic reading is the same whether what you read is in a traditional textbook, e-book, or online. You look at how the author organized information and focused attention on ideas within it. You find, understand, and organize key information for future reference and use. Many of the same features used in print content (e.g., headings/subheadings; boldfaced terms; graphics) are also found in online content. Thus, the same techniques used to read and understand print apply to online content. If you have an e-book version of your text, the techniques are exactly the same because the e-book format is the same as the print version.

Wouldn't it be nice if someone could read information aloud to you as you commute, do household chores, or get ready for work or class? Now someone can. Free software that you can download online converts text to speech. You can use it to create files for your computer or MP3 player. Different voices and dialects are available as well. Either search for "free text to speech downloads" or go to the links at this textbook's website.

Some online books and software require special plug-ins (special applications designed to run with your Web browser to let you view content). If these are needed, your instructor will inform you or the computer will prompt you how to download them.

Marking, labeling, and organizing online content for future use is just as important as doing so in your texts. There are several free online services that allow you to electronically highlight and bookmark Web content for your use. You can also use it to mark graphics and take notes. Other online tools allow you to label Web pages and organize and search your notes for future reference. If you like to use sticky notes to show important information, you will love virtual stickies. They can be attached to websites as well as documents so they only show when the page is onscreen. You can find these tools and more by searching for "online highlighters," "online Web notes," or "virtual stickies." You'll also find links for these tools at the text website.

TIPS FOR ONLINE READING

1. **Know your instructor's (and thus, your) purpose for using the site.** Your instructor included each site for a reason. If the site is listed as a resource with no specific directions, the purpose is probably to provide background or supplementary information. Other purposes include case study or personal perspective, collection of data, current news, contrasting perspective, multimedia content, interactive content (e.g., surveys, assessments, exercises), demonstrations, or collections of hyperlinks to other online content.

2. **Know what you need to do with the site's information.** Once you access the site, reread the assignment reading prompt (e.g., *Read this in preparation for this week's discussion posts*; *Read this as background for this week's online chat,* etc.). This helps you set a purpose for reading. Look for additional information from the instructor that tells you how you are to respond. For instance, the discussion prompt might be: *After reading Smith's commentary on global warming, identify a potential flaw in his thinking as your original post to the discussion. Do not replicate any of the flaws identified in prior original posts. In a reply post, provide the textbook information that explains the flaw. Reference the textbook information by page number.*

3. **Adapt SQ3R for online use.** Survey any features included on the site. As in reading print materials, read a section at a time. Stop after each one to summarize and check understanding. Look for the information that meets your purpose. Restate in your own words for your discussion or assignment.

Marking and Labeling Online Content
activity 4

Imagine that your instructor has asked you to choose what you think are the top three Web pages for new students at your college's website. Use the 5C process—Define the **C**hallenge; Identify **C**hoices; Predict **C**onsequences; **C**hoose an option; **C**heck your outcome—to select one of the online tools (or a similar online tool) identified in this module. Use it to mark what you think is important and make notes on the Web pages explaining your choice.

GROUP APPLICATION: In small groups, decide which tool was best to use. Be prepared to demonstrate the tool to the class.

How is critical reading different from the way I usually read?

Critical Reading and Thinking

Reading and thinking are alike in that they are invisible processes. You don't really know what people do when they read. You can't actually see how someone thinks about something. Reading and thinking are alike in other ways. Both occur at literal, inferential, and critical levels. At the *literal* level, you read for the stated, most obvious meaning in a text. When you think at literal levels, you think about the most basic, salient characteristics of an idea. For example, suppose you read these sentences: "Abraham Lincoln's wife Mary was from the South. Her stepbrothers fought as Confederates." These facts might be new to you or not, but they are just facts.

Figure 7.7 Bloom's Taxonomy.

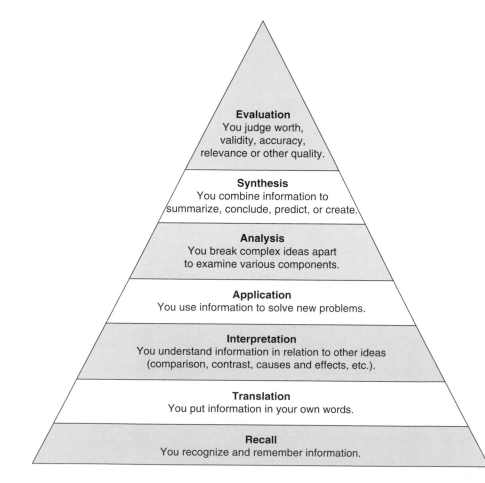

Evaluation
You judge worth, validity, accuracy, relevance or other quality.

Synthesis
You combine information to summarize, conclude, predict, or create.

Analysis
You break complex ideas apart to examine various components.

Application
You use information to solve new problems.

Interpretation
You understand information in relation to other ideas (comparison, contrast, causes and effects, etc.).

Translation
You put information in your own words.

Recall
You recognize and remember information.

When you read at *inferential* levels, you read between the lines. That is, you read to infer relationships and draw conclusions about the text. When you think inferentially, you question relationships, "think outside the box," and hypothesize conclusions about what you see, hear, and experience. You ask questions about what you are reading. For instance, "Since Mary Lincoln was from the South, her family fought against the Union her husband pledged to preserve." On reading these lines, you might think, "How did this affect President and Mary Lincoln's marriage? Did people in Washington, D.C., hold her family against her? Which side of her family did she support?"

When you read *critically,* you examine the text from as many angles as you can to question its meaning, purpose, or truth. Similarly, when you think critically, you look at people, issues, and ideas from as many angles as you can to question their meanings, purposes, or truths.

Psychologist Benjamin Bloom created a **taxonomy,** or a list of groups that lets you identify differences and similarities among the groups (see Figure 7.7), that applies to these levels of reading and thinking. It shows how thinking changes as you consider a subject in more and more depth.

You can use Bloom's taxonomy to identify different learning tasks depending on the nature of your assignments. You can use it to set learning goals at different levels by the questions you ask. The tasks and questions in Table 7.3 provide examples of how you might use this thinking tool.

As a college student, you use different levels of the taxonomy depending on the learning tasks you need to complete. These levels explain why the same subjects you took in high school seem so different in college.

Many high school texts and exams focus more on lower levels—recognition and recall of information, the ability to express stated information in different words (translation), and sometimes, identifying relationships (interpretation) or using information in new situations (application).

taxonomy
A list of ordered groups or categories that lets you identify differences and similarities among the groups.

Table 7.3 Using Bloom's Taxonomy to Set Learning Goals

Level	Tasks	Example Questions
Recall	Recalling vocabulary Memorizing lines of poetry Playing musical notes or melodies Recalling mathematical facts (for example, multiplication tables) Remembering rules of grammar	What does *casa* mean? Recite the first verse of the poem. Play the first sixteen measures of the song. What is the formula for the area of circle? How should the sentence be punctuated?
Translation	Paraphrasing information Creating a chart, diagram, or other visual device based on written information Describing art, music, process, or other event	In your own words, define *postsecondary education.* Create a timeline of the key events in the American Revolution. How would you characterize impressionistic art?
Interpretation	Comparing and contrasting Determining causes and effects Identifying denotations and connotations	How is poetry like music? How is it different? What happens when you mix an acid and a base? What does *college* mean to you?

Table 7.3 Using Bloom's Taxonomy to Set Learning Goals (*Continued*)

Level	Tasks	Example Questions
Application	Using a theory or formula to solve problems Grouping or classifying information Solving word problems	What formulas will I use on the test? In which category does this word fit? If tax is 8%, what is the total cost of a $6.73 item?
Analysis	Identifying stated or inferred details that support a main idea or conclusion Examining the form or style of music, poetry, literature, or art Identifying a math or science problem by type Identifying information relevant to the solution of a problem Identifying statements of fact, opinion, or expert opinion Identifying figures of speech Identifying gaps in logical sequences of arguments	What led you to that conclusion? How did the poet create a feeling of sadness? What kind of problem is #3? What do you need to solve the problem? Which of the statements are factual? Underline the metaphors in the passage. Why is the argument flawed?
Synthesis	Writing creatively or from research Composing music Creating works of art Designing an experiment	Write an essay that describes your college experiences. Write a song about yourself. Draw a picture that expresses your feelings about your family. What is the point of the experiment?
Evaluation	Determining consistency Making decisions Judging worth	Do the descriptions agree? What is your choice? Which answer is best?

College faculty assume you can read and think at those levels. They focus on higher levels of reading and thinking. They, too, expect you to draw conclusions (interpretation) or solve problems (application). Instructors also want you to break complex concepts into parts (analysis). They ask you to create new ideas (synthesis) and make judgments (evaluation).

So, how do you meet the expectations of college faculty? First, you have to understand what you read at *literal* levels. You should know the definitions of words and state their meanings. You should be able to paraphrase or summarize what you've read. If you don't know meanings, stop and refer to the text glossary or a dictionary. If you can't put information in your own words, you need to reread. Next, you make *inferences* to find main ideas and relationships among details. You draw conclusions. These reorganizations of ideas often form your text labels. If you can't reorganize ideas, you reread, see your instructor, or talk about information with your study group.

Now, you are ready to *think critically*. These levels are rarely achieved when you first read or think about new information. In fact, you may not get there until your second or third reading. Rather, this level of thinking happens over time as you review and rethink information.

For instance, consider how your thinking about college has changed since the start of the semester. Before you began, your idea of "college class" may have been pretty basic. After attending a few classes, you probably found that your understanding of a "college class" was changing. You now see relationships between the lectures and text assignments. You've found relationships between the ways you prepare for different classes. You see how future courses might build on what you are currently learning.

You probably assume that higher-level classes are harder than your first year coursework. And you are right. But you will most likely make better grades in more advanced courses in your major than you will in freshman coursework. Why? Because you will have learned how to apply what you know to new subjects. You will have learned to think about information in more complex ways. For example, you will analyze your classes and know what really makes a good class or instructor. You may have to create (synthesize) presentations. You might even critique or evaluate presentations that other students give. You will be a critical thinker.

Thinking and discussing content are more exciting than memorizing content and better for you!

Thinking Critically about Text Content

activity 5

Look at the newspaper text you labeled or marked as important in Activity 3. Use the examples of questions from the list in Table 7.3 to create learning questions about the labeled text that will help you read. Be sure to ask one question for each level of Bloom's taxonomy.

GROUP APPLICATION: Exchange your learning questions with a partner. While your partner evaluates your questions, check his/hers to see if there is one at each level of the taxonomy. Which questions would be the easiest to answer? Which would be the hardest?

chapter review

Respond to the following on a separate sheet of paper or in your notebook.

1. What aspect of preparing to learn is most challenging for you?

2. Which type of organizational format do you most prefer? Why?

3. What aspect of textbook reading is most difficult for you? Why?

4. Do you tend to overmark or undermark your texts? Why?

5. What information should be marked in a textbook? How does this relate to the information that should be labeled?

6. What are some strategies for reading outside materials? Which do you feel would work best for you?

7. How is reading online different from reading print materials? How is it the same?

8. Give an example of something you've done—either for school, work, or home—at each level of Bloom's taxonomy.

9. Identify three times during a typical class day when you have at least five minutes to read over text labels you have recently made. Be specific.

10. How does decision making apply to reading course materials? At the most basic level, the decision is to read or not and the consequences are probably pretty obvious. But other decisions about the reading and studying process are less clear. Use the 5C process—Define the **C**hallenge; Identify **C**hoices; Predict **C**onsequences; **C**hoose an option; **C**heck your outcome—and what you have learned in this chapter to identify what you think might be your biggest reading problem and a possible solution.

did you decide?

Did you accomplish what you wanted to in this chapter? Check the items below that apply to you.

Review the *You Decide* questions that you identified at the beginning of the chapter, but look at them from a new direction. If you didn't check an item below, review that module until you feel you can confidently apply the strategies to your own situation. However, the best ideas are worthless unless they are put into effect. Use the 5Cs to help you decide what information you found most helpful in the chapter and how you plan to use it. Record your comments after the statements below.

☐ 7.1 I know how to prepare for learning.

_____

_____

☐ 7.2 I have a good method to highlight and mark key information in print materials.

_____

_____

☐ 7.3 I understand how to read and note information from nontraditional sources.

_____

_____

☐ 7.4 I can take notes from online readings.

_____

_____

☐ 7.5 I know what it means to think or read critically.

_____

_____

perspectives

Find your passion, remember you are unique, and don't listen to people who say you can't succeed. Tompkins Cortland Community College (TC3) alumnus Robert DuBois delivered that message to the Class of 2008 in a speech titled "Following Your Own Unique Path."

Respond to the following questions:

1. What is an aquatic ecology? How much do you think this field has changed since Dubois graduated?

2. What kind of student do you think you are? Is that the same as the kind of student you were in the past? Why or why not?

3. What is the passion that drives your life?

4. How do you think Dubois defines success? Is this different from the success Lewis suggests? How is it similar or different from your personal definition?

5. Choose the most difficult course in which you are enrolled. Describe how you can use the 5C process to make decisions about success in the course.

   A. What challenge is affecting your passion for success in this course?

   B. What key **C**hoices are open to you?

   C. What would be the major **C**onsequence(s) of each choice?

   D. What option will you **C**hoose?

   E. How can you **C**heck the outcome of your decision?

Robert DuBois, a liberal arts and sciences graduate from TC3's class of 1979 who is now a leader in his field of aquatic ecology, talked to the graduation class about how TC3 shaped his life. "I was a terrible student in high school," he said. "Statistics show that only one out of every 100 people in the world gets a chance at a college degree. I had squandered several chances before coming here and learning how to learn."

After graduating from TC3, he went on to earn a bachelor's degree from Cornell University. He is very successful in his career, and he offered some simple advice to graduates. "I learned how important it is to find your passion in life," DuBois told the graduates. "We're all poised to make a unique contribution in life. Finding your passion means finding a career that is a good fit for who you are."

He said the key to happiness is doing something that matters to you. "Once you've found your passion, head for it like a heat seeking missile and don't let anyone tell you that you can't achieve your dreams," said DuBois. "My wish for you is that you will find your passion, persevere through obstacles, and through it all, maintain your enthusiasm."

The audience also heard from a member of the graduating class. Justine Lewis talked about what she learned at TC3 and what she hopes for her classmates. "We can use the degree we've earned here at TC3 to gain wealth or power, or we can use it to achieve the most coveted type of success . . . the one I hope you carry with you, tucked in your heart. It's all about really living our lives, never forgetting that this life is not a dress rehearsal."

reflecting on decisions

Now that you have read this chapter, can you think of ways to improve what you learn from your reading assignments?

SHARING YOUR LOVE
OF BOOKS

Just like practice makes you a better athlete or musician, you become a better reader when you practice reading. Reading for fun, or recreational reading, lets you gain both practice and background information with which to make your reading stronger. Do you have any books that you enjoyed but no longer want? www.BookCrossing.com is a site where many people in many countries share their love of books. You join them by registering a book on the site and then leaving it somewhere a new reader could find it—a classroom, bus seat, or coffee shop. You then log onto the site and track the book on its journey around the world.

❮ CHOOSING TO SERVE

REVIEW

Skim the notes you made throughout the chapter. How does the content fit together? What information is still unclear? Were your learning goals met? Can you answer the review questions and define terms?

❮ CHOOSING TO BE AN ACTIVE LEARNER

CHAPTER **EIGHT**

Decisions about Study and Test Taking

Tests often seem like obstacles to overcome. In reality, they are a measurement of what you know and how well you know it. They allow you to show or prove that you know and understand the material. How do you decide what to study?

YOU DECIDE

To *wonder* means to think or have curiosity about. Things and ideas you wonder about often mask a need for a decision. Check the items below that apply to you.

In terms of studying and test taking, I've been wondering . . .

☐ 8.1 What do I need to prepare to study?

☐ 8.2 How do I get my notes, text content, and other materials organized?

☐ 8.3 How do I remember what I need to know on a test?

☐ 8.4 What online tools can help me prepare for an exam?

☐ 8.5 How do I keep from getting stressed before and during tests?

☐ 8.6 What can I do to maximize my success on exams?

☐ 8.7 What can a returned test tell me?

Each of these decision points corresponds to the numbered modules that follow. Turn to the module for immediate help.

CHOOSING TO BE AN ACTIVE LEARNER

SURVEY

Before reading this chapter, prepare for learning. Purposefully skim the title, introduction, headings, and graphics. As you survey, decide what information you already know and what information is new to you.

QUESTION

Change each section's heading into a question. This forms your learning goal for reading.

READ

Read the section without marking. Reread and mark key information that answers your question.

RECITE

Stop after each section and make sure you understood the content. Organize or summarize content and make notes.

Decisions about Study Preparation

studying

The purposeful acquisition of knowledge or understanding.

Although the goal of college is learning, you often show what you learned by how you do on tests. Such preparation is called **studying,** or, in terms of SQ3R, Review. Although you might think of review as passive repetition of content, it's actually much more. It is an active decision to learn. You start through your decisions about preparation. This includes knowing when, where, what, and how much to study as well as if you should study alone or with others.

Deciding When and Where to Study

Deciding when and where to study puts you in control of your learning. This control lets you make the most of your study sessions. You start by setting a regular time and place for study. This helps you focus attention through conditioning. It creates a "worksite" where you know your job is to study rather than relax or do other things. Just as distractions in the classroom cause you to lose focus, distractions and disorganization at your study site (e.g., noise from family or others; messy work areas) sabotage study time. Look for a secluded study site away from visual, auditory, and moving stimuli. If your study site is cluttered, you'll find your concentration split. Remove extra materials and keep out only what you need. If you use your computer to take notes while you study, close other applications.

Similarly, the same thoughts—worry, boredom, procrastination and so on—that distract your attention during class also affect study time. Setting learning goals and using time management strategies help. Analyzing and then organizing what you need to learn help you focus. For instance, when you can divide a large job (e.g., learning 10 chapters for a history exam) into smaller, more manageable tasks, it becomes easier to stay on task. Varying activities and using active study strategies keep you from getting bored. For instance, you might read for 20 minutes and then create a timeline that shows the time periods you covered. Studying using your learning style helps maximize memory as well. For example, if you are visual learner, mapping content or drawing pictures may help you recall information more easily. If you are an auditory learner, create study tapes or digital audio files to listen to. If you are a kinesthetic learner, make learning hands on by typing, drawing, or creating flash cards you can manipulate. Finally, pace yourself. Cramming produces panic and keeps you from concentrating fully.

Deciding How Much and What to Study

You decide how much you need to study. Like other decisions you make, you base your choices on your goals and values. There may be times when family, work, or other coursework comes before study. But such choices must be conscious ones you can live with. For instance, if you need to work, you may decide that making a B, C, or even a D grade is OK from time to time. The key is knowing your level of comfort. If you feel you need an A in every course, you must be prepared to make the decisions that will let you to do that. If your life requires you to balance other responsibilities with study, you may need to reconcile yourself to less than perfect grades sometimes.

Once you make your choices, answer the following questions to help you decide what to study. Your responses to these questions will help you create a study checklist of specific topics and chapters to address.

1. **What does the test cover?** The scope of the information often helps you decide how many details you need to know. The more information an exam covers (e.g., numerous lectures, several chapters, other materials) or the fewer the questions on the exam, the broader the questions will be. Tests over fewer chapters or that have more questions may be more detailed.

   For instance, if a test over six short stories consists of only three essay questions, your responses should fit several concepts into each answer. You may have to find broad relationships among several stories in each essay. On the other hand, a multiple-choice test of 50 questions over the same information often requires you to isolate and analyze information more specifically.

2. **Is the test comprehensive?** Comprehensive exams include all information from the beginning of the course. Tests that are not comprehensive cover all information discussed since the last exam.

3. **What is the format of the test: objective (e.g., matching, multiple choice, true-false) or subjective (essay or short answer)?** Objective tests require you to recall and use information to solve problems and choose answers from given choices. Subjective exams require you to produce written responses—usually in paragraph or essay form—to questions.

4. **What levels of thinking will I be expected to use?** In general, you will be asked few, if any, questions requiring simple recall of memorized information. Most questions require you to interpret, analyze, and apply what you've learned (recall our discussion in Chapter 7).

5. **How much does the test count in my final grade?** This helps you decide how much time and effort to devote to test preparation. For instance, perhaps you have the same average in two courses. The final for one course counts for 10 percent of your grade. The final for the other exam counts for 25 percent of your grade. If you must make decisions about what to study, you would be better served by studying for the second exam.

6. **What special materials will I need for the test?** Some materials (e.g., calculator) may be permitted for an exam (check with your instructor).

TIPS FOR STUDYING FOR AN EXAM

1. Have a regular place to study that is free from distraction. Keep all your study materials there.

2. Synthesize (combine) lecture, textbook, and other notes.

3. Make a test review that includes the following:
   - Points emphasized in the textbook
   - Points stressed during class lecture or other content
   - Questions in study guides, old quizzes and tests
   - Review questions from the end of textbook chapters
   - Lists of terms and their definitions

4. Once you know what you need to study, separate it into tasks. Divide the tasks into the number of days you have before the exam. Set and stick to deadlines. Schedule specific times to study and identify learning goals for each of your study sessions.

5. Plan each study session to include breaks.

6. Create a practice test several days before your exam is scheduled. Take the practice test on the day before your exam. Review only the information you miss.

study group
Two or more students who work together to learn information.

Other materials (e.g., #2 pencils, blue book, standardized answer form) are essential to your ability to take the test. Don't wait until the morning of the exam to ask what supplies you should bring.

7. **What time constraints affect my study time?** Compare how much study time you think you need to get the grade you want with the amount of time you have to prepare. If needed, find ways to shift priorities to reallocate to study time. Schedule specific times to study and identify learning goals for each of your study sessions.

Deciding Whom to Study With: Alone or in Groups

Studying on your own has advantages. Finding mutually beneficial times to meet is not a problem in that case. Missing a study session affects no one but yourself. You don't have to worry about the possibility of group members letting you down by not doing their share of the work. Studying on your own can also have disadvantages. You have no one to depend on but yourself. If you miss a study session, you miss out. You don't have anyone to help share the load. In truth, studying with others has many other benefits as well.

A **study group** is a valuable way for you to meet others and get involved in campus life. But the highest value of a study group is what study groups actually do: actively discuss and share information and study. Therefore, members of a study group need to have good communication skills, a common purpose, the ability to set goals, and the skills to achieve those goals. Creating and maintaining such groups are often easier said than done.

Research suggests that study groups provide optimum learning opportunities. For instance, small-group learning works better than studying in large groups, independent study, or in some cases one-to-one tutoring from a faculty member. Why?

Study groups let you see, hear, and practice your problem-solving, communication, and learning skills. They ensure active learning through participation. They allow you to observe the way other people think and to hear what they think about course content. Being in a study group also focuses your attention. You are less likely to let your mind wander when engaged in a discussion. Study groups force you to keep regularly scheduled study times. You will experience less stress because study group members encourage and support each other.

Getting the Most from Your Study Group

1. **Select group members who have similar academic interests and dedication to the success of the group.** Friends do not always make the best study partners. Study group members need to be prepared to discuss the topic at hand, not what happened at last night's party. If you aren't sure which class members want to form a study group, ask your instructor to make an announcement, place a sign-up sheet on a nearby bulletin board, or e-mail the class through your course management system.

2. **Seek group members with similar skills and motivation.** The group functions best when each member adds to the overall learning of the group and no one uses the group as a substitute for personally learning information. Dismiss members who fail to live up to their time, preparation, or participation commitments.

3. **Limit group size to five or fewer students.** You need to feel comfortable with and actively participate in a study group. Too many people limit participation. In addition, scheduling meeting times for a large number of members tends to be an impossible task.

4. **State the purpose and lifetime of the group.** Some groups tend to drag on without a real focus or end. Instead, the group should begin by answering some key questions: What do we want to do and how long will it take? Will we meet until the next test, the completion of a project, or the end of the course? Will we focus on problem solving, conceptual development, or a class project? Group goals require measurable outcomes and

deadlines. Each session needs a purpose. Feelings of achievement and closure at the end of each study session and at the end of the group's life span add to your academic success.

5. **Schedule regular group meetings at the same time and place.** Meetings should start and end on time. Although needless interruptions should be discouraged, you should schedule breaks in study sessions as long as the group agrees to return to the task.

6. **Get acquainted.** As a group member, you invest a lot of time and effort with the members of your group. Although you don't need to know their life histories, it does help to know something about each member's level of ability in a course (Are they majoring in history or is this their first course?), their current commitments (Do they have jobs, family, social, or other activities that affect the time at which they can and cannot meet?), and their expectations for the group (Do they want to prepare for the next exam, work on problems, or share reading assignments?). At the very least, exchange names and contact information (phone numbers; e-mail addresses) so that you can reach members in case of an emergency.

activity 1

5Cs and Test Taking

Use the 5C approach—Define the **C**hallenge; Identify **C**hoices; Predict **C**onsequences; **C**hoose an option; **C**heck your outcome—to determine your biggest test-taking problem and find a solution for it.

Organizing Study Materials

Now that you are prepared to study, it's time to get organized. Organizing with **charts** and **maps** helps you actively divide and conquer the materials you need to learn through association. Charts and maps show how you mentally think about and structure information. Much of your learning occurs as you think about and create your charts and maps.

chart
Information presented in columns and rows.

map
A graphic representation of main ideas and details.

Charts

Charts summarize and categorize information. They help you identify and compare or contrast the same factors across differing elements. Making these comparisons lets you find trends. Charts also condense and simplify information. They arrange information by order or time. They emphasize important points. Figure 8.1 shows an example of a chart. The following are the main steps in charting information:

1. Make a vertical list of the concepts you want to compare.

2. List horizontally the factors you want to use in comparing each concept.

3. Draw a grid by sketching lines between each concept and each factor.

4. Locate and record the information that fills each box of the grid.

Explorers and Discoveries

Who?	From Where?	Discovered What?	When?
John Cabot	Italian	Newfoundland	1497
Vasco da Gama	Portugal	Sea route to India	1498
Francisco Fernández de Córdoba	Spain	Yucatan peninsula of Mexico	1517

Figure 8.1 Sample Chart.

Concept Maps

Concept maps organize ideas graphically by showing relationships among them. They show how you organize and think about information. These maps help you integrate notes with text information, gaining greater depth and understanding. This forms your synthesis, or understanding, of the topic as a whole. Concept maps can be created in different ways and show many kinds of information. For instance, they can show rankings of details by branching out from the central topic. Or, maps can show how details relate to a topic by showing a progression of steps or chronological order of events or historical periods. Processing information with maps helps you prepare for all sorts of test questions. Figure 8.2 shows some different mapping structures you might use. The following are the steps in creating a map:

1. Choose a word or phrase that represents your subject or topic (might be a chapter title, purpose-setting question, heading, objective, main term, etc.).

2. Write that word or phrase at the top or center of a page.

Type	Example of Elements	Content Area Applications	Visual Structure
Introductory/ Summary	main ideas supporting details	applicable to any content area	

Subject Development/ Definition	definitions
	supporting details
	examples
	characteristics
	types or kinds
		scientific concepts
		psychological, medical
		   educational, or other
		   case studies
		genres of literature
		styles of music
		political philosophy	

Enumeration/ Sequence	main points details steps elements procedures	mathematical process historical chronology literary plot scientific method computer science programs	
Comparison/ Contrast	similarities pros cons opinions time periods	authors composers case studies political philosophies psychological treatments educational principles scientific theories	
Cause/Effect	problems solutions	historical events scientific discovery mathematical principles scientific principles health and nutrition sociological conditions psychological problems	

Figure 8.2 Mapping Structures.

3. On a separate sheet of paper, list information about the topic (details, components, steps, functions, reasons, etc.). If you feel unsure about how information connects, complete step 3 on separate cards or sticky notes and arrange and rearrange to discover relationships.

4. Examine the elements. How do they relate to each other?

5. Choose the type of idea map that best represents the relationships you identify. (See Figure 8.2.)

6. Lay out the information.

7. Draw lines or arrows to indicate relationships.

Charting and Mapping

1. Create a chart that compares charting and mapping in terms of purpose and format.

2. Using what you read and learned in Module 8.1 in this chapter, create a concept map that shows how to prepare to study in terms of *when, where, what, how much,* and *who.*

3. Which process do you like better, charting or mapping, and why? Do you think that charting and mapping would work better for different subjects? Why?

GROUP APPLICATION: In groups, identify your learning style preferences and your mapping or charting preferences. Are there any surprises? Why might this be so?

How do I remember what I need to know on a test?

Choices for Practicing and Remembering Content

Memory is a skill, like playing baseball or playing the piano. No team or band waits until the night before the big game or concert to prepare. Why? They know practice over time is more effective than cramming at the last minute. Although people think practice makes perfect, that's only true if what you practice is correct. What practice does is make permanent. Thus, memory also needs frequent practice.

What's the best way to use practice to improve memory? First, practice needs to be an active process. Say and/or write what you need to learn. Creating and using flash cards, revising concept maps, discussing information and taking self-tests are part of the active process you need to learn. Second, practice in the form you expect to face during your exam. For instance, if a classroom test includes essay questions, make sure your practice includes actually writing a response by hand in standard essay format. If your test will be timed, practice answering questions with time limitations. Third, be realistic about the amount of time that you can concentrate. No matter what you think, the reality is that you can concentrate for about an hour at a time. Trying to do so for longer results in your attention wandering.

What exactly can you accomplish in an hour of study? Plenty. First, spend the first few minutes of the hour setting a learning goal(s). You should be able to identify what you intend to do during the given time. For instance, you might want to review note cards, create a concept map or outline an essay response. Second, practice actively for approximately 40 minutes. Write, talk, or physically manipulate (e.g., flash cards, mapping, writing, word processing) what you want to remember. Next spend five minutes reviewing what you practiced. Finally, take a break. The break gives your brain time to assimilate information, provides closure and feelings of accomplishment, and gives you a fresh start on your next practice session.

Need an extra boost to recall that formula or term that you always seem to forget? **Mnemonics** are memory tricks that cue your recall. Have a look at Table 8.1. Try several until you find the one(s) that work best for you for the content you need to remember.

Mnemonics
Set of techniques for improving your memory skills.

Table 8.1 Common Mnemonics

Acronyms	Create a "word" from the first letter of the concepts you're trying to recall	*FACE* (spaces on the treble clef in music), *ROY G. BIV* (colors of the rainbow), and *HOMES* (names of the Great Lakes: Huron, Ontario, Michigan, Erie, and Superior)
Acrostics	Create a "sentence" from the first letter of the concepts you're trying to recall	*Every Good Boy Does Fine* (lines of the treble clef in music: E, G, B, D, F), *Please Excuse My Dear Aunt Sally* (order of operations in math: parentheses, exponents, multiplication, division, addition, subtraction).
Association	Link what you need to know with a cue. Think of a humorous or extreme cue.	Green notebook (GO on a traffic light) is notebook for first class on Monday. Yellow notebook (color of the sun) is notebook for astronomy. Black notebook (sum of all colors; night) is planner.
Location	Think of a route you commonly take (e.g., from home to school). As you visualize the route, mentally "place" information you need to know at landmarks along the route. You can also use location by visualizing "where" information is in a book or notes. Adding other visual cues (e.g., exclamation points, highlights in colors, sketches, etc.) makes it more memorable.	You need to recall chemical symbols. You think about the route you take on campus from Building 1 to Building 5. You assign one of the symbols (e.g., Iron = Fe) to each of the buildings.

Patterns	Create an image or record your mental image in written form; this is also called a mnemonigraph (e.g., exclamation points, highlights in colors, sketches, etc.).
	
	Look for ways that concepts are alike or different (e.g., all concepts start with the same letter, end in *ing*, or have similar meanings).
		For example, to remember that similes use *like* or *as*:
		A
		S I M I L E
		     I
		     K
		     E

Word Games	Think of a rhyme, song, limerick, jingle, or saying.	"*I* before *E* except after *C* or when sounded like *A* as in *neighbor* or *weigh*."

Creating Your Own Mnemonics

activity 3

Identify three concepts you need to learn for your next exam in this course. Develop a mnemonic to recall each one.

GROUP APPLICATION: Compare the mnemonics you created with others in your group. Which do you like best? The mnemonics you create for yourself are generally more memorable that those you learn from others. Do you think that is true for you? Why or why not?

What online tools can help me prepare for an exam?

Using Online Tools for Test Preparation

Get a headstart on concept mapping. If you like to create your own, search for concept mapping software on the Web. If you prefer to fill in standard concept mapping templates, search for graphic organizer maker or graphic organizer templates. These allow you to print ready-to-go maps that you can complete. The text website provides links to online concept mapping and graphic organizers sites.

Flash cards no longer have to be written by hand on 3 × 5 note cards. Search for online flash card generators. These allow you to make, use, store, print and even share flash cards. Some also let you practice content in test question formats and as games. Virtual flash cards can also be developed for your iPod and cell phone that allow you to create, organize, and practice content. See the text website for links to flash card generators.

Some cell phones have applications that help you study. More are being developed every day. Visit the website of your cell phone provider and search for study applications. You may be surprised by what you find.

activity 4

Mobile Learning Apps

Use Google, another search engine, or your cell phone to identify three iPod or cell phone apps that you could use for learning. List each, the cost, and the pros and cons of their use.

GROUP APPLICATION: Compare the mobile learning tools you found with others in your group.

Overcoming Test Anxiety

Remember the first day of school? Not college . . . but your first day in kindergarten or first grade. Children are excited to be "big kids" and get to go to school. Generally, most are excited and eager to learn. That soon changes as some children realize that they don't measure up. They don't get the stars on their papers. They get red F's and a note to take home. The pressure to perform—and the anxiety that goes with it—starts early and often continues through elementary and high school years. Or, perhaps you were one of those students that got the stars and the A's on your paper. But you've found the demands in college to be greater. At times, you don't do as well as you'd hoped and the fear sets in.

For some reason, humans most often remember and believe the worst rather than the best about themselves and others. You, too, might find yourself dwelling on past embarrassments, problems, and failures. In similar situations, you think that the same disasters will recur. Your anxiety mounts, you lose confidence, and the cycle repeats itself.

Anxiety about coursework is one of these cyclical processes. When prompted, you feel pressure from within and without. You lack the confidence to succeed. Voices echo in your mind. Examples of this self-talk include statements like, "If I fail this test, I know I'll fail the course." "What if I freeze up?" "I must, I must, I must but I can't, I can't, I can't."

The secret to combating anxiety is twofold. First, figure out what stresses you and why. Is the voice you hear your own? Is it a ghost from your past? Can you believe what is being said? Is it true? Have you *never* performed well under pressure? Have you *never* been able to recall information? What is reality? What is not?

Second, replace negative messages with positive ones (see Chapter 5 for information about self-talk). Consider the coach of a team sport. The coach doesn't say, "Well, our opponent is tough. I don't see any way we can win." Instead, the coach acknowledges the opponent's worth. Then he or she says, "Well, our opponent is tough. But we've practiced hard all week, and I know we're prepared. We can beat them." The coach's talk before a game motivates players to excel even in stressful situations. You can take steps to fight a negative mindset. Success messages help you motivate yourself to succeed.

Remember, however, that the best messages are those you create for yourself. They are personal and meaningful. They help you prepare for success. To be effective, you need to practice them. For example, during a test, make sure your self-talk focuses on the task rather than on yourself: *What is the question I have*

TIPS FOR OVERCOMING MATH ANXIETY

Students who have math anxiety often try to memorize rules and formulas rather than understand the process of math. Once that happens, anxiety takes the places of numbers and letters. Math is a linear process, and understanding that process is absolutely essential. Once you realize you know the process, it's easy to overcome math anxiety.

- Be positive. Use self-talk.

- Be brave. There's no such thing as a dumb question. Ask questions. Make sure you understand the process. Ask for sample problems, illustrations and/or demonstrations.

- Practice. Practice. Practice. Work sample problems until you can do them without looking at the solutions. Then immediately work them again. If you can't immediately rework the problem correctly, you didn't understand it.

- Don't be shy. Go to your instructor's office, visit the learning center, get a tutor or work with a study partner or group.

to answer? What do I need to do? I know information about it. I know worry won't help. This is not a life and death situation. One task at a time. I can do this. Once the test is over, reinforce your coping mechanisms and successes. Your self-talk might be one of the following statements: I did it! I answered every question. The test wasn't as bad as I thought it would be.

Visualization takes positive self-talk one step further. Instead of imagining the worst and seeing yourself fail, you imagine success. Visualization is a powerful process that can produce results through practice. Start your visualization by closing your eyes. Imagine yourself in class. Picture yourself as a confident student who understands lectures and participates actively in class. Watch yourself study for the course. See yourself actively reading and understanding text information. Imagine yourself preparing for a test. You do not feel anxious or tired. Feel yourself learning and feeling good about what you learn. After all you've done your homework. You can expect to do well.

The feeling grows stronger. You feel prepared. Imagine yourself closing your books and gathering your notes. Picture yourself falling asleep. Feel yourself waking up refreshed and ready. Watch yourself review the information. You are calm and prepared. See yourself going to the class in which you have an exam. See yourself walking into the class and sitting down. Visualize yourself being calm and collected. Watch your instructor give you your test. Imagine yourself carefully listening to the verbal instructions and estimating the time needed to complete each section. Watch yourself take the test. You are calm and confident. You think logically. You remember accurately. Watch yourself complete the test and turn it in. Visualize yourself leaving the room. You feel pleased with yourself and your performance. Yes, you *can* do it.

"Relax, you won't feel a thing," say many nurses right before they give you an injection. And, while you're sure to feel the needle going in, it really does hurt less if you can ease the tension in your body. Similarly, **relaxation** eases nervousness and stress. Even in the middle of an exam, you can relax.

relaxation
A positive feeling created through the loosening of muscles.

You relax your muscles by doing a physical body check. Whenever you feel tense, stop and see if any muscles are involved that really don't need to be. For example, suppose you feel your shoulders tense as you take or prepare for a test. Since shoulder muscles play little part in test taking, make a conscious effort to relax them. Finally, conscious, deep breathing also relaxes the body.

memory blocks
Sudden losses of memory for a specific piece of information.

Suppose you fail to control your anxiety, and you "block" information while taking the test. Everyone experiences **memory blocks.** The trick is to prepare for them. When you get hit by a memory block, take a few deep breaths to regain your composure, make your best guess, and continue with the test. Maintain appropriate self-talk so that you stay confident and focused. "Of course I know that, I'll think of it in a minute," relieves stress better than, "What is the matter with me? I must be an idiot! If I can't remember this, I won't be able to remember anything else."

As you continue the test, your brain generally continues processing and looking for the information. If you've ever wracked your brain to think of a name and given up only to recall it later, you've experienced such processing. In addition, as you continue the test, information in other questions may cue your recall. When you return to the question, take a deep breath, think logically, and review everything you know about the topic. Associations of various kinds—recall of when or where you heard or read information, recall from different points of view and so on—often serve to trigger the memory. Sometimes saying the alphabet slowly will unlock the memory of a specific fact. Ask yourself, does it start with *A*? *B*? and so on.

Measuring Your Test Anxiety

How much test anxiety do you have? Answer the following questions with "True" or "False."

_____ **1.** While taking an important exam, I find myself thinking of how much brighter the other students are than I am.

_____ **2.** If I were to take an intelligence test, I would worry a great deal before taking it.

_____ **3.** If I knew I was going to take an intelligence test, I would feel confident and relaxed.

_____ **4.** While taking an important exam, I perspire a great deal.

_____ **5.** During class examinations, I find myself thinking of things unrelated to the actual course material.

_____ **6.** I get to feeling very panicky when I have to take a surprise exam.

_____ **7.** During a test, I find myself thinking of the consequences of failing.

_____ **8.** After important tests, I am frequently so tense my stomach gets upset.

_____ **9.** I freeze up on things like intelligence tests and final exams.

_____ **10.** Getting good grades on one test doesn't seem to increase my confidence on the second.

_____ **11.** I sometimes feel my heart beating very fast during important exams.

_____ **12.** After taking a test, I always feel I could have done better than I actually did.

_____ **13.** I usually get depressed after taking a test.

_____ **14.** I have an uneasy, upset feeling before taking a final examination.

_____ **15.** When I'm taking a test, my emotional feelings do not interfere with my performance.

_____ **16.** During a course examination, I frequently get so nervous that I forget facts I really know.

_____ **17.** I seem to defeat myself while working on important tests.

_____ **18.** The harder I work at taking a test or studying for one, the more confused I get.

_____ **19.** As soon as an exam is over, I try to stop worrying about it, but I just can't.

_____ **20.** During exams, I sometimes wonder if I'll ever get through school.

___ **21.** I would rather write a paper than take an examination for my grade in a course.

___ **22.** I wish examinations did not bother me so much.

___ **23.** I think I could do much better on tests if I could take them alone and not feel pressured by time limits.

___ **24.** Thinking about the grade I may get in a course interferes with my studying and performance on tests.

___ **25.** If examinations could be done away with, I think I would actually learn more.

___ **26.** On exams I take the attitude, "If I don't know it now, there's no point in worrying about it."

___ **27.** I really don't see why some people get so upset about tests.

___ **28.** Thoughts of doing poorly interfere with my performance on tests.

___ **29.** I don't study any harder for final exams than for the rest of my coursework.

___ **30.** Even when I'm well prepared for a test, I feel very anxious about it.

___ **31.** I don't enjoy eating before an important test.

___ **32.** Before an important examination, I find my hands or arms trembling.

___ **33.** I seldom feel the need for "cramming" before an exam.

___ **34.** The university should recognize that some students are more nervous than others about tests and that this affects their performance.

___ **35.** It seems to me that examination periods should not be made such intense situations.

___ **36.** I started feeling very uneasy just before getting a test paper back.

___ **37.** I dread courses where the instructor has the habit of giving "pop" quizzes.

Scoring with the Test Anxiety Scale is very easy. The total number of TRUE answers is your test anxiety score. A score of 12 or below ranks in the low test anxiety range. A score of 12 to 20 ranks in the medium range. Any score above 20 signifies high test anxiety. Scoring 15 or greater is a good indication you experience considerable discomfort about taking tests.

activity 6 — Anxiety and Performance

Identify one course in which stress affects your test performance. Specify the aspect of the course that causes the most anxiety. This is your challenge. Now use the remainder of the 5C process (Define the **C**hallenge; Identify **C**hoices; Predict **C**onsequences; **C**hoose an option; **C**heck your outcome) to find a solution you can use to combat this stress.

GROUP APPLICATION: Share individual answers with your group. What similarities and differences do you discover among your group's answers? What factors might contribute to these similarities and differences?

Choices for Exam Success

You've done the work. You're prepared for the test. Now all you have to do is take it, right? It's not always as easy as it sounds, but there are choices you can make to maximize your performance and your grade. Some test formats (e.g., multiple choice, essay) require special strategies. Other strategies work for all kinds of tests.

First, make sure you are mentally prepared. Be sure you have the materials you need for the test (e.g., #2 pencils, calculator, test forms, etc.). Otherwise, you'll feel panicked. Avoid personal conflicts prior to the test. Getting upset destroys your focus. Get a good night's sleep and eat something nourishing before the exam. Getting physically ready helps you be more mentally ready.

Second, get to the exam on time. If you arrive early, avoid talking to others. Their fears tend to be contagious. If you arrive late, you may miss important verbal directions or you may feel rushed and anxious.

Third, read the exam directions carefully. Although it might seem like a given, many students are so focused on answering the questions that they skip over the directions. However, directions often provide key information you need. Thus, once you get your exam, read the directions. Underline key terms and steps in the directions to ensure that you read them carefully.

Fourth, preview the test. Note total number of questions and variations, if any, in point values. Estimate the amount of time you plan to spend on each item and plan to spend the most time on questions receiving the most credit.

Fifth, answer the easiest questions first. This builds your confidence and triggers your memory for other information. Also, if you run out of time, you will have answered the questions you know. Mark difficult questions, but skip them and go on. Return to them when you have more time to consider them. If there is no penalty for guessing, attempt to answer every question. Make your responses as neat and legible as possible.

Sixth, work at your own pace. Don't worry if some students finish and leave before you do.

Seventh, if time permits, review your questions and answers. Be sure you understood the question and have marked the answer you intended. Some students think it's better to stick with their first response. Actually, that depends on your past performances on tests. Some students find their initial nervousness results in their

Answers come to all who wait . . . whether they're correct or not depends on preparation.

misreading directions or questions. After-exam analysis helps you determine what your decisions should be.

Taking Objective Exams

objective test

A test in which you select an answer from several choices provided by an instructor.

One of the two types of exams given most often in college is the **objective test,** a test in which you select an answer from several choices provided by an instructor. Objective tests require that you recognize or reason out information from the options you are given. There are some ways you can maximize your performance on an objective test.

You need to begin by looking at the stem (the question part) and trying to create an answer before reading the distractors (choices you select from). This helps you focus your thoughts and keeps you from being led astray by **attractive distracters,** that is, incorrect choices that seem plausible. For instance, which of the following presidents left office before impeachment? A. Bill Clinton; B. John F. Kennedy; C. Richard M. Nixon. While you may recall that Clinton's and Kennedy's reputations with the ladies were questionable, and that Clinton faced impeachment, it was Richard Nixon who left office before he was impeached for the Watergate incident.

attractive distracters

Incorrect choices on objective tests that seem plausible.

Even if you don't know the answer to the question, take a guess and go on to the next question. If the question is one you can answer with a little work, take your best guess, mark it, and go on. Return to the question when you have more time.

Often all of the responses are correct in some way. You may be looking for the best choice of the group—check your instructions. It's easy to confuse the first correct answer you see with the *best* choice of correct answers.

The wording of the question affects responses. Look for small words like *not* or *except* that completely change the meaning of the question. Double negatives cancel each other. For example, *not un*lucky means *lucky.* Words that set limits (e.g., *few, sometimes, often*) are more likely to be correct than those that are all inclusive (e.g., *all, none, always, never*).

You should also watch for responses that are essentially the same. Usually this means that neither answer is correct. For example, in the following question answers B and C are synonymous; therefore, neither can be correct.

The _____ branch is the part of the government responsible for interpreting laws.

A. executive

B. legislative

C. congressional

D. judicial

A final suggestion, should you find yourself confused, is make your exam a true-false exam. To do this, you use the stem (the question part) and each possible choice as a true-false question when you feel confused by similar choices. This helps you isolate answers in a logical manner.

Answering Essay Questions

subjective questions

Prompts which require you to write answers in essay or paragraph form.

Although instructors may give objective tests, they may also ask you to respond to **subjective questions.** Some specialized tips help maximize your performance.

First, you should consider choosing a title for your essay or response. Even though you don't actually entitle an answer, a title helps you focus your thoughts and narrow your subject. It will help if you know what information your instructor is asking for. The list in Table 8.2 describes common question/instruction words in essay tests, examples of how they might be used in a question or instruction, and strategies for responding to them. In addition, the key words help you identify the transitions you need for clarity.

Table 8.2 Answering Essay Questions

If You Are Told . . .	As in This Example . . .	Take This Action . . .
Explain, discuss, describe, delineate	Explain how to set up and run a business.	Write as much detail as possible about the topic in a clear, concise, complete manner.
Compare, find the similarities	Compare businesses in the U.S. to businesses in another country.	Discuss the ways in which the two topics are alike.
Contrast, find the differences	Contrast businesses in the U.S. to businesses in another country.	Discuss the ways in which the two topics are not alike.
Criticize, critique, evaluate, review	Criticize current U.S. economic policy toward small business owners.	Discuss the positive and negative aspects of the topic, and conclude with a summary that makes a judgment based on the pros and cons cited.
Justify, support, give a rationale	Justify the need for government aid to minority businesses.	Give facts and figures to defend the topic.
List, enumerate, name, outline	List the three laws that pertain to business.	Give a detailed, numbered list of the items requested.
Summarize	Summarize the major principles that support the North American Free Trade Agreement.	Construct a clear, concise statement that includes all main ideas.
Paraphrase	Paraphrase the following ad copy for a business.	Reword a selection expressing the main ideas in synonymous terms.
Define, clarify, interpret	Define the following terms: entrepreneur, collective bargaining, Consumer Price Index.	Explain the meaning.
Elaborate	Elaborate on the following statement: "U.S. import tariffs should be abolished."	Explain in great detail.
Classify	Classify businesses according to sector of the economy.	Organize in categories.
Trace	Trace the development of accounting ethics in a specific company.	Explain the sequential development of the topic.
Illustrate, diagram, chart	Illustrate the relationship between earnings and taxes.	Draw a graphic representation.
Label	Label the categories of entrepreneurs in the following figure.	Name each part.
Calculate or compute	Using a company's financial statements, calculate its total assets and current liabilities.	Solve a problem.

Next, take a few minutes to outline your response or list a few main points before you begin. An outline keeps you from omitting important details. Write this outline somewhere on your bluebook or paper. Even if you run out of time, your instructor will be able to see where the essay was going. You might receive partial credit.

Standard essay format matters. Using it makes you seem like a more prepared student and a better writer. Introduce your subject, develop the topic, and summarize.

Finally, you need to do a final reading to make sure that your response answers the question that was asked. You need to check organization, coherence, and clarity. It's also important to proof your work. You should check spelling, grammar, and punctuation.

Taking Math and Applied Science Exams

Math and applied science exam preparation begins with your class notes and textbook. To be sure you understand completely, first you need to re-examine the notes you took while your instructor was demonstrating how to solve each problem and the homework problems you have completed. Look for similarities and differences among problems, especially those with which you are having difficulty. Sometimes your understanding of one problem helps you see how to solve another one.

Second, your textbook provides example problems for your practice. You need to study these just as you studied class work and homework examples. In addition, as you work through the examples, you need to identify the concepts, formulas, methods, steps, and rules each example uses. Consider defining these using a list of concepts, and so forth, possibly on index cards. You need to write definitions in your own words, accompanied by a sample problem.

Finally, you need to find additional problems and create for yourself a test similar to the one you think your instructor will give. Then, take it a step further and test yourself under realistic conditions. Give yourself the same amount of time you will have for the real test. It might even help reduce test anxiety if you take your practice exam in the math or applied science classroom.

On the math or science exam itself, you need to solve problems. That's what most math and science instructors want to see. Following are steps in taking math and applied science exams:

1. Quickly examine the exam to locate difficult problems and estimate how much time problems will take.

2. Work in this order: easiest and highest point value; second easiest and highest point value; difficult and highest point value; and difficult and lowest point value.

3. Read each phrase of the problem and underline or write all pertinent information.

4. In your own words, identify what the problem wants you to do.

5. Ask yourself "What do I need to do to solve this problem?" Note relationships among data and relevant formulas.

6. If you get stuck, try one or all of these:

   - Recall an example problem similar to the one you are working, and write the sample problem on paper so you can better study it.

   - Break the problem into parts and work the parts you can. Look for a relationship between what you understand and what you don't.

   - If you cannot work the problem, skip it and go on.

7. Check your solution. Make sure you have the answer in the proper form, and use any checking method you like to double-check your work.

8. Show all your work. Some instructors give partial credit. Even if an instructor doesn't, he or she might indicate where your thinking went astray. This is valuable information for the next exam.

Taking Online Exams

In many ways, taking an online exam is the same as taking a paper and pencil one. The same tips you use for objective, subjective, math, and science questions apply. However, there are a few differences.

If the exam is part of your course management system, be sure you know how to access and find your way around it. There may be special instructions for submitting responses that, if not followed, mean that your exam is never submitted. You may be able to see all the questions at once or you may only get one question at a time. Check and double-check the availability of the exam. Most have specific times at which they open and close. Check to see if the exam is timed. This helps you manage your time.

If you are taking the exam in a testing center, the same rules of conduct apply. You will probably not be allowed to use your text or other materials. But if the exam is one that you can take on your own time at home or in a computer lab, it may be an open-book exam in which you can use course materials. Such exams might seem easy since you can look up the answers. However, instructors often ask more complex questions on open-book tests which require you to find related information, understand it, and apply it to a new situation. Although you don't necessarily need to memorize and practice what you learn, you do need to understand and know where to find it prior to the test.

Ethical Academic Behavior

You know when you are acting ethically or are being your best self. **Ethics** are standards of behavior that tell us how human beings ought to act in certain situations. One type of ethics is called *virtue ethics*. Honesty, integrity, fairness, and self-control are all examples of virtues. Virtue ethics asks of any action, "What kind of person will I become if I do this?" or "Is this action consistent with my acting at my best?"

In all classrooms, and particularly in testing situations, instructors trust you to decide to act according to virtue ethics. They count on you to value your honesty or moral integrity more than your course grade. Instructors also assume that you realize at least two other consequences of cheating. First, getting caught means a failing grade. Failing grades lower your GPA. Second, it's embarrassing and troubling for both you and your instructor. In some cases, cheating can lead to expulsion.

ethics
Standards of behavior that tell us how human beings ought to act in certain situations.

Cheating takes many forms. It includes using cheat sheets (in print or technological form), getting answers from others during tests, and stealing copies of exams. Using your cell phone to get information during an exam (even if it's only the dictionary to check spelling) is cheating. You want to avoid any appearance of cheating. When in doubt, ask yourself, "What would my instructor say?" If you think an instructor would disapprove, it's probably cheating.

Each college has a written code of conduct. It clearly states what it expects of you in terms of ethical behavior. Your college's code of conduct is on the campus website and in the college catalog.

activity 7

Test-Taking Strategies

1. Reflect on the information contained in this module. Rewrite the "no" answers you gave on the text anxiety scale as positive statements.

2. Use the 5C approach (Define the **C**hallenge; Identify **C**hoices; Predict **C**onsequences; **C**hoose an option; **C**heck your outcome) to determine your biggest test-taking obstacle and develop a plan for overcoming it.

After-Exam Analysis

What can a returned test tell me?

You finished the exam, turned it in, and got a grade. What can you possibly learn from that exam? A lot, depending on what you do when a test is returned to you.

Reviewing your test helps you decide which of your study and test-taking strategies work and which do not. You can use this information to improve future test preparation and performance. Figure 8.3 shows a form for examining

Test Item Missed	Insufficient Information					Test Anxiety						Lack of Test Wisdom						Test Skills					Other
	I did not read the text thoroughly.	The information was not in my notes.	I studied the information but could not remember it.	I knew main ideas but needed details.	I knew the information but could not apply it.	I studied the wrong information.	I experienced mental block.	I spent too much time daydreaming.	I was so tired I could not concentrate.	I was so hungry I could not concentrate.	I panicked.	I carelessly marked a wrong choice.	I did not eliminate grammatically incorrect choices.	I did not choose the *best* choice.	I did not notice limiting words.	I did not notice a double negative.	I changed a correct answer to a wrong or e.	I misread the directions.	I misread the question.	I made poor use of the time provided.	I wrote poorly organized responses.	I wrote incomplete responses.	
Number of Items Missed																							

Figure 8.3 Worksheet for Examining Returned Tests.

your test paper. To use it, list the number of each item you missed in the first column. Then mark an X under the description that best explains why you missed a question. Sometimes you will mark more than one reason for a question. Next, add the number of X's under each reason. These numbers indicate the areas of study and test-taking strategies that need more attention.

After you use the form to analyze your study and test-taking habits, look for information about how your instructor constructs exams. Look for patterns in the types of questions asked. See if your instructor emphasized text or lecture information. This information helps you prepare for the next exam.

strategic planning
A design that gathers, analyzes, and uses information to make decisions.

Strategic planning, a buzzword in the corporate world, is important in college as well. Strategic planning is a decision-making process that involves setting goals, devising a plan for achieving them, evaluating the results, and then rethinking your plan to be sure it's the most effective, efficient way to reach your goals. You are in the process of strategically planning your college career. You've made decisions about the goals you want to achieve and how you plan to accomplish them. Course exams help you determine where you stand in your attainment of your goals; however, it's your after-exam evaluation that helps you assess the effectiveness of the plan you've selected.

activity 8

Your After-Exam Follow-Through

1. Photocopy the after-exam worksheet contained in Figure 8.3. Use this worksheet with a recent exam from one of your courses.

2. On a separate sheet of paper or in your notebook, answer each of the following:

   a. How much time did you study for this exam?

   b. Specifically, what did you do to prepare for the exam?

   c. Were you satisfied with your score? Why or why not?

   d. What have you learned about the way your instructor creates exams?

   e. What have you learned about yourself in terms of test preparation and/or test-taking skills?

   f. What problems have you identified in terms of test preparation and/or test taking?

   g. How can you use the 5C approach (Define the **C**hallenge; Identify **C**hoices; Predict **C**onsequences; **C**hoose an option; **C**heck your outcome) to confront this problem?

chapter review

Respond to the following on a separate sheet of paper or in your notebook.

1. What aspect of planning to study causes the most difficulty for you? Why? How can you solve this problem?

2. What kinds of negative self-talk affect your study and test performance? Why? What is your plan for changing it?

3. What is the difference between charting and mapping? Which do you prefer? Why?

4. Which mnemonic do you use most often? Why?

5. Do you tend to get better scores on objective or subjective exams? Why?

6. Which method for controlling anxiety have you used before? Never used? Which one are you most likely to try? Why?

7. How do personality and learning style affect how you study?

8. What can you learn from returned exams?

did you decide?

Did you accomplish what you wanted to in this chapter? Check the items below that apply to you.

Review the *You Decide* questions that you identified at the beginning of the chapter, but look at them from a new direction. If you didn't check an item below, review that module until you feel you can confidently apply the strategies to your own situation. However, the best ideas are worthless unless they are put into effect. Use the 5Cs to help you decide what information you found most helpful in the chapter and how you plan to use it. Record your comments after the statements below.

☐ 8.1 I know what I need to prepare to study.

_____

☐ 8.2 I understand how to get my notes, text content, and other materials organized.

_____

☐ 8.3 I have some ideas to help me remember what I need to know on a test.

_____

☐ 8.4 I am aware of some online tools that can help me prepare for an exam.

_____

☐ 8.5 I have a plan to keep from getting stressed before and during tests.

_____

☐ 8.6 I know how to maximize my success on exams.

_____

☐ 8.7 I understand the things a returned test can tell me.

_____

perspectives

They can be seen wandering zombie-like, bleary-eyed, sleep hair sticking up on their heads, or slumped over their keyboards. What are we talking about here, hangovers? No, they are sleep-deprived Glendale Community College students, and missing too much sleep can affect one intellectually, physically and emotionally.

Sixty-three percent of college students do not get enough sleep, according to a recent study by the National Sleep Foundation. "Studies have shown that chronically sleep-deprived people believe that they have adapted to their lack of sleep while actually their test performances continue to deteriorate," said Michael H. Silber, president of the American Academy of Sleep Medicine. "We can't keep as many things online at any one time when we're sleep deprived. Sleep deprivation significantly impairs attention, working memory performance, our ability to drive. It has the same effect as alcohol does," said Dr. Sean Drummond, who works with the University of California at San Diego.

To keep themselves alert, students have increased their caffeine intake. Caffeine is starting to come in many different forms; Jolt, the highly caffeinated soda, now has a gum. Its big selling point is that the caffeine gets into your blood stream quicker because it is absorbed through the tongue. You can also buy Umph tablets. They are described as effervescent caffeine tablets that you can pop into any of your favorite beverages. Milk that can get you wired?

Caffeine may do the trick for a little while, but there is no substitute for sleep. "We have done lab studies on healthy people who are sleep-restricted and find they are memory-impaired. We know the more they sleep the better. Eight hours are good; 10 hours are better," says Dr. David Hudgel, of Henry Ford Hospital's Sleep Disorder Clinic in Detroit. Researchers have found that interruption of sleeping patterns can lead to depression. In addition, "The body needs to adjust and recuperate from sleep deprivation, which takes more than just a few days. It can take up to a month to see a real change; sleep resets emotions," according Dr. Peter L. Franzen, a researcher at Western Psychiatric Institute and Clinic.

To combat sleep deprivation: Avoid stimulants; avoid caffeine after 2 p.m. (coffee, tea, colas); the stimulant effect of caffeine can last up to 12 hours. Alcohol might help onset of sleep, but later withdrawal effects can lead to sleep disruption. Avoid all-nighters: Remember that memory is very dependent on adequate sleep. Studying late into the night can be detrimental to learning if sleep is reduced. The best preparation for an exam is a good night's sleep.

Light: Bright light in the morning helps you to be "awake"; darkness at night helps you to sleep.

GCC photography students Nate Harris and Daniela Behm both value sleep before play; but they do not always get their 8–10 hours every night. Nate Harris say he tries to get 6–7 hours sleep a night. His priorities are school, work, sleep, and play. Though he sometimes feels drowsy, he rarely falls asleep. He uses energy drinks to stay awake. Daniela Behm says, "Tuesday and Thursday I only get about five to six hours, and the rest of the week less than eight hours a night." As far as priorities go, she says, "Sleep is number one, even though I do not get as much as I should! If I do not get enough sleep, I feel in a fog for the rest of the day. School takes up a lot of time. I also just moved here from Michigan so I am still trying to get used to the new lifestyle. I always have times during the day where I feel like I need a nap!"

Students that are unable to get 8–10 hours of sleep at night should think about taking a nap. Sleep specialist Dr. Maas maintains, "Brief naps taken daily are far healthier than sleeping in or taking very long naps on the weekend." They are also far better than caffeine as a pick-me-up. "Consumption of caffeine will be followed by feelings of lethargy and reduced R.E.M. (or dream) sleep that night," Dr. Maas writes. "A debt in your sleep bank account is not reduced by artificial stimulants."

reflecting on decisions

Now that you've learned about studying for and taking tests, how will that affect decisions about the tests you take?

END WORLD HUNGER ONE
ANSWER AT A TIME

What if you could learn and help end world hunger at the same time? With Free Rice, http://www.freerice.com/, you can! The goals of this site are (1) free education for all and (2) free rice for hungry people. This site provides multiple-choice questions for learning vocabulary and other subjects (e.g., foreign languages, chemistry, English). Each answer you get right generates ten grains of rice which are paid for by the site's sponsors. Ten grains per response isn't much until you multiply it by the thousands of people who might be using the site at one time. The site provides totals of how much rice is generated by year, month, and day. You can help feed hungry people . . . one right answer at a time!

◀ CHOOSING TO SERVE

REVIEW

Skim the notes you made throughout the chapter. How does the content fit together? What information is still unclear? Were your learning goals met? Can you answer the review questions and define terms?

◀ CHOOSING TO BE AN ACTIVE LEARNER

CHAPTER **NINE**

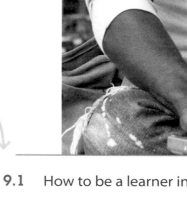

LEARNING **OUTCOMES**

In this chapter you will learn

9.1   How to be a learner in the Digital Age

9.2   Ways to integrate the Internet and the Web into your coursework

9.3   Whether what you are reading online is actually valuable information

9.4   How to access course information and campus services through e-mail and other electronic sources

9.5   How to avoid plagiarism

9.6   How to decide if you should take a course that delivers content through distance learning formats

Making Choices about Today's Technology

With the arrival of the Internet, the World Wide Web, e-mail, and cell phones, access to education now occurs almost anytime or anyplace. As a result, education is available to more people more of the time. Just about any information you might need is literally at your fingertips 24/7. But you can't use all of it. This chapter shows you how to make informed choices about using technology to maximize your college experience.

YOU DECIDE

To *wonder* means to think or have curiosity about. Things and ideas you wonder about often mask a need for a decision. Check the items below that apply to you.

In terms of technology, I've been wondering . . .

- [ ] **9.1** How much computer experience do I need to be successful in college?
- [ ] **9.2** How can I use the Web to help me succeed?
- [ ] **9.3** How do I decide if what I find on the Web is worthwhile?
- [ ] **9.4** In what ways will I use electronic course content, e-mail, and campus portals?
- [ ] **9.5** What rights and responsibilities come with using technology?
- [ ] **9.6** Are distance learning courses right for me?

Each of these decision points corresponds to the numbered modules that follow. Turn to the module for immediate help.

CHOOSING TO BE AN ACTIVE LEARNER ➤

SURVEY
Before reading this chapter, prepare for learning. Purposefully skim the title, introduction, headings, and graphics. As you survey, decide what information you already know and what information is new to you.

QUESTION
Change each section's heading into a question. This forms your learning goal for reading.

READ
Read the section without marking. Reread and mark key information that answers your question.

RECITE
Stop after each section and make sure you understood the content. Organize or summarize content and make notes.

How much computer experience do I need to be successful in college?

Learning in the Digital Age

When were you born? In 1991, the Bureau of Transportation reported that approximately 120 million Americans had cell phones. A decade later almost 300 million (91 percent of the U.S. population) owned a cell phone. Google started as one of many search engines in 1998. By 2006, Google was added to the Oxford English Dictionary as a word meaning "to use the Google search engine to obtain information on the Internet." Over 2 million Google searches are now made per minute (3 billion daily). Facebook started in 2004 and had 400 million subscribers six years later. The first video was uploaded to YouTube in 2005. Today 65,000 videos are uploaded daily with over 10 billion videos viewed each month. Twitter, created in 2006, had only about 500 thousand tweets per quarter in 2007. Now 65 million tweets are made per day. How does life in the Digital Age affect the choices *you* make? The world has changed and it has changed in your lifetime. You not only access information; you create it.

College websites . . . campus portals . . . course management systems . . . e-mail . . . online library catalogs. . . . Today's colleges rely on technology to deliver information. They depend on you to know how to access and use it. Just as college students have varying levels of knowledge and skills in academic subjects, they have varying degrees of computer expertise.

If you already feel confident about your technology skills, look for ways to apply your expertise to learning. If, however, you feel less than confident, you're not alone. Many people starting college—or returning to it after years away from school—have not had extensive experience with computers. Every campus offers a range of computer courses, help desks, workshops, and computer labs for users. Each of these is expressly designed to help you in different ways. Ask your instructors, advisor, or other students to help you find the one(s) that best meet your needs.

Assessing Your Computer Skills and Attitudes

PART 1: Your Computer Knowledgability

Respond to each of the following using the following scale:

0. This does not describe me.

1. I've done this a couple of times, but I'm not confident about my ability to do so again.

2. I think my knowledge or ability to do this is OK.

3. This describes me very well.

COMPUTER USAGE

_____ **1.** When I have a minor problem with my computer, I know how to fix it.

_____ **2.** I know how to use basic editing functions (e.g., copy, paste, delete).

_____ **3.** I own a computer or have regular access to one.

_____ **4.** I know where I can use a computer on campus.

_____ **5.** When my instructor gives assignments that involve computer applications (e.g., word processing, spreadsheet), I know what to do.

_____ **6.** I easily understand computer terms and know how to use these functions (e.g., start, document, file, folder, save).

Now add up your total responses and divide by the number of questions:

TOTAL POINTS: ____ /6 = _____

INTERNET/ WEB USE

_____ **1.** I use the Web almost every day.

_____ **2.** I know what a URL is and how to use it to find a specific website.

_____ **3.** I know how to follow links from one Web page to another.

_____ **4.** I know how to navigate backward and forward among many Web pages.

_____ **5.** I know how to download a document.

_____ **6.** I know how to create favorites of sites I visited.

TOTAL POINTS: ____ /6 = _____

FINDING AND EVALUATING INFORMATION

_____ **1.** I know what kinds of information are available on the Internet.

_____ **2.** I know how to use a search engine to locate information.

_____ **3.** I know how to use a subject directory to locate information.

_____ **4.** I know how to evaluate a website to determine if it is credible and valid.

TOTAL POINTS: ____ /4 = _____

ELECTRONIC ACCESS AND COMMUNICATION

_____ **1.** I have accessed and used my college's website.

_____ **2.** I know how to use the campus library electronic catalog and databases.

_____ **3.** I have used a course information system (e.g., Blackboard, WebCT, Moodle, Angel) to access information about one of my classes.

_____ **4.** I have an e-mail account.

_____ **5.** I send and receive e-mail almost every day.

_____ **6.** I know how to attach a document to send to someone via e-mail.

TOTAL POINTS: ____ /6 = _____

ETHICAL USE OF DIGITAL CONTENT

_____ **1.** I know how to identify copyright information on the Web.

_____ **2.** I can cite information from a website correctly.

_____ **3.** I use, but do not abuse, technology.

_____ **4.** I know the basics of "netiquette."

TOTAL POINTS: ____ /4 = _____

SCORING
If your total score is less than 2 for any part, you need to look for resources and ways to increase your knowledge, skills, and confidence.

If your total score is 2 for any part, you probably have average or satisfactory knowledge and skills in that area.

If your total score is greater than 2 for any part, your knowledge and skills are strengths for you.

PART 2: Where Do You Go from Here?
Choose the section in the quiz above in which you had the lowest scores. Apply the 5C process—Define the **C**hallenge; Identify the **C**hoices; Predict the **C**onsequences; **C**hoose an option; **C**heck your outcome— in order to improve your score. What do you need to learn about computers and the Internet and how will you do so?

GROUP APPLICATION: Compare answers with others in your class. What contributed to similarities and differences in challenges? What other options did your classmates identify? Find someone in your class who has a high score in an area that poses a challenge for you. What tips or suggestions does that person have for increasing your skill level?

Choices for Successful Use of the Internet and the Web

The Internet does for information what the U.S. interstate highway system did for people and products. That is, it increases access and the speed with which information travels. When you use the Internet, you access a worldwide network of millions of educational, government, commercial, and personal computers. As a student, you'll use the Internet to locate information for your courses, complete assignments, and communicate with your faculty and fellow students.

The World Wide Web, also called the Web, is composed of **websites** owned by a person, company, or organization containing collections of documents called **web pages** that can include information in graphic, audio, video, animated, or other formats.

websites
Sites (locations) on the Web owned by a person, company, or organization that have a home page, the first document users see when they enter the site, and often additional documents and files.

web pages
Specially formatted documents that support links to other documents, as well as graphics, audio, and video files.

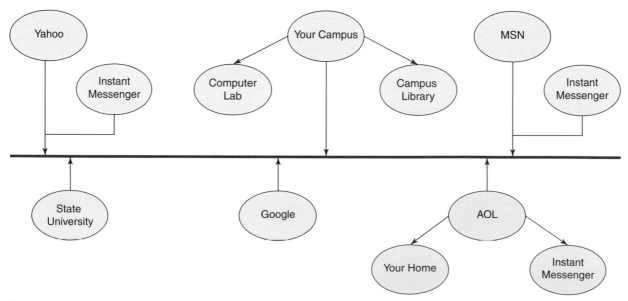

Figure 9.1 Diagram of the Internet Network.

Through the Web you can access resources that were once available only in library or museum holdings or through traditional classroom instruction. In addition, Web pages use special links called **hyperlinks** between parts of a document or between files. These let you automatically access more information at another location—either within the document or in a different document or site.

Have you ever heard someone say that looking for something was like looking for a needle in a haystack? Finding information on the Internet is a little like that. There are billions of websites with no system of organization. There are, however, several ways to find what you need.

Often your course textbook or instructor can suggest a good starting point. From there, you can **browse,** or follow links in a Web page, or explore without specific direction as the spirit of what you see or read moves you, until you find what you want. This strategy, however, can be less productive because you are depending on luck to find exactly what you want. It is better to use a search strategy.

Search strategies are more productive because they allow you to target your needs more specifically. Dr. Bernie Dodge at San Diego State University recommends a *Step Zero* to precede your search. In this *Step Zero*, Dodge suggests that you start by identifying the specific question you're trying to answer and generating a list (e.g., people, terms, organizations, places, objects) that might be in a response.

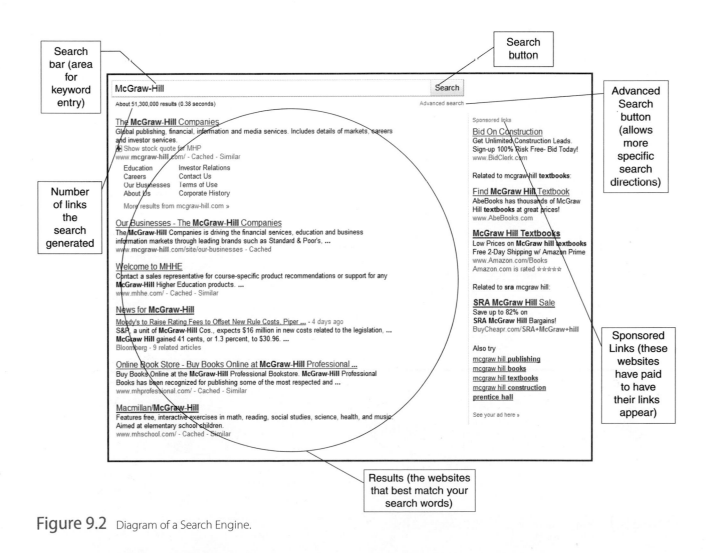

Figure 9.2 Diagram of a Search Engine.

Next, Dr. Dodge says you create a 3M list of MUSTS (words that you think would definitely appear in Web content on the topic), MIGHTS (words that are relevant or synonyms that could appear in Web content), and MUSTN'TS (words that use some of the words you want but that are incorrect in terms of context). When you enter the terms in your **search engine,** put a + in front of MUST terms and a − in front MUSTN'T terms. You don't need to mark MIGHT terms in any special way.

As you search, Dr. Dodge recommends use of a second search strategy abbreviated as NETS. First, use the 3M plan to **N**arrow your search and specify **E**xact terms. Once you get to a site, **T**rim the URL by deleting part of the address bit by bit to see other pages at the site (For example, http://www.finaid.org/loans/parentloan.phtml could be trimmed to http://www.finaid.org/loans/parentloan; http://www.finaid.org/loans; or http://www.finaid.org.) Finally, click on the **S**imilar pages link for hits you find particularly interesting.

Some of the most commonly used search engines are http://www.google.com, http://www.search.aol.com, http://www.bing.com/, http://www.altavista.com, http://www.excite.com, http://www.hotbot.com, http://www.lycos.com, http://www.northernlight.com, and http://www.msn.com.

A **subject directory,** or a set of topical terms that can be browsed or searched by using keywords, is another specialized Internet tool. Unlike search engines that use electronic robots to identify information, subject directories use humans—often experts in their fields—who look for the best and most relevant sites for each category. In some cases, the information may also be more up to date because human researchers often update topics of special interest (e.g., new information about different sports during the Olympics).

To use a subject directory, you identify the broad category from a list or enter a search term. You continue browsing in subcategories or searching until you find the information you need. Common directories include http://www.yahoo.com/, http://search.looksmart.com, http://www.academicinfo.net, and http://about.com/.

Once you find what you want, you can read it on your computer screen, print a hard copy, **bookmark** it for future reference, or, in some cases, **download** it.

search engine
An Internet program that searches documents for specified keywords and returns a list of the documents where the keywords were found.

subject directory
A set of topical terms that can be browsed or searched by using keywords.

bookmark
To mark a document or a specific address (URL) of a Web page so that you can easily revisit the page at a later time.

download
To copy data (usually an entire file) from their main source to your own computer or disk.

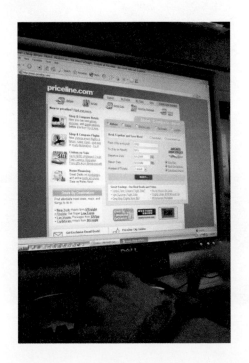

activity 2

Applying 5Cs to Internet and Database Searching

Using a textbook chapter from one of the classes in which you are now enrolled, identify a topic that you want to know more about. This is your **C**hallenge.

PART 1: The 5Cs on the Internet

Use the rest of the 5Cs—Identify the **C**hoices; Predict the **C**onsequences; **C**hoose an option; **C**heck your outcome—to find what you need on the Internet.

PART 2:

Again, using the rest of the 5Cs—Identify the **C**hoices; Predict the **C**onsequences; **C**hoose an option; **C**heck your outcome—search for the same information on your library database or at WorldCat.org and determine if there are libraries near you that have what you want.

GROUP APPLICATION: Compare your results with others in your group. Which search (Internet versus WorldCat databases) provided better results? In what way were they better?

Evaluating Worth

There's no one place where the Internet exists. It's really just a connected collection of computers around the world. Thus, no one owns or manages the Internet. As a result, no one checks the accuracy of what's on it. What you find could be truly worthy or just worthless. It may be legitimate news or just advertising. It may be obsolete or even obscene. Even sites sponsored by reputable institutions may contain inaccurate or flawed information. Thus, you have to evaluate every site you find. To do so, seek answers to some basic questions.

First, examine the source. Real people with real information generally don't mind putting their names or the names of their sponsors on their work. The site should also tell you how to reach the author or sponsor (physical address, phone number, or e-mail address). Credible sites often provide information that supports or verifies the information they contain. This might include a list of references or the professional experience or educational background of the author. If that information is unavailable, look at the sponsor's credentials.

For instance, perhaps you find information written by J. Doe as part of the NASA government website. Although you might not know who J. Doe is, you know that NASA is a credible source of information. If you don't recognize the author's name, try using it as the term on a search engine or search the Library of Congress Online Catalog (http://lcweb.loc.gov/catalog) or an online bookstore such as Amazon.com. A credible author often has several articles or books on the topic.

Next, determine the site's apparent purpose and target audience. Does it seem to be informational or commercial? Is it written in easily understandable language or technical jargon? Analyze the tone, or attitude, of the site. Is it serious (includes specific facts and data), humorous (provides outrageous details and ideas; spoof or hoax), or emotional (creates fear, anger, or sorrow)? Purpose also involves deciding if the site's content is nonacademic or academic. Nonacademic information is more general. Online encyclopedias (e.g., Britannica, Wikipedia) provide informational overviews, but are too general to use as resources at the college level. Academic resources are subject area journals and materials written by experts in the field. Your campus librarian can help you identify academic sources appropriate for the kind of research you need.

Third, note when the information was published. The importance of this factor depends on your purpose. Is what you need well-known and stable information (e.g., list of works by Mark Twain, names of state capitals), or do you need the latest news or research? Credible sites often include a *last date page updated* notation to show how current the information is. Also look at the links within the site. If you find several links that are no longer functioning (called "dead links"), then the site is not regularly maintained.

Fourth, assess the accuracy of the information. Consider how what you find in one site compares with information in other sites or in print materials. Determine if it includes facts and data or generalizations and suppositions. Check to see if the content has been reviewed or edited by others.

Finally, examine the content for evidence of bias. Ask what the author or sponsor wants you to do or believe and why. Look for ways in which the author or sponsor could profit from your actions or beliefs. If you have questions or concerns, e-mail the site's author/sponsor. You can also consult a librarian at your institution's library or ask your instructor for assistance.

activity 3

Evaluating Websites

Go to the following websites, and evaluate each in terms of validity of the source, purpose of the site, recency of information, accuracy of information, and evidence of bias. Identify the spoofs and tell how you knew they were spoofs. *HINT: Two of the sites are spoofs intended to fool the reader.*

George Bush Presidential Library   http://www.bushlibrary.tamu.edu

National Rifle Association   http://www.nra.org

The Onion   http://www.theonion.com

The Green Party of the United States   http://www.gp.org

Dihydrogen Monoxide Research Division   http://www.DHMO.org

Choices in Electronic Access

Most colleges now have websites for the general public. However, colleges also have other online services such as grades, scheduling, or course-specific information that are only for enrolled students. Sometimes websites with campus-only information are called "portals."

Portals give you, the student, access to a vast array of information from current campus events to schedules of final exams. You access these from a computer terminal by using a log-on identification number (log-on ID) and a password. If you don't have these or have questions about using them, ask your instructors or advisor to refer you to the appropriate campus service.

Some faculty use **course management systems** such as Blackboard or WebCT as integral parts of their course delivery. These are also accessed by a log-on ID and password. The management system looks like a kind of website and is used to facilitate course-specific communication and interactions. The instructor places assignments, resources, review questions, lecture notes, and other course materials there for student use. Students can also post comments and questions to the site. Other students can access comments and questions from other students and respond. The instructor adds to the discussion, clarifies questions or comments, and posts other messages for the entire class such as "Don't forget Friday's test," or "Class canceled on Wednesday." The instructor may require that students place electronic copies of completed assignments on the site. Exams can be taken online and scored as soon as the test is completed. The instructor can even ask students to meet online and discuss a topic together in a special chat area. If your instructor utilizes a course management system, it's important to know how to access and use it well before the time when an assignment is due or an exam is available. If you have problems, ask your instructor for help.

A library's holdings are the collection of books and other reading materials. They are available through a catalog either from computer terminals within the library or online from another site. You can search for documents or books by author, subject, or title. If you can't find what you need, you can contact your library's staff for help. Some libraries also provide links to instant message chats with librarians for immediate assistance.

In addition, libraries often subscribe to online database services that provide access to other science, social science, and humanities materials. You can have more confidence in the credibility of what you find because libraries specifically choose materials for their content and scholarly value. Because each library differs in the way its catalog is used and the other electronic services it provides,

course management system
An electronic message center that serves groups with similar interests.

brief library orientation programs are often available. Library staff members are always on hand to answer questions and help you find what you need. Experts in the contents and use of your campus's library, library staff also know about materials and services of other libraries and can help you secure materials through an interlibrary loan. You can generally reach your campus librarian by e-mail or instant message as well as onsite.

activity 4 | Information Access Scavenger Hunt

Access your campus portal to answer the following questions:

1. What is the name of your campus portal?

_____

2. List three kinds of information available on it.

_____

_____

_____

If you use a course management system in one or more of your classes, answer questions 3–6. Otherwise, skip to question 7.

3. What communication tools are available?

_____

4. How do you submit assignments?

_____

5. How do you access your grades?

_____

6. What other tools are available?

_____

Access your campus library Web page to answer the following:

7. What are the library's hours?

_____

8. What is the policy on overdue books?

_____

9. Other than books, what materials can be checked out of the library?

_____

10. List three materials available on the library's electronic catalog.

_____; _____; _____

Rights and Responsibilities of Digital Citizenship

Digital citizenship involves the rights and responsibilities of technology use. The decisions you make about the use—or abuse—of technology or digital content define the kind of digital citizen you are. Ethical behavior regarding content on the Web and communication with others ultimately affects yourself.

❯ Choices in Using and Citing Content

Once you find information that is relevant and credible, what do you do with it? Some students use the computer's edit tools to copy and paste information until they have all the information they need. In practically no time, their papers are complete . . . aren't they?

Copying and pasting is fine as you collect information. But all Internet information is copyrighted at the moment of its creation whether it contains a specific copyright symbol or not. The content (everything from websites to e-mail communications) belongs to the person who developed or wrote it. "Borrowing" information by cutting and pasting it into your own document or electronic format without **citing** it is no different than using print information without referencing it. You must summarize what you find and cite electronic materials just as carefully as you would print materials.

Summarizing is much like recording the main ideas in your notes during a lecture (see Chapter 6). Both require you to record main points but there is a key difference. In lecture notes, you record all the main points. In summarizing, you record only what's important to your topic. Thus, you decide what to include. What you choose depends on its **relevance** or importance to your topic.

You do not, of course, need to reference ideas that are your own. You also need not reference information that is commonly known (such as the dates of the American Revolution, a math formula, or symbols for chemical elements). When in doubt, your best bet is to cite the information you use. The same websites you used to find ways to cite online information can be used to get guidelines for citing print materials.

citing
Telling the source of information.

relevance
Importance to your topic.

There are rules about how much you can borrow from a source without citing it. Become familiar with those guidelines so that you don't plagiarize someone else's work.

Just as there are ways to cite different kinds of print materials, there are ways to cite different kinds of electronic ones. The format you use depends on style manuals (e.g., APA Style, www.apa.org; MLA Style, www.mla.org; Columbia Guide to Online Style, www.columbia.edu/cu/cup/cgos/idx_basic.html). Ask your instructor to identify the one you should use. No matter which format you use, include the author (if known), the page's title, any publication information available (e.g., sponsor/publisher, date), URL, and the date you accessed the material. If the name of the author or the owner is not readily found, you can delete ending information from the URL to find the site's homepage. Usually, this means that you delete everything after the first slash (/) in the address.

To make sure that you do choose to act ethically by citing resources, many faculty require students to submit papers to online sites such as TurnItIn.com. This is used to reveal **plagiarism.** Plagiarism can be either unintentional or intentional. Unintentional, or accidental, plagiarism occurs through inaccurate note-taking, by incorrect citing of references, and/or from poor writing ability. Intentional plagiarism is deliberate, premeditated theft of another person's work or published information. Intentional plagiarism includes getting a paper from a friend or from a term paper service or copying information from a website and using it as your own. It results from poor time management, fear of not doing well, and pure laziness. While the motive for unintentional and intentional plagiarism differs, the punishment is the same.

Netiquette

Just as etiquette applies to proper rules of social behavior, **netiquette** describes expectations for proper behavior online. How you use the Internet to communicate and interact makes a difference to others and to yourself.

In terms of the format of an e-mail, include your full name and section identification (e.g., 2:30 T/TH class or online class 43897) in the body or subject line of your e-mails when corresponding with your instructor or classmates. They may not know you by your user name (e.g., JSmith34), or they may have more than one JSmith in their classes. Use the subject line to label the contents of your correspondence. This helps the recipients to whom you are writing gauge the response that will be required to your message without having to open your note. These subject labels are not as important when you are sending an e-mail within your course management system. Such e-mails are often part of an **intranet** which includes only those individuals in your course section.

Beware of sending out jokes or personal notices to lots of recipients at once. Such "spam" is annoying to many people. Make sure that anyone you send this kind of information to really wants to receive it. Finally, don't mark e-mail as "urgent" or "priority" unless it really is.

The tone of your e-mails can be as important as what you write about. It's always a good idea to write, think, and revise before you send. Don't write anything that you wouldn't say in person. If you write in anger or frustration, reread your message *before* sending. Better yet, save your message and reread when you feel calmer.

plagiarism
Stealing another person's work and presenting it as your own.

netiquette
Abbreviation for Internet etiquette.

intranet
Internal network.

Don't assume e-mail communications are private. Most electronic communications are stored somewhere on your computer and can be accessed at later times. Don't write anything you would not want everyone to see. Avoid using all-caps—it's perceived as yelling. Overuse of emoticons such as :) or :(can be annoying to some readers.

Because much of today's communications take place solely online, you can't always assume that people are who they say they are. Tabloids and TV news are filled with stories of people who formed relationships online only to find that their online "friends" took their money, love, identity, or even their lives. Unless you know someone in person, you should be wary. Beware of anyone or any company that asks for personal information or money or that seems "too good to be true."

In some ways, proper use of the Internet and other technologies also applies to yourself. Spending too much time online, missing work or school due to online activities, obsessive checking of e-mails and social networking sites, constant text messaging can affect relationships with others as well as your performance and productivity. Although it may seem like you're multitasking, you may actually be addicted to technology use. If you have a problem, awareness of it is the first step toward regaining the balance between your actual and virtual lives.

Defining Plagiarism

activity 5

For each of the following situations, circle Y (yes) if you think it is cheating or plagiarism, N (no) if you think it is NOT cheating, or D (depends) if there are specific circumstances under which the situation might or might not be considered as a form of cheating or plagiarism.

1. You are typing a paper for a friend who doesn't have time to finish the paper due to a work shift. As you type, you realize that the paper has a lot of misspelled words and quite a few grammatical mistakes. In addition, you think the paper lacks a good conclusion. As a helpful friend, you make the changes and add a couple of concluding paragraphs.   **Y   N   D**

2. You are taking a history course with Dr. Smith. Your roommate had Dr. Smith last semester and kept copies of Dr. Smith's exams. You use them to study for your tests.   **Y   N   D**

3. You are writing a term paper. You find many resources on the Internet. You copy sections from government websites because you know they are owned by the public and don't need to be cited. You paste them into your document and add a few transitional sentences of your own.
Y   N   D

4. Your instructor uses a personal website to provide your class with information. Prior to each class, the instructor posts a file which contains PowerPoint slides of key points in the lecture. You download the file to your own computer and print a copy.   **Y   N   D**

5. Your instructor does not have an attendance policy. You skip class because you prefer to sleep late. You get a copy of the notes from your roommate who never misses a class.   **Y   N   D**

GROUP APPLICATION: Compare your answers with other students in your group. Are your responses the same? Why or why not? What surprised you about the results? What did you learn?

Deciding to Become a Distance Learner

hybrid courses
Blend of distance learning and face-to-face formats.

synchronously
Hybrid course content delivered at the same time.

asynchronously
Hybrid course content delivered not at the same time.

Distance learning sounds like a dream come true. You can log on to the class when you want. You can wear what you want. Bad weather and heavy traffic are no longer problems. What could be easier?

Although online classes do offer convenience, most distance learners report that they are actually harder than face-to-face ones. Rather than a free-flowing course that you can complete on your own time, most online classes feature weekly content with scheduled tests, assignments, and assessments. The complexities of the course information systems sometimes result in technological glitches. Posted websites and content are not always available. Content that seemed clear in a lecture sometimes seems less organized in technological forms. You have to be vigilant in keeping up with due dates for responding to discussions, taking tests, or submitting assignments. Questions and comments have to be delayed until the instructor or other student responds to an e-mail. In addition, there's always something else at home or at work that needs to be done. Family and friends don't always see your online time as in-class time.

Many colleges offer courses in **hybrid** formats that blend face-to-face and distance learning. The distance learning component can consist of online, media (video or audio), print, or another source. Depending on how your college defines hybrid, the alternative format provides one-fourth to one-half of the content **synchronously** (at the same time) or **asynchronously** (not at the same time). Hybrid classes can form a good transition to fully online courses. They provide some classroom support while allowing opportunities to complete other activities independently.

Becoming a distance learner can be the best—or the worst—decision you make. Taking a traditional face-to-face class that also uses the course management system to deliver some content can provide you with experience, and experience is one way to learn more about the format. Talking to your advisor or other students can provide other insights about distance learning at your college.

Are You Ready to Be a Distance Learner?

Are online courses for me? Take this quick questionnaire to find out.

1. My need to take this course now is:

   a. High. I need it immediately for degree, job, or other important reason

   b. Moderate. I could take it on campus later or substitute another course

   c. Low. It's a personal interest that could be postponed

2. Feeling that I am part of a class is:

   a. Not particularly necessary for me

   b. Somewhat important to me

   c. Very important to me

3. I would characterize myself as someone who:

   a. Often gets things done ahead of time

   b. Needs reminding to get things done on time

   c. Puts things off until the last minute

4. Classroom discussion is:

   a. Not necessary for me to understand what I have read

   b. Sometimes helpful to me

   c. Almost always helpful to me

5. When an instructor hands out directions for an assignment, I prefer:

   a. Figuring out the instructions myself

   b. Trying to follow the instructions on my own, then asking for help if I need it

   c. Having the instructions explained to me

6. I need instructor comments on my assignments:

   a. Within a few days, so I can review what I did

   b. Within a few hours, or I forget what I did

   c. Right away, or I get frustrated

7. Considering my job and personal schedule, the amount of time I have to work on an online class is:

   a. More than enough for a campus class or a distance learning class

   b. The same as for a class on campus

   c. Less than for a class on campus

8. When I am asked to use computers, voice mail, or other technologies that are new to me:

   a. I look forward to learning new skills

   b. I feel apprehensive, but try anyway

   c. I put it off or try to avoid it

9. As a reader, I would classify myself as:

   a. Good. I usually understand the text and other written materials without help

   b. Average. I sometimes need help to understand the text or other written materials

   c. Needing help to understand the text or other written materials

10. As a writer I would classify myself as:

    a. A strong writer. I am comfortable with writing and have strong organizational, grammar, punctuation and spelling skills

    b. An average writer. I am moderately comfortable with writing and occasionally need help with organization, grammar, punctuation and spelling

    c. Needing help with my writing, especially with organization, grammar, punctuation, and spelling

11. I have dropped a college class after the term has started:

    a. Never

    b. Once

    c. More than once

Scoring: Add 3 points for each "a" that you selected, 2 for each "b," and 1 for each "c." If you scored:

28 and over: You may be a self-motivated independent learner, and on-line courses are a real possibility for you.

15–27: Online courses may work for you, but you may need to make a few adjustments in your schedule and study habits in order to succeed. On-line courses take at least as much time and effort and in some cases more than traditional face-to-face classes.

14 or less: Online courses may not be currently the best alternative for you. Online courses take at least as much time and effort and in some cases more than traditional face-to-face classes.

chapter review

Respond to the following on a separate sheet of paper or in your notebook.

1. How does the concept of community college access relate to learning in the digital age?

2. What did you learn about yourself as a learner in the digital age?

3. Why is evaluation often a more important skill for Internet information than for print information?

4. What should you include when citing an Internet source?

5. Describe the process for using your college's library catalog.

6. Does your community college use course management systems to deliver some of its courses? How could you find out?

7. Describe the Dodge search processes of 3M and NETS. How would they enable you to search more effectively?

8. What is your college's plagiarism policy?

9. What technology do you use most often? How can you adapt this for use in studying?

did you decide?

Did you accomplish what you wanted to in this chapter? Check the items below that apply to you.

Review the *You Decide* questions that you identified at the beginning of the chapter, but look at them from a new direction. If you didn't check an item below, review that module until you feel you can confidently apply the strategies to your own situations. However, the best ideas are worthless unless they are put into effect. Use the 5Cs to help you decide what information you found most helpful in the chapter and how you plan to use it. Record your comments after the statements below.

☐ 9.1 I know the computer skills I need to improve to be successful in college.

_____

☐ 9.2 I know how to search the Web to help me succeed.

_____

☐ 9.3 I understand how to assess the value of what I find on the Web.

_____

☐ 9.4 I am able to use electronic course content, e-mail, and campus portals.

_____

☐ 9.5 I grasp the rights and responsibilities that come with using technology.

_____

☐ 9.6 I know whether distance learning courses fit my needs.

_____

perspectives

As a college student, you will probably use the Internet and other electronic formats to learn and communicate.

As you read the following article from a college newspaper by Richard Okagbue ("The Internet: A Friend Made to Look Bad"), consider the following questions:

1. Do you see the Internet as "good" or "bad" for society? For students? Why?
2. What kind of "friend" is the Internet to you?
3. Where does the writer put the blame for the "bad" things on the Internet? Do you agree? Why?
4. This article was written in 2002. How has the role of the Internet changed in the last decade?
5. Imagine that you have friend who is concerned about Internet security. Use the 5C process to convince your friend that this concern is unfounded.

   A. What is your **C**hallenge?

   B. What **C**hoices does a person have in terms of using the Internet (both safely and unsafely)?

   C. What is the major **C**onsequence(s) of each choice?

   D. What would be the best **C**hoice?

   E. How could he outcome of the decision be **C**hecked to address security concerns?

Imagine the Internet as a human being, with all the features of humans including the ability to experience different emotions and to speak out to protect itself. Then, take about 30 minutes each morning to browse various news websites and read all the bad stuff that is being said about the Internet. Next, get back to your imagination that the Internet is a human being.—What do you think its response is to all that is said about it?

My opinion is that the Internet is crying out, "I am a friend, please stop making me look bad," or a variation of that because so much is blamed on the Internet every day. Once in a while, the Internet receives some praise for the good it has delivered to our lives. Nevertheless, when compared to how much it is criticized and made to look bad, I wouldn't consider any of the positive comments regarding the Internet as any form of praise.

It seems everything bad is blamed on the Internet lately, including children accessing pornography, children going to chat rooms and newsgroups and learning all sorts of bad stuff there, people having their credit cards accessed by strangers who use complex computer skills to steal their credit card numbers, extramarital affairs resulting from Internet chats, etc. The list goes on forever and may never end.

Like I already said, the Internet is our friend, and a very welcome one at that. A friend that delivers all that it promises and much more. A friend that never really wants anything from us but is always willing to give us nearly anything we want. I don't think there are any friends like that in this world. The Internet is one of a kind.

Let's face it, the Internet is perhaps the very best thing that has happened to the computer industry during the 90s. In fact some people deeply involved in the computer industry have such high regard for the Internet that they named it the best thing to ever happen in the history of computing. And since the involvement of computing in our lives has increased immeasurably during the 90s, one wouldn't be so wrong in saying that the Internet is also one of the best things to ever happen to our lives.

Then, why do we have this hostile treatment towards it? Is it some unknown problem with us humans that makes us unable to appreciate such a good thing as the Internet? I don't know and I suppose nobody knows, but any form of explanation would be greatly appreciated.

We can't blame *anything* bad on the Internet! Are your kids now able to view pornography on the Internet? Well, if your answer to the above question is yes, then you better supervise their Web activities. Various software packages are available which can monitor all the websites visited on a computer. If you tell your kids to stop viewing pornography and they don't, *get rid of the Internet from your home computer.* It won't kill them, or you. Before we unleash any complaints on the Internet, we should remember one important thing: nobody is forcing us to use it.

We use it by our own choice and as a result we bear all the risks associated with its usage. If some Web hackers are able to obtain someone's credit card number and use it for their own personal gain, then as much as that is unfortunate to that person, it is a risk he or she takes once they use their credit card online. It's just like our daily activities.

When someone uses his or her credit card in a supermarket and it gets stolen, then it is pretty much the same story. But rarely do we blame the supermarket for the loss of our cards because we know that no one forced us to shop there with them instead of using cash or check. Additionally, we know that truly the loss of our credit cards is not the supermarket's fault.

However, chances are that if a Web hacker uses one's credit card number he/she will complain about it and blame it on the Internet. Why does the Internet have to get the bad treatment? Well, for one thing, it can't speak out to defend itself, it can't sue us for our bad, unfair comments against it, and generally speaking, it can't do anything about the way we treat it. In other words we just keep blaming all sorts of bad things on the Internet because it can't react back, it is helpless.

The Internet was created by human beings and is also used by human beings. Since this is so, we should expect all the risks we face in our daily lives to exist on the Internet. In fact the risks are greater on the Internet because it is such a great medium that it allows everyone to do whatever they want to do to the best of their abilities.

This means that hackers get to do great hacking and people who just intend to improve their lives by using the Internet also get to improve their lives a great deal. It's a two-way deal: if you want the good things online then you have to risk the bad things along the way.

Another thing we can expect and do experience on the Internet is its lack of perfection. When you really get to think about it, you will realize that the Internet isn't perfect because it was created by human beings and is used by human beings. Since we ourselves aren't even close to perfection, the Internet will remain imperfect. We are the ones who create all the bad websites that are unhealthy for our children. We are also responsible for the creation and distribution of all those viruses.

We shouldn't blame anything on our dear friend the Internet. We should be blaming everything on ourselves.

reflecting on decisions

Now that you have learned about using the Internet for class, what kinds of decisions will you be making about information on the Web?

DONATING BY SEARCHING

Search engines help you find the information you need on the Internet. To finance their work, most search engines use advertisements. Some socially conscious search engines donate a part of their advertisement revenues to charity. These search engines work just like Google or Yahoo in terms of what you see. So using one of these search engines is a no-cost way you can support a favorite cause. Visit the sites, choose a search engine, and begin donating.

- CatchTommorow (http://catchtomorrow.com/) Supports public education in your state

- Clicks4Cancer (http://www.clicks4cancer.com/) Supports cancer research and charity

- Click4TheCause (http://searchandgive.com/) Supports your choice of over 900,000 charities or schools

- GoodSearch (http://www.goodsearch.com/) Supports a school or charity of your choice

- GoodTree (http://goodtree.com/) Supports a variety of causes of which you choose a selection

- MagicTaxi (http://www.magictaxi.co.uk/) Supports charity of your choice

- Ripple (http://www.ripple.org/) Supports one of four social issues in third world countries

- SearchKindly (http://searchkindly.org/) Supports a variety of nonprofit organizations

◄ CHOOSING TO SERVE

REVIEW

Skim the notes you made throughout the chapter. How does the content fit together? What information is still unclear? Were your learning goals met? Can you answer the review questions and define terms?

◄ CHOOSING TO BE AN ACTIVE LEARNER

CHAPTER **TEN**

LEARNING **OUTCOMES**

In this chapter you will learn

10.1 How to create a budget

10.2 Strategies for financing your education

10.3 The differences between cash, credit, and checking accounts

CHOOSING TO BE AN ACTIVE LEARNER

SURVEY

Before reading this chapter, prepare for learning. Purposefully skim the title, introduction, headings, and graphics. As you survey, decide what information you already know and what information is new to you.

QUESTION

Change each section's heading into a question. This forms your learning goal for reading.

READ

Read the section without marking. Reread and mark key information that answers your question.

RECITE

Stop after each section and make sure you understood the content. Organize or summarize content and make notes.

Making Financial Decisions

What impact does your enrollment in college have on how you decide what to buy or how to spend your money?

YOU DECIDE

To *wonder* means to think or have curiosity about. Things and ideas you wonder about often mask a need for a decision. Check the items below that apply to you.

In terms of financial decisions, I've been wondering . . .

- [ ] 10.1 How can I create and stick to a budget?
- [ ] 10.2 How can I pay for college?
- [ ] 10.3 Where does my money go?

Each of these decision points corresponds to the numbered modules that follow. Turn to the module for immediate help.

Your decision to go to college wasn't just a career or life choice. It was a financial choice as well. Just as new college responsibilities impact your time and the ways you choose to spend it, they also affect your finances and how you choose to use them. Although the college pays off in more job opportunities, greater fulfillment, personal satisfaction, and higher pay in the future, it does come at a cost. How you choose to spend your money during college affects you now and, if you have school loans, can continue to affect you for years to come. To make the best choices about how you spend your money, you need a **budget** and a plan for paying items within it.

How can I create and stick to a budget?

budget
A plan for the management of income and expenses.

income
The amount of money or its equivalent that you receive during a period of time.

expenses
The amount of money or its equivalent that you spend during a period of time.

Budgeting

What is a budget? Some describe it as an attempt to live below your "yearnings." In practice, a budget is a kind of estimate of both **income** and **expenses.** In other words, a budget tracks how much comes in, how much goes out, and where it goes.

While the idea of making a budget may sound dull, consider the consequences of *not* having one. You could run out of money before the month is out, bounce checks, have to borrow from family or friends, or worse. Making a budget is a fairly quick task that saves you a lot of grief and embarrassment during your college years. Keeping a budget consists of three steps: estimating income and expenses, creating a financial plan, and keeping records. For most people, a monthly budget makes the most sense. As a college student, you may need to do a term budget as well.

Estimating Income and Expenses

The word *budget* comes from *bougette,* the old French word for *bag* or *wallet.* The first step in keeping your money in your *bougette* is to gather facts about your income and expenses.

What are your income sources? Like most college students, you probably get funds from one or more sources. These might include your family (spouse, parents, grandparents, etc.), financial aid (grants, scholarships, loans), savings, or employment.

In planning your budget, record the amount that comes from each source. Is this amount the same each month? Does it change depending on how many hours you work or how much you get from other sources? If you aren't sure of the exact amount you'll get from a source, estimate it as closely as you can or take an average.

Next, predict your expenses. You should include everything you can think of that you spend money on. Typical expenses include tuition, books, groceries, other food costs (e.g., meals or snacks), health costs, housing costs (e.g., rent, utilities), transportation costs, insurance, personal items, and entertainment. If you have a family, you may have additional costs for child care or other needs. Although it may seem impossible to save money when you're going to college, it's a good idea to think of saving as a kind of expense. Including saving money as part of your budgetary expenses lets you plan for emergencies.

Creating a Financial Plan

Once you have a clear sense of your income and expenses, your next step is to make a plan to *balance* them. That means your totals for income and expenses should equal each other. If you have more income than expenses, you have no pressing financial worries. The amount left over can be saved for a rainy day— an unforeseen expenditure.

INCOME	Projected	Actual	Difference
Wages & Tips	2,000.00	2,000.00	-
Interest Income			-
Dividends			-
Gifts Received			-
Refunds/Reinburcements			-
Transfer From Savings			-
Other			-
Other			-
Total INCOME	2,000.00	2,000.00	-

HOME EXPENSES	Projected	Actual	Difference
Mortgage/Rent	1,100.00	1,100.00	-
Home/Rental Insurance	56.00	56.00	-
Electricity	50.00	67.00	(17.00)
Gas/Oil	43.00	52.00	(9.00)
Water/Sewer/Trash	7.00	7.00	-
Phone	25.00	25.00	-
Cable/Satellite	35.00	35.00	-
Internet	15.00	15.00	-
Furnishings/Appliances	0.00	150.00	(150.00)
Lawn/Garden	0.00	0.00	-
Maintenance/Supplies	50.00	20.00	30.00
Improvements	0.00	0.00	-
Other	0.00	0.00	-
Total HOME EXPENSES	1,381.00	1,527.00	(146.00)

TRANSPORTATION	Projected	Actual	Difference
Vehicle Payments			-
Auto Insurance			-
Fuel			-
Bus/Taxi/Train Fare			-
Repairs			-
Registration/License			-
Other			-
Total TRANSPORTATION	-	-	-

HEALTH	Projected	Actual	Difference
Health Insurance			-
Doctor/Dentist			-

MONTHLY BUDGET SUM	Projected	Actual	Difference
Total Income	2,000.00	2,000.00	0.00
Total Expenses	1,381.00	1,527.00	(146.00)
NET	619.00	473.00	(146.00)

DAILY LIVING	Projected	Actual	Difference
Groceries			-
Personal Supplies			-
Clothing			-
Cleaning			-
Education/Lessons			-
Dining/Eating Out			-
Salon/Barber			-
Pet Food			-
Other			-
Total DAILY LIVING	-	-	-

ENTERTAINMENT	Projected	Actual	Difference
Videos/DVDs			-
Music			-
Games			-
Rentals			-
Movies/Theater			-
Concerts/Plays			-
Books			-
Hobbies			-
Computers/Electronics			-
Sports			-
Outdoor Recreation			-
Toys/Gadgets			-
Vacation/Travel			-
Other			-
Total ENTERTAINMENT	-	-	-

SAVINGS	Projected	Actual	Difference
Emergency Fund			-
Transfer to Savings			-
Retirement (401k, IRA)			-
Investments			-

Figure 10.1 Sample Budget.

Unfortunately, having more money than you need happens less often than you might like. If your expenses outweigh your income, which is more likely, you will have to adjust your spending. You do this by carefully and objectively separating **discretionary costs,** or nonessential items over which you have discretion, or choice, from **nondiscretionary costs,** fixed expenses over which you have no discretion, or no choice.

Discretionary costs are your "wants," not your "needs." The plan for discretionary expenses is flexible. It can increase or decrease depending on what you have to spend. For instance, entertainment costs are discretionary. You can choose whether to buy movie tickets or rent a movie to watch at home. It's a good idea to rank your discretionary costs and use that list in choosing how to spend your money. The key is in planning your expenses in advance rather than spending money without thinking.

Nondiscretionary costs are unavoidable. These prices change very little. Tuition, books, insurance, and utilities are nondiscretionary budget items. Rent and car payments are also examples of these.

discretionary costs
Nonessential items over which you have discretion, or choice.

nondiscretionary costs
Fixed expenses over which you have no discretion, or no choice.

There are creative ways to cut costs. You may be able to use books placed on reserve in the library or buy used books. Purchasing and downloading ebooks may be cheaper than buying print ones. Bringing a lunch from home instead of buying it and using coupons can cut food costs. Carpooling or public transportation may be cheaper than personal transportation. But part of your decision involves the trade-offs among time, usability, and money. You may have to wait to get books at the library or you may not be on campus when you need them. Ebooks may not be as convenient to use. You may not have time to get to the store get lunch supplies. Carpooling and transportation might limit your flexibility. Thus, there's no one best way to cut costs. The choices you make need to be ones that work for you.

Auditing Your Budget

Once your budget is in place, you need to check how well you kept the financial plan you made. You can do this by regularly auditing your budget—keeping careful records and making sure your records agree with your bank's records. This is known as *reconciling*. It is best if this happens monthly.

The only way to account accurately for money spent is to keep records. Record all checks you write in your checkbook. Keep fee receipts, sales slips, and canceled checks. Make records of cash you take from your ATM or purchases you make with your debit card. Retain all of your pay stubs, too. It's a good idea to file your records each month in labeled envelopes or folders. On the front of the envelope or folder, list the month and year of the receipts and any major expenses for which you have receipts. Or, you can file them by income or expense type, rather than by month.

If you're computer savvy, you can do all this using a spreadsheet. As you collect receipts, periodically take time to record your income and expenses on the computer. Remember to back up your data so that you don't lose it in a computer crash.

Once you gather your monthly receipts, look at them in light of your budget. Did you overspend? Underspend? On what items? If you overspent, make a plan for limiting future spending. What can you give up? If you've underspent (congratulations!), you know you have a little breathing room for the next month. Whether you've overspent or underspent, reconciling your budget helps you watch your spending before any overwhelming problems occur. When you finish your budget reconciliation, file a copy of it with your receipts for the month.

activity 1

Using a Budget

Using Figure 10.1 as a template, create your own budget. Label each cost D for discretionary items or N for nondiscretionary items. Keep in mind that some fixed or nondiscretionary costs may really be discretionary (e.g., cable television, daily lattes). Think about this. Rank your list of discretionary items. Which ones can you live without? Compare your estimated income and expenses. If the numbers are not balanced, adjust your figures (get more income or cut discretionary wants) to make things balance.

What did you learn from completing this budget? How might what you learned affect your future spending or work decisions?

Financing Your Education

No one denies that going to college is an expensive decision. But you should reap the rewards of education in higher salaries and more opportunities in the long run. The challenge is how to pay for school and everything else in your life right now. Too many capable, qualified students drop out of college because of money problems. Knowing about funding sources for college will help you make ends meet.

Working

Working is an obvious choice for funding college. But working full- or part-time and going to school full- or part-time means you have two jobs. If you are married and/or have children, you also have work to do as a spouse or parent. If you have elderly parents or grandparents who need care, you also have work as a caregiver. Juggling all these roles takes time, energy, and commitment. It brings great rewards as well as great demands, great sacrifices, and great stress.

One way to reduce the stress of working and going to school is to work on campus. Working on campus saves you commuting time. Plus you may be able to schedule your work around your classes more easily with an on-campus job than an off-campus one. Many schools have **college work-study programs**— federally funded job programs for students who can prove financial need. Students in these programs work on campus 10 to 20 hours per week in academic, administrative, or other departments. The amount of money they earn varies. Your college's financial aid office can tell you what you need to qualify.

Beyond work-study, there are also part-time jobs in campus offices and departments. To learn about them, check with the dean of students, financial aid office, food service providers, college newspaper, and/or college bulletin boards, computerized and otherwise.

Most working students, however, are employed off campus. Many employers support college attendance by rearranging schedules and, in some cases, providing tuition assistance. Employer tuition assistance often comes with requirements. These can range from maintenance of a specific GPA to payment only for courses that are relevant to the company. If you are looking for off-campus employment, check your campus career services office. It often keeps lists of employers who are looking for workers.

college work-study programs
Federally funded job programs for students who can prove financial need.

Financial Aid: Grants, Loans, and Scholarships

Financial aid is administered by your college. This aid "package" comes from available resources. The amount of aid in a package depends on financial need, aid from other sources, and the availability of funds at your school. Because funds are limited, most aid packages do not cover all costs. There are three types of financial aid: grants, scholarships, and loans.

Both grants and scholarships are financial aid sources that do not have to be repaid. Federal and state grants are based on financial need. Some states, colleges, and organizations offer grants and scholarships based on need, scholarship, or both. High school counselors, college financial aid offices, college catalogs, websites, and local libraries provide sources for scholarships. Because finding and applying for them is time-consuming, some scholarships often go without recipients to take them. By doing some research, you can take advantage of opportunities that other students have missed.

Many college scholarships are given on behalf of the person that funded them. Those people can set the qualities they want in the recipients. Such scholarships often target specific qualifications. For instance, a scholarship might state that the recipient must be a female nontraditional sophomore student from Smith County majoring in horticulture with a minimum 3.0 GPA. You might be the only person that fits the qualifications. Your college catalog or financial aid office can help you identify scholarships available on your campus. Even if you aren't eligible now, you'll know what you need to have and when the deadlines will be. Some scholarships ask that you write an essay explaining why you deserve to get one. It's always a good idea to let other people read and critique your essay or visit your campus writing center for help. Many scholarships require letters of reference from faculty who can vouch for you and your work. First, contact former professors and ask if they are willing to be your reference. If you are applying for more than one scholarship, let them know. Second, give them a brief written summary of your background, major, and interests as well as a stamped envelope, addressed to where the reference should be mailed. Finally, identify the deadline for sending the letters. Be sure to give the people you ask plenty of time to write the letter. A thank-you e-mail or note lets faculty know you appreciate their time and effort.

School loans may be obtained from government and/or private sources and must be repaid. Lenders, especially those from private sources, make getting school loans easy. And they are easy to get . . . but not always so easy to repay. Consider these examples. You borrow $2,500 a semester for two years for a total of $10,000. Your interest rate is very low—only 5 percent. But if you pay the money back over five years, your payments are $188 per month. Given that you should be making more money with a degree than without one, this amount might seem reasonable.

But because borrowing the money is so easy (and the time at which it must be paid seems so far away), some students borrow to pay for all of their expenses: rent, car, tuition, and so on. So, maybe you borrow $15,000 per year for a four-year degree for a total of $60,000. If your interest rate is 6 percent you would have to make monthly payments of approximately $430 for the next 20 years to pay off your student loans. And even if you file for bankruptcy in the future, student loans are exempt and must still be repaid. The key is get as much money from grants and other sources as you can and borrow as little as possible.

Although payment plans are not really forms of financial aid, they do help you manage your college expenses. Paying for books, tuition, and fees at the same time is costly. Check to see if your college requires payment for all tuition and fees before the term starts or if you can make monthly payments.

TYPES AND SOURCES OF SCHOLARSHIPS

Institutional scholarships. Awarded from the college's endowed funds on the basis of academic potential and/or financial need.

Local scholarships. Awarded by civic groups, local organizations and churches, high schools, and private foundations on the basis of academic potential and/or financial need.

Merit scholarships. Awarded from private sources, colleges, and national competitions to students with appropriate experience and talents based on accomplishments in fields like sports, music, and science.

Military scholarships. Awarded from the Army, Navy, Marine Corps, or Air Force ROTC programs to students who have been in the military or plan to join the military for a given time period after graduation.

Minority scholarships. Awarded from a college's special scholarship fund for minority students on the basis of financial need.

Restricted scholarships. Awarded from monies set aside for students who meet specialized criteria in terms of where they are from or what they plan to study. Many of these scholarships go unawarded every year.

tips

TIPS FOR FINDING FINANCIAL AID INFORMATION

Here are some online resources for financial aid:

FAFSA (Free Application for Federal Student Aid)
http://www.fafsa.ed.gov/
Information for starting the financial aid process. *Note:* If your parents count you as a dependent, both you and your parents must apply for a PIN number to start the process.

FinAid! The SmartStudent™ Guide to Financial Aid
http://www.finaid.org/
Financial aid information, advice, and tools.

Federal Student Aid Portal
http://studentaid.ed.gov/PORTALSWebApp/students/english/index.jsp
U.S. Department of Education source for funding education beyond high school.

Pay for College
http://www.collegeboard.com/student/pay/
Information and tools for finding scholarships and other forms of financial aid.

Financial Aid
http://www2.ed.gov/finaid/landing.jhtml?src=ln

Fastweb
http://www.fastweb.com/
Scholarship opportunities.

BORROWING MONEY? ANSWER THESE QUESTIONS FIRST!

1. **How many terms will you attend school (including the possibility of graduate school)?** Graduate school may seem a distant, highly unlikely decision, but try to predict your future plans.

2. **How much money do you need to graduate with a degree (two year, four year, or graduate)?** You can determine this by reexamining the budget you set for this term and multiplying that amount by the number of terms you plan to attend school. You may want to add a cushion factor. (For instance,

assume that costs will rise 5 to 10 percent while you are in school or that you may need to go to school a term more than planned.)

3. **What will your monthly payments be when you repay the loan?** The amount you will owe each month depends on the amount you borrow and the lending agency.

4. **When do you have to repay the loan?** This, too, is determined by the amount you borrow and the lending agency. Perkins and Stafford Student Loans must be paid within 10 years (120 payments). It can, however, require you to pay in less time.

5. **Considering your career goals and possible starting salary ranges, will you be able to start repaying the loan as soon as you graduate?** One way to calculate this is to estimate your future take-home salary. You can do so by looking at the Department of Labor's *Occupational Outlook Handbook* (http://www.bls.gov/OCO/). Another way is to ask a professor in your major or a person in your field the reasonable amount you could make. Don't forget taxes. Deduct a percentage for local, state, and national taxes from the gross annual income, and divide the remainder by 12. This is the money you will take home each month. It's also the amount you will have to live on as well as repay your student loan.

6. **Is getting a loan the right choice for you?** The answer to this question lies in the answers to all the other questions. If your answer is yes, you need to explore the types of low interest loans available to you.

TYPES OF LOW INTEREST LOANS

Institutional loans. Funded by alumni and friends of the college, these loans are sometimes restricted to students in particular majors.

Insured supplementary loans. Funded by local banks or credit unions, these loans require you to begin repayment within 60 days of leaving school, and interest rates change each year. Financial need is not a requirement to get the loan. The agency in your state that guarantees the loan may charge an origination fee of up to 5.5 percent of the loan principal.

Perkins loans. Insured by the federal government and given at very low interest rates, these loans require that you show financial need and sign a promissory note. Repayment begins nine months after you graduate, leave school, or drop below half-time status. If you serve in the Peace Corps or Vista or teach in what is designated as a disadvantaged area, part or all of your loan may be canceled. If you attend graduate school, loan repayments may be deferred.

Stafford student loans. Insured by the federal government and administered by local banks and credit unions, these loans require that you show financial need. Interest rates fluctuate, depending on how long you take to repay the loan.

Finding Scholarships

Look at your college catalog or website or visit your campus financial aid office to find two scholarships for which you are eligible and that you are not currently receiving.

Complete the following chart.

Scholarship Name	From Whom?	Amount of Aid?	Application Requirements	Date Due

Use the 5Cs—Define the **C**hallenge; Identify the **C**hoices; Predict the **C**onsequences; **C**hoose an option; **C**heck your outcome—to create a plan for financing the remainder of your education.

Managing Your Money

In the last 10 years, according to the International Credit Association, 24 million consumers were in some sort of financial trouble, and 3 million of these were about to go bankrupt. The Federal Reserve Board has found that the increased number of bankruptcies seems to correlate with increased consumer debt—in other words, people owed money that they were unable to repay. Financial crises in the United States and in the world have contributed to this.

As a student, you may feel that consumer debt has little to do with you. But if you have a student loan or a credit card with an outstanding balance, you are a consumer debtor. Like a bad cold, debt strikes everyone to some degree or another. And that's the issue—the degree to which you allow consumer debt to invade and control your life.

❯ Credit Cards

Americans possess over 840 million forms of plastic money including general cards such as VISA, MasterCard, Diner's Club, American Express, and Discover; department store cards like Sears, Macy's, and J. C. Penney; and oil company cards like Shell and Exxon. With the right card, Americans have access to everything from automobiles to zucchini.

You, like many college students, probably get many credit card applications in the mail or even at your college. You may have been tempted—or even succumbed to the temptation—to request a card. After all, they're good to have for emergency purchases. They also let you shop without carrying a lot of cash.

If you charge only those items within your budget, you can pay off your credit card balance each month. Most cards add no finance charges on such purchases. Like using cash or writing a check, you pay only for the item you purchased. Unlike using cash or writing a check, you've delayed payment on that item until a more convenient time.

Suppose you buy an object more costly than you have allowed for in your budget. If your budget has room for more than a monthly payment, allowing you to pay the entire sum off when the bill arrives, you're in a minority. Sixty-six percent of Americans leave balances on their credit cards each month, accumulating high costs in the form of interest on their unpaid balances.

The finance charges are calculated on unpaid balances. That's a problem if you are using credit cards because credit cards charge anywhere from 9 to

21 percent interest on outstanding amounts. If you can afford to make only minimum payments each month, the final cost of your purchases will be far greater than you expect. Some companies add a penalty for a late or incomplete payment. Interest and late fees turn what seemed like a great buy into a burden.

For instance, let's say that you owe $5,000 on a credit card with an 18.9 percent interest rate. You make a payment of $100 per month. How long will it take you to pay off your debt? Eight years and four months. That's if you don't charge anything else to the card! And you'll pay almost as much interest as what you owe: $4,911.

Read the list of debt danger signals below. If any of the statements apply to you, you may be on the road to financial trouble. If so, contact a nonprofit credit counseling service. These services provide free or low-cost advice on financial management. To find the nearest nonprofit credit counseling service, check the National Foundation for Consumer Credit (NFCC) (www.nfcc.org/).

As a college student, you may be doing everything you can to get from day to day. But re-evaluating your expenses—especially in credit expenses—is always a good idea. Most people find that at least some of their purchases are for wants instead of needs. Stop putting your wants on a credit card.

The first caution you need to observe in credit card use, then, is: Don't purchase more than you can reasonably afford.

A second caution involves financial identify theft. If someone steals your car, wallet, or other valuables, you know immediately. But someone can take your financial identify and use it without your even realizing it. Before you know it, your credit is ruined and your account is emptied. Once stolen, recovery of your

TIPS FOR PHONE PURCHASES

1. **Only make purchases in which you initiate the call to a reputable company.** Don't give credit card numbers to telemarketers that call you.

2. **Don't give out credit card or other personal information if you are in a public place.** People that overhear you can take your identify.

financial identity may take hundreds of hours of effort, if you can do it at all. As a credit card holder, you must guard against the dishonesty of others.

It's a good idea to check your credit report. Although there are a number of valid sites, there are also some that have hidden fees or membership costs. The Federal Trade Commission (http://www.ftc.gov/freereports) links you to AnnualCreditReport.com (https://www.annualcreditreport.com/cra/index.jsp) which is described as "the ONLY authorized source for the free annual credit report that's yours by law." Why? This law—the Fair Credit Reporting Act—gives you access to your credit report at no cost from each of the three nationwide credit reporting companies once a year.

What affects your credit score? Your credit score is based on the number and kind of accounts you have, how old they are, late payments, and debt. The lower the score, the more risky you are as a borrower. As a result, you might face higher interest rates or denial of future credit cards or loans. Paying bills on time and in full, using less than 25 percent of your available credit, and steady employment increase your score. Late payments, too many requests for new lines of credit, using too much credit, or too many inquiries about your credit can lower your score. You might see ads or websites that promise to "fix" your credit scores. The truth is . . . they can't. Only you and your financial choices affect your future credit score.

Credit Debt Danger Signs

1. You do not think of credit card balances as debt.

2. You frequently pay your bills late because you don't have money to pay them.

3. Creditors call or write asking for payment.

4. You have little or no savings.

5. You have little or no idea what your living expenses are.

6. You have more than two or three credit cards with outstanding balances.

7. You carry several cards in your wallet and use them impulsively and often.

8. You pay only the monthly minimum on each account.

9. You don't know the sum of your debts.

10. You have to borrow money or get a cash advance to pay creditors.

11. You spend more than 20 percent of your take-home pay on credit card payments.

12. If you're married, you use all of your or your spouse's income to make payments on credit cards.

13. It will take you more than a year to pay off your credit card debt.

14. You've considered consolidating your payments into one loan.

15. You lie to friends or family about your spending or what you really owe.

16. You've been denied credit.

17. You frequently bounce checks or overdraw your account.

18. You have one or more credit cards that are at or near their spending limits.

Protecting Your Financial Identify against Theft

1. **Sign your card as soon as you get it.**

2. **Keep your credit card in a safe place, and don't give it or lend it to others including friends or family.**

3. **Keep your PIN safe.** Store your PIN separate from your card, and don't tell others where or what it is.

4. **Shred or tear up any credit card offers you receive in the mail.** This keeps others from using them.

5. **When you use your credit card, shield it from others' view.** This keeps someone from copying the numbers or taking a picture of it with a cell phone.

6. **Keep your credit cards separate from your wallet.** If your wallet is stolen, your credit cards will still be safe.

7. **Keep a list of all your credit cards and numbers in a safe place.** If your credit cards are lost or stolen, you will know whom to call and what accounts to close. One easy way to do this is to photocopy your cards. Since this copy serves only as a record, several cards can be copied on one page. Photocopying your driver's license, insurance cards, and other forms of identification is a good idea, as well. Store these in a safe place.

8. **Check your credit card statements**. Call your credit card company, and dispute any charges you don't recognize or have record of.

TIPS FOR FACE-TO-FACE PURCHASES

1. **Check your receipt before signing.** Before you sign a sales draft, make sure the amount that's printed on the sales draft is the same as the amount of your transaction. Keep your credit card sales draft so that you can match it with the credit card statement/bill.

2. **Make sure that the merchant staff return the credit card to you.** Dishonest employees can take your card and return one that's not yours but looks just like it.

TIPS FOR INTERNET PURCHASES

1. **Send secure e-mails.** Don't send your credit card information by e-mail at all.

2. **Check site security.** Don't give out your credit card number(s) online unless the site is a secure and reputable site. Sometimes a tiny icon of a padlock appears to symbolize a higher level of security to transmit data. This icon is not a guarantee of a secure site, but might provide you some assurance. Also, URLs for secure sites are noted as https or shttp rather than http.

3. **Know from whom you buy.** Make sure you are purchasing merchandise from a reputable source. Don't judge people/companies by their website and don't trust a site just because it claims to be secure.

4. **Be proactive.** Don't respond to unsolicited e-mails or cell phone calls that try to sell you something or ask for personal or banking information. Sending such communication is termed "phishing" and can result in theft of your identity. E-mails or calls from reputable companies *never* ask for personal information. Also, reputable companies will refer to you by name rather than "Dear Customer." If you have any doubts, search for the company on the Internet and initiate contact.

TIPS FOR USING DEBIT CARDS

1. If you lose your debit card or it is stolen, contact your bank and report the loss immediately.

2. If you think your debit card is being used by someone other than you, contact your bank immediately.

3. Take your receipts. Don't leave them for others to see. Your account number may be all someone needs to order merchandise through the mail or over the phone.

4. Create an unusual PIN number. Don't use your phone number or birthday.

5. Memorize your PIN number. Do not keep your PIN number with your card.

6. Never give your PIN number to anyone.

7. Always know how much money you have available in your account.

8. Deduct debits and any transaction fees from the balance in your check register immediately.

9. Keep the receipts in one place and remember to record them in your check register.

10. Keep your debit card in a safe place and never let anyone else use it.

Debit Cards

While you pay credit cards later, debit cards take money from your checking or saving account and pay now. You use your debit card just like you use a credit card but it is essentially plastic cash.

Some debit cards work only with a PIN (personal identification number). Others can be used with either a PIN or your signature. Cards that can work both the PIN and PIN-less methods offer more flexibility, especially when dealing with businesses that do not have the equipment needed to process PIN transactions. In either case, the money will be taken from your account immediately or fairly quickly.

Checking Accounts

Checks offer a pay-as-you-go alternative to credit and are accepted almost universally as long as you have proper identification. Most banks charge fees depending upon the number of checks you write or the amount of money you keep in the account. Minimum-balance accounts charge nothing per check, as long as you maintain a specified balance in your account. If your balance falls below this amount, you pay a service charge. Special checking accounts charge both a monthly maintenance fee and a fee for every check you write. If you write very few checks, this is probably the best account for you. Another type of account involves your paying a fee for a variety of services. These services could include any or all of the following: free personalized checks, unlimited check writing, free traveler's checks, free money orders, a MasterCard or VISA card, a 24-hour ATM (automated teller machine) card or a debit card, free term life insurance, a safe deposit box, overdraft protection (the bank puts cash from your savings account or advances from your bank credit card in your account should you write a check for an amount over your available funds), and special interest rates on personal loans.

Checks are convenient and help you avoid the cycle of credit card debt. Because you have a finite amount of money in your account, you can only write checks within your current means. However, there are some

BANK OF SUCCESS
Joe Student
Address
City, State, ZIP
Phone Number

101

Date _01/31/2012_

Pay To the Order Of _City Electric_ _$48.95_

Forty-eight and --95/100 DOLLARS

MemO: _January Electric Bill_

AUTHORIZED SIGNATURE

123456789 II 12345678 II 101

Bank routing number | Account number | Check number

Figure 10.2 Sample Check.

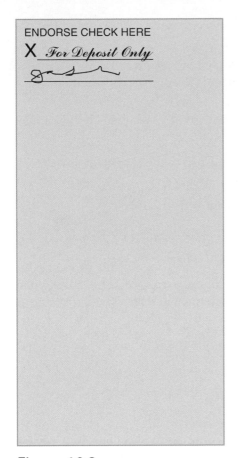

Figure 10.3 How to Endorse a Check.

tips

QUESTIONS TO CONSIDER IN SELECTING OR CONTINUING WITH A BANK

1. How many checks do you plan to write each month? Is there a service charge?

2. How much money will you keep in the account? Is there a service charge below a certain amount?

3. How convenient is the location of the bank to the campus?

4. What bank services do you really need?

5. Which bank offers these services for the least money?

things to watch out for. For instance, avoid writing checks payable to *cash.* Doing so isn't a good idea unless you stand in front of the person who's going to cash the check. When a check is made out to *cash,* anyone can cash it.

When you write a check, try not to leave spaces before and after the words and numbers. Doing so leaves your check open to possible alterations that increase its worth. If your check is written for "20.00" and if there is space, someone could put a 1 in front of the 2, changing the amount to 120.00.

When you endorse a check (which allows you to deposit it or cash it) write either the words "Payable to the order of XX," "For deposit to account XX," or "For deposit only" on one line and your name on a second line. This prevents others from being able to cash your check should you lose it before you get it to the bank.

When you pay bills by check, mail them from the post office rather than from home. This prevents people from stealing and "washing" your check for reuse.

Finally, avoid overdrafts. The best way to do so is to balance your checkbook each month. If you have an agreement with your bank to authorize payments of overdrafts, you will probably be charged interest at an agreed rate and/or a fee of some sort. If you do not, your account will be charged the amount plus the overdraft fee.

How to Balance Your Checking Account

1. Write checks in the order in which they are numbered. Record each check by number and actual amount (not rounded figures) in your checkbook register when you write it. If you are married or have a joint account, make sure each of you records checks as they are written.

2. Keep all debit/ATM receipts, and write records of your transactions in your checkbook register, including dates and times of transactions. Additionally, call the bank as soon as possible if you make a mistake that cannot be corrected at the ATM.

3. Keep all deposit receipts.

4. Give deposits 24 to 48 hours to clear.

5. When you receive your monthly bank statement, mark each check that has been posted by the bank.

6. Go through your checkbook register, and add to the statement any checks that have not cleared the account.

7. Subtract the amounts of these checks from your balance.

8. Add to the balance any deposits you've made that aren't posted.

9. Deduct any bank service charges from your checkbook register.

10. If your final figure and the bank's final figure aren't the same, check your math. If you find no errors, take your statement and checkbook register to the bank, and ask for help.

11. File all canceled checks if your bank sends them to you. They are legal receipts of payment.

Cash

One way to manage your budget is to consider using cash instead of writing checks or using a debit card. While this may seem old-fashioned, using cards may make you forget that it is real money you are spending. Having the amount of money you can spend in your wallet and stopping when it's gone forces yourself to stay on budget.

The problem lies with how you think about and keep up with your spending. When you buy coffee, gas, and lunch, the money adds up. By swiping a card, you may forget how much you actually spend. If you are using cash, you'll know quickly when your money is gone.

activity 3

Money and the 5Cs

What money management issue or goal is of most concern to you? Using credit? Paying off credit cards? Overspending? Paying for tuition or books? Inability to meet basic needs? Saving for an emergency? What else? Use the 5Cs—Define the **C**hallenge; Identify the **C**hoices; Predict the **C**onsequences; **C**hoose an option; **C**heck your outcome—to make a decision that addresses your concern.

chapter review

Respond to the following on a separate sheet of paper or in your notebook.

1. What's the difference between income and expenses?
2. Provide three examples each of discretionary and nondiscretionary costs.
3. Consider your income and expenses. Where do your financial problems lie?
4. In what two forms does financial aid come?
5. Explain the differences among grants, scholarships, and loans.
6. What are the dangers of using credit cards?
7. What are the benefits of using a debit card? List any liabilities.
8. What should you consider in selecting a bank?
9. List advantages to using checks over debit/credit cards.
10. Explain how using cash can help you manage your budget.

did you decide?

Did you accomplish what you wanted to in this chapter? Check the items below that apply to you.

Review the *You Decide* questions that you identified at the beginning of the chapter, but look at them from a new direction. If you didn't check an item below, review that module until you feel you can confidently apply the strategies to your own situation. However, the best ideas are worthless unless they are put into effect. Use the 5Cs to help you decide what information you found most helpful in the chapter and how you plan to use it. Record your comments after the statements below.

☐ 10.1 I can create and stick to a budget.

_____

_____

☐ 10.2 I have good ideas about how to pay for college.

_____

_____

☐ 10.3 I know exactly where my money goes.

_____

_____

perspectives

The decisions you make about money can have lasting effects. The following letter to the editor from a community college newspaper ("Fairy Tale Becomes Reality: Credit Disenchantment") provides one perspective on credit card use.

Think about and answer the questions that follow.

1. What are the advantages of having credit cards? What are the disadvantages?
2. What is your biggest problem in money management?
3. Are you for or against legislative reforms regarding a credit card company's solicitation of credit cards to high school and college students? Explain your point of view.
4. Jennifer Brown says she has many friends who are in the same situation as she was—young and finishing college with unmanageable debt and bad credit. Use the 5C approach to identify a strategy for ridding a person of debt and poor credit.
   A. What is the **C**hallenge?
   B. What **C**hoices does a person have in terms for eliminating debt and bad credit?
   C. What is the major **C**onsequence(s) of each choice?
   D. What would be the best **C**hoice?
   E. How could he outcome of the decision be **C**hecked?

September 6, 2002

TO WHOM IT MAY CONCERN:

My name is Jennifer Brown and I am a student at Austin Community College (ACC) who will graduate from St. Edward's University this spring. I am 23 years old and I have had a credit card since I was 17.

After reading a recent article in the *Austin American-Statesman* about college students getting into debt using credit cards, I decided to write a letter to the ACCent editor to share my story as a personal testimonial to illustrate why serious legislative reforms are needed to regulate credit card companies' solicitation of high school and college students.

I was only 17 years old when I graduated from high school and within two months after graduation, I started receiving credit card solicitations in the mail. I earned less than $2,500 per year at a part-time job. The majority of these companies offered a starting credit limit of $500 to be increased after making timely payments for a certain period. Like any immature 17-year-old whose main concern was shopping, I happily accepted the card. Over a period of five and a half years many more credit cards came in the mail.

I began to get further and further into debt. At a time in my life when I might have been establishing good credit and learning to manage my finances, I was sliding deeper into debt with each attractive offer of larger credit limits and more credit cards. The best credit card offer was yet to come!

I was a 20-year-old, totally dependent on my parents financially and only working a part-time job paying $8 per hour. I remember opening the mail one day, and Yahoo! Visa had sent me an offer for a card with a $5,000 dollar limit! WOW!

I am now 23 years old and have more than $6,000 of credit card debt. I still have a part-time job, and I am about to graduate from college in May. Three months ago when I realized that I could no longer make the minimum monthly payments, which totaled more than $350 per month, I joined a debt management program.

At 23, I have terrible credit and [what could have been] avoidable debt. I take full responsibility for accepting the credit cards and making the charges. For the next three years, until they are paid off, I will remember every month the consequences of my actions. Because so many credit card purchases are impulse purchases, I rarely remember the purchases; however, I cannot forget the debt.

I believe that most young adults who are still fully dependent on their parents have no business with credit cards. Directors and managers of companies that solicit to college students surely realize this, but they do not care because they are making millions of dollars from interest and late charges.

I have many friends who are in the same situation as I am—young and finishing college with unmanageable debt and bad credit. If a credit card company says it does not solicit to college students, then I ask: "Why do you set up stands on the most popular spring break beaches in the U.S. and offer free T-shirts to sign up for a credit card?" "Why do you pelt young graduates of high school and college with endless mailings of credit card offers?"

I commend the people who stand up to credit card companies and ask our government to enact legislation regarding this issue! Every day more and more college students are accumulating debt. This is a serious issue and serious reforms need to be made.

Sincerely,

Jennifer Brown
ACC Student
Austin, TX

"Fairy tale becomes reality: Credit disenchantment." *ACCENT*, Austin Community College, Vol. 5, #2, Oct. 2002. Copyright © 2002. Used with permission.

reflecting on decisions

Now that you've read this chapter, how does what you learned affect your financial decision making?

LOAN **FORGIVENESS**

Did you know that you can serve the public and help pay off your student loans?

The College Cost Reduction and Access Act of 2007 established a program that provides forgiveness of federal education loans after 10 years of full-time employment in public service. First you make 120 payments while the loans are in the direct loan program and while employed in public service. After the end of the 10-year period, any remaining outstanding principal and interest are forgiven. For more information, go to http://www.finaid.org/loans/publicservice.phtml.

❮ **CHOOSE TO SERVE**

REVIEW

Skim the notes you made throughout the chapter. How does the content fit together? What information is still unclear? Were your learning goals met? Can you answer the review questions and define terms?

❮ **CHOOSING TO BE AN ACTIVE LEARNER**

CHAPTER **ELEVEN**

Choosing Health and Wellness

"Early to bed, early to rise, makes a (wo)man healthy, wealthy, and wise." What lifestyle decisions make you healthy, wealthy, and wise? Which ones are counterproductive?

YOU DECIDE

To *wonder* means to think or have curiosity about. Things and ideas you wonder about often mask a need for a decision. Check the items below that apply to you.

In terms of my health and wellness, I've been wondering . . .

☐ 11.1 Why do I feel so stressed?

☐ 11.2 How do I cope with stress and crisis situations?

☐ 11.3 What can I do to be more physically fit?

☐ 11.4 What do I do if I think someone (maybe even me) is having a health problem?

☐ 11.5 What is important in practicing "safer sex"?

☐ 11.6 How can I stay safe?

Each of these decision points corresponds to the numbered modules that follow. Turn to the module for immediate help.

CHOOSING TO BE AN ACTIVE LEARNER

SURVEY

Before reading this chapter, prepare for learning. Purposefully skim the title, introduction, headings, and graphics. As you survey, decide what information you already know and what information is new to you.

QUESTION

Change each section's heading into a question. This forms your learning goal for reading.

READ

Read the section without marking. Reread and mark key information that answers your question.

RECITE

Stop after each section and make sure you understood the content. Organize or summarize content and make notes.

One word that most students agree describes their first term in college is *new*. New experiences such as the first day of class, the opportunity to pursue your career, and meeting different people are exciting. But new and different experiences also present new and different demands such as finding the right classrooms, deciding what to major in, and getting to know others. Another way to describe a reaction to a new demand is **stress.** The newness of the college environment and the rigors of college courses can take a toll on you unless you pay attention to your physical and mental health and manage your stress.

Stress is only one aspect of health. This chapter also focuses on other wellness issues: nutrition, exercise, and sleep; sexually transmitted diseases and mental disorders; and crime-prevention tips for campus living.

What Is Stress?

Have you ever wished you had no stress in your life? Wouldn't that be wonderful, you might think. Hans Selye, a stress researcher, says, "To be totally without stress is to be dead."

There are two types of stress. When most people think of stress, they think of the first type: *distress*. Distress is the body's reaction to a perceived negative demand. Such demands can be major—such as failing a course, getting a serious illness, or losing a job. They can also be minor—such as sleeping through your alarm, getting in a traffic jam, or losing money in a vending machine. The second type of stress is *eustress*. Eustress is the body's reaction to a perceived positive demand. Such demands can also be major—getting a new job, graduating from school, starting college. Eustress can be minor as well—playing intramural sports, having a birthday, playing a musical instrument at a concert.

Oddly enough, according to Selye, the body's physical reaction to any kind of stress—good or bad, large or small, distress or eustress—is much the same. The body prepares for the demand through both physical and biochemical reactions. These reactions affect the physical body, thinking, and emotions. A relaxation response should follow a stress response. The relaxation response allows physical and biochemical states to bounce back to normal. If the relaxation responses do not occur, the biochemicals the body needs for good health are depleted. This affects the immune system. The person—you—is more susceptible to illness and mental burnout.

Table 11.1 Common Sources of Stress

Classification	Explanation
Intrapersonal Conflict	Inner turmoil resulting from decisions about goals, values, and priorities.
Interpersonal Relationships	Stress resulting from interaction with others outside your family (e.g., friends or peers) as you deal with individual differences and learn to communicate and compromise.
Family	Although a major source of support, families also create stress as the result of strong emotional ties and judgmental interactions.
Work and School Demands	Involves your satisfaction with your work and meeting standards expected of you. Sarros and Densten (1989) identified the following as the top stressors of college students: Number of assignments, taking course exams, size of assignments, low grade on the exam, assignment due dates, class presentations, course workload, own expectations, and spacing of exams.
Money Concerns	Always with you, especially as a college student, money problems are usually not a matter of having enough to survive (although it may seem like that at times) but how to prioritize spending.

The new and changing demands of being a college student—both good and bad—create both eustress and distress. So, stress is okay. The key is how you handle it. The actions you take or don't take affect how well you cope. The first step is recognizing which stressors you have in your life.

activity 1

Lifestyle Inventory

Health and lifestyle choices affect your stress level.

Mentally, respond to each of the following questions on a scale of 1 (almost always) to 5 (never), according to how much of the time each statement is true of you.

1. I eat one hot, balanced meal a day.
2. I get 7 to 10 hours of sleep at least four nights a week.
3. I give and receive affection regularly.
4. I have at least one relative or friend within 50 miles on whom I can rely.
5. I exercise to the point of perspiration at least twice a week.
6. I smoke less than half a pack of cigarettes a day.
7. I take fewer than five alcoholic drinks a week.
8. I am the appropriate weight for my height.
9. I have an income adequate to meet basic expenses.
10. I get strength from my religious beliefs.
11. I regularly attend club or social activities.
12. I have a network of friends and acquaintances.

Based on your ratings, identify one statement you feel is the greatest Challenge for you in terms of stress. Then use the 5C approach to create a way to increase your wellness in this area.

Coping with Stress and Crisis Situations

Some stress is just part of life. Stretching money from one payday to the next, balancing work and school, and taking care of elderly or sick parents or children are all examples of life situations that happen as a part of normal life.

When faced with stress, you have essentially four ways to cope with it. You can accept the stressor, avoid the stressor, change the stressor, or change the way you think about the stressor. The coping method you use depends on the stressor and how you choose to handle it. For instance, you might not like to get up in front of others to make presentations. Acceptance of the stressor might mean that you enroll in courses even though you know presentations are course requirements. Or, maybe one of your stressors is the traffic when driving to campus. You could avoid this stressor by taking classes at a different time or by taking online classes. Perhaps one of your stressors is overspending. You could change this stressor by evaluating your spending and separating wants from needs. Or, perhaps you are a perfectionist who gets stressed when your grades are less than 100 percent. If your grades are still acceptable (e.g., 95 percent), you could choose to think that an A is an A and be happy with your success.

But some stress comes when a problem flares up without notice and becomes a crisis situation. A crisis always seems to come at the worst possible time and results in stress overload. You can't schedule unexpected family problems, financial concerns, illnesses, and interpersonal dilemmas when or how you want to.

How do you define crisis? In his April 12, 1959, address future President John Kennedy said, "When written in Chinese, the word *crisis* is composed of two characters—one represents danger and the other represents opportunity." The word *crisis* comes from the Greek word *krisis*, which means "decision." One positive way to look at a crisis, then, is as another chance to use the 5Cs—Define the **C**hallenge; Identify the **C**hoices; Predict the **C**onsequences; **C**hoose an option; **C**heck your outcome—in decision making.

Sometimes what seems like a major stressor or crisis actually becomes a chance to learn and grow. Lack of money, disagreements with others, difficult children or other family members, poor performance in courses, job loss, and

Table 11.2 Stress and Crisis Situations You Can Control

Crisis	Alternatives for Solutions
Communication problems (e.g., assertiveness, parenting skills, personal relationships)	• Take a course in interpersonal communication. • See a counselor or therapist. • Consult self-help books.
Money management	• Share expenses. • Cut current expenses. • Seek financial aid. • Work part time. • Assess priorities. • Create a budget.
Study skills and time management	• Consider dropping a course; form a study group. • See a counselor. • Visit campus learning assistance center. • Take a study skills/orientation course. • Attend campus seminars.
Job loss	• Visit campus career center. • Look into retraining. • Activate network of support (faculty, friends, other employees/employers) to help locate job options.
Self-doubts (own high expectations, family pressures, concerns about career choices, class presentations, low exam grades, academic competition)	• Practice test taking. • Avoid cramming. • Take stress-management course. • Practice relaxation exercises. • Seek counseling services. • Hire a tutor.
Interpersonal relationships (family conflicts, love decisions, social pressures, family responsibilities, sexual pressures/fears, religious conflicts, job conflicts)	• Seek counseling services. • Talk to family and friends. • Examine values and priorities.
Intrapersonal conflicts (social anonymity, loneliness, depression, anxiety)	• Seek counseling services. • Attend campus activities. • Join campus organizations. • Volunteer your services.

other problems often seem devastating at the time. Once the issue is resolved, life continues, for the most part, the same as it did before—but maybe better. In other words, some stresses and crises are really situations you can control and change for the better.

Other stressful and crisis situations—death, illnesses, family problems, accidents, and crime—are outside your control. How do decision-making skills help you cope with such events? Your values and goals (see Chapters 3 and 4) factor into your decision. For instance, perhaps, due to no fault of your own, you become seriously injured in an accident. Although you are hospitalized for several weeks, you return to school, ready to finish. You find that you cannot catch up, but you feel that resigning is a cop-out. However, when you reexamine your goals, you realize that your goal is to finish and do well—not finish in a hurry. Although you may not be able to control the problem, what you can control is the way you view the problem—your thoughts, attitudes, and resulting behavior. Often, the most important thing you can do is come to such a realization and let go of the problem.

What if the problem is one that you can't let go of? Then you need tools and techniques to cope. Meditation and relaxation techniques help you manage stressors—large or small. Although they seem simple, with practice they do work and help you regenerate the biological chemicals that can allow you to cope with other future stressors and crisis situations.

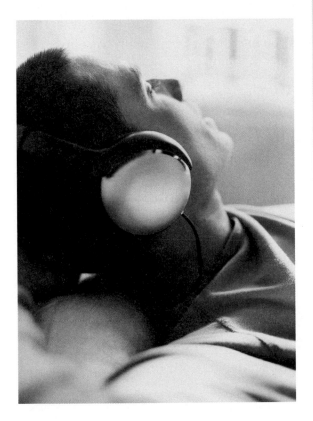

COPING WITH PROBLEMS OUTSIDE YOUR CONTROL

1. **Take it one day at a time.** Letting go doesn't mean that you don't cope with the problem. Problems that might overwhelm you if you confront them as if they lasted for a lifetime can be handled for 24 hours. Take them one day at a time.

2. **Talk it out.** Talk to others. Friends, faculty and staff, mentors, family, and others can advise you, support you, and listen to you. Problems that seem impossible appear less difficult when shared with others.

3. **Run away for a time.** While you can't run away forever, you can escape for a while. Getting away helps you regain perspective. If you can't physically leave town, escape to a movie, a new place to eat, a park, or a different place to study.

4. **Act normal.** Do something you regularly do. A crisis is an abnormal event. Simple, everyday activities like grocery shopping, taking a walk, or studying can take the edge off and help regulate the situation.

5. **Be a busybody.** Regular physical activity (e.g., exercise, yardwork, cleaning, etc.) burns excess energy. Mental activity (e.g., reading, studying, puzzles) occupies your mind and prevents you from worrying.

6. **Make time for fun.** Schedule time for recreation. Recreation literally means to re-create or renew. Like an escape, it breaks the tension and provides a vacation from the problem at hand. Laughter improves any situation.

7. **Golden rule.** Do something nice for yourself or for others. You deserve it and they probably do, too.

8. **Peace.** Meditation is another form of relaxation. It involves narrowing your conscious mind until anxiety wanes. One type helps you lower anxiety levels by focusing on peaceful, repetitive stimuli. Combining this focus with the repetition of a spoken phrase, relaxing sounds or music also helps you cope.

activity 2   Meditation and Relaxation

Part 1: Try Meditation

Follow the instructions below to begin meditating once or twice a day for 10 to 20 minutes.

1. Find a quiet, nondisruptive environment. Don't face direct light.

2. Don't eat for an hour beforehand. Avoid caffeine for at least two hours beforehand.

3. Assume a comfortable position. Change it as needed. It's okay to scratch or yawn.

4. Use a device to help you concentrate. This could be a plant, a candle, or some other item.

5. As you breathe out, say mentally to yourself, "stress." As you breathe in, say mentally to yourself, "peace." Try to visualize sending stress out of your body and bringing peace into your body.

6. If you find yourself thinking disruptive thoughts, refocus your thoughts on your breathing and the words *stress* and *peace* as you breathe out and in.

7. Take what you can get. If meditation is new to you, you may be unable to meditate for more than 10 minutes at first. As you practice meditation, you will be able to increase the time and its benefits.

Part 2: Try Relaxation

You need to practice relaxation at least once each day. Below is the general order of muscle groups to be relaxed. Do each exercise twice, concentrating on the difference between tension and relaxation.

First, tense up muscles in the area mentioned and then relax that area as completely as possible.

1. Relax your hands and arms by

    a. making a fist with your right hand and then releasing it.

    b. making a fist with your left hand and then releasing it.

    c. bending both arms at elbows, making a muscle, then straightening both arms.

2. Relax your face, neck, shoulders, and upper back by

    a. wrinkling your forehead and releasing.

    b. frowning and creasing your brows and releasing.

    c. closing your eyes tightly and then opening them.

    d. clenching your jaws, biting your teeth together and releasing.

    e. pressing lips tightly and releasing.

    f. pressing back of neck down against a chair and releasing.

    g. pressing chin against your neck and releasing.

    h. shrugging shoulders.

3. Relax your chest, stomach, and lower back by

    a. holding breath for a period of time, then exhaling.

    b. tightening and releasing stomach muscles.

    c. pulling stomach muscles in and releasing.

4. Relax your hips, thighs, and calves by

    a. tightening your buttocks and thighs and releasing.

    b. straightening your knees, pointing feet and toes downward away from your face.

    c. bending your feet toward your face and releasing.

5. Relax as you imagine a calm scene by closing your eyes and visualizing a quiet, relaxed outdoor setting. Pay attention to the sounds and sights in this scene. Try to feel the breeze; try to see the sun, clouds, birds, and trees; try to hear the birds, water, and wind.

GROUP APPLICATION: Discuss with your group how these different relaxation techniques affected you. Which do you think you'd use again? When?

What can I do to be more physically fit?

Physical Fitness

No matter how smart you are or how hard you work, you won't do as well if you aren't physically fit. Caring for your body isn't just important to your physical fitness, it's essential for your academic success. Everything—what you eat, how you sleep, and what you do—contributes to your physical fitness and your success as a college student.

❯ Nutrition

nutrition
The process by which you take in and use food and drink.

Nutrition affects your physical well-being. It also affects your study habits and grades by affecting your stamina and behavior. A balanced diet supplies the nutrients you need. It serves as the basis of good health and helps you store energy.

As a college student, classes, work, and study interfere with regular mealtimes. Fast food is, by definition, a fast solution. Vending machines also seem like a quick fix for hunger. When you're in a rush, feeling stressed, and wanting some quick "comfort food," it's easy to turn to junk food for sustenance.

But burgers and fries or chips and a candy bar will eventually, sooner rather than later, catch up to you in weight gain, sluggishness, and overall poor health. If you want to stay at the top of your game, you need a plan for getting good nutrition even when you miss meals or eat at weird times. For instance, suppose you have a night class, from six to nine, and you find you are always rushing to get there from work with no time for a meal beforehand. Eating a later lunch and a light, healthy snack after class can help you cope. You could carry some fruit, cheese, or low-fat snacks in your backpack for a between class snack or a snack to eat during the break, if all else fails. Carry a water bottle instead of relying on coffee or sugary drinks. Drinking plenty of water keeps you hydrated and is important for your overall health.

Rest and Relaxation

In addition to nutritious food and lots of water, you need adequate rest. What's adequate? It depends on two factors: your physical condition and the tasks you undertake.

High degrees of fitness, interest, or skill help you achieve more with less fatigue. Methods of avoiding fatigue vary in quality and effectiveness. For instance, you may enjoy football or tennis. That means you can play a game for an hour without getting tired or bored.

Sleep is the most obvious way to get rest. The National Sleep Foundation (NSF) *Sleep in America* poll found that 74 percent of American adults experience a sleeping problem a few nights a week or more; 39 percent get less than seven hours of sleep each weeknight; and more than one in three (37 percent) are so sleepy during the day that it affects daily activities.

College students are among the most sleep-deprived people in the country. This may be due to the irregularity of their sleeping habits. According to a recent study, over 63 percent of college students have poor sleep quality. If sleepiness interferes with or makes it difficult to do your daily activities, you probably need more sleep. Although sleep experts generally recommend an average of 8–10 hours per night, some people can get along with less while others need as much as 10 hours to feel alert the next day. Studies

TIPS ON SLEEP

- First, relax! Read a book or watch television until you become drowsy, and then try to fall asleep. Because your purpose is to relax, do not choose a textbook or an overly simulating movie.

- Keep a notebook by your bed, so that you can keep a list, similar to the one you use in class to keep you from losing concentration during lectures. Your problems are on paper, and you can stop worrying about forgetting something.

- Avoid or limit caffeine and nicotine which can keep you awake.

- Avoid or limit alcohol which may interfere with your rest.

- Exercise during the day but not in the 6 hours before bedtime.

- Avoid long naps. Long naps (over 30 minutes) can interfere with a good night's sleep.

- Stay on schedule. Try to go to sleep and wake up at the same time every day. A regular sleep pattern reduces insomnia, and increases your alertness during the day.

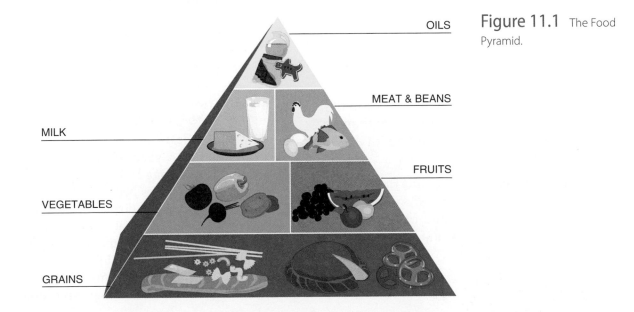

OILS

MEAT & BEANS

MILK

FRUITS

VEGETABLES

GRAINS

Figure 11.1 The Food Pyramid.

TIPS FOR GETTING EXERCISE

- Make it a habit. Never skip exercising for two days in a row. You can skip a day, but the next day, you *must* exercise no matter how inconvenient. If playing tennis is your way of exercising, you must play at least every other day.

- Commit to 30 days. Make a commitment to exercise every other day for one month. This will solidify your exercise habit.

- Get a partner. Like a study partner, an exercise partner who expects you to show up at a certain time and complete certain exercises will make you less likely to skip your workout. The social interaction will also make exercise more enjoyable.

- Set goals but not weight loss goals. Don't link exercise to weight loss to motivate yourself. Instead, use exercise as a way of uplifting your mood or enhancing your performance of a difficult task.

- Look for affordable ways to make exercising more pleasant or satisfying. Downloading some new music to listen to as you exercise may help you stick to a schedule. Purchasing new shoes or getting a coach may be just what you need. Exercise should be a priority in your life, so budget some money to make it happen.

- Mix it up. Don't stick with the same routine or the same machines. Look for ways of exercising that you enjoy. Look at less traditional methods for working out—dancing, yoga, Pilates, karate, Wii Fit, and so forth.

- Make use of campus resources. Many campuses offer credit classes, noncredit courses, and fitness facilities.

- Exercise whenever and wherever you can fit it in. Ten minutes of exercise a day is better than no exercise at all. Park in the last parking lot and walk. Take the stairs.

- Keep a record. List the date and time you exercised and what exercise you accomplished. This list will help you see the results of your exercise as you increase time and stamina.

show that lack of sleep leads to problems completing tasks, concentrating, and making decisions.

Sleep, however, is not the only way to rest. Changing activities—such as studying different subjects—also rests your mind. Recreational activities help you relax. These might include exercising, listening to music, talking to friends, or reading a book. Meditation also provides a way to rest and relax.

Sleep and relaxation are essential to a clear and active mind. If you think that it's always more important to study than to sleep, think again. Without adequate sleep, your study time is less efficient. Don't fall into the trap of thinking that you have to be on the go all the time. Make it your goal to establish a pattern of regular, healthful sleep. You will find that you're much sharper when you sit down to study.

Exercise

Exercise also plays a role in reducing stress. It helps you work off excess adrenaline and energy. Exercise releases physical and emotional tension in the body. It also releases endorphins that make you feel happy and less anxious.

Some forms of exercise allow you to be social, which can also be great for stress reduction. Other forms of exercise can allow you to get into a meditative state. Exercise can also raise feelings of self-esteem and bring other benefits that improve life quality. Paradoxically, exercise also increases your energy level. As a result, you better cope with stress because you feel less exhausted or overwhelmed.

Exercise tends to have a positive effect on your lifestyle. If you exercise regularly, you'll probably find yourself drinking, smoking, and/or overeating less. This, in turn, causes you to feel and look better. If you worry about your appearance, as do many people, exercise eliminates this potential stressor as well. Exercise increases strength and flexibility while it decreases your chances of cardiovascular or skeletal-muscular problems. Finally, exercise tends to slow the natural aging process.

Taking Care of Your Health

Complete the following wellness log for at least one week. Copy it so you can complete each copy for one day each. Write an associated daily journal that reflects on how these activities are affecting your ability to cope with stress.

DAILY WELLNESS LOG		
DAY: M T W Th F Sa Su		**DATE:**

SLEEP LOG
Hours: <4   4   6   8   10   >10

	DIET LOG	
Time	**Food**	**Calories**
1		
2		
3		
4		
5		

Cups of Water Consumed:

	EXERCISE LOG		
Time	**Activity**	**Distance/Reps**	**Intensity**
1			
2			
3			

RELAXATION	
Activity	**Time**

Making Decisions about Health Problems

You don't have to look far to see someone (maybe even you!) who appears to be having some sort of problem with health. Some people eat too much. Others eat too little. Some seem depressed. Others drink or use other substances to change their mood.

Problems with Food

eating disorder

Any of various psychological disorders, such as anorexia nervosa, bulimia, or chronic dieting, that involve insufficient or excessive food intake.

The National Institute of Mental Health (NIMH) reports that 10 percent of college-age women have a clinical or near clinical **eating disorder.** More males are thought to suffer in silence than females because eating problems are often not talked about among men. Commonly recognized eating disorders include anorexia nervosa, bulimia, binge-eating disorder, and chronic dieting.

Many students with eating disorders hide the disorder and don't talk to others about it. Check with your campus advisors or student services professionals to learn about the resources for help available in your community. The important thing to know is that eating disorders are illnesses that cannot be solved easily without treatment, but they can be treated and cured. Signs of an eating disorder are

- Obsession with food, weight, nutrition, or dieting
- Wide fluctuations in weight or severe weight loss
- Wear baggy, loose-fitting clothes, often with long sleeves
- Frequent complaints about feeling cold
- Fainting or dizzy spells
- Grade fluctuations
- Fine downy hair
- Feelings of isolation, anger, sadness, irritability
- Unusual eating habits (skipping meals, food rituals, or overeating)

- Hoarding or stealing food

- Frequent trips to the bathroom

Problems with Mood: Depression

One common college experience that one in seven college students faces is **depression.** Why? Biology is one reason. Full-blown depression most often starts in adulthood. A second is circumstances. The stress and demands of being a student, worker, spouse, child, and all the other roles you fill daily make you more susceptible. Remember that stressors deplete the brain's store of chemicals. If the chemicals become too depleted, they can't regenerate. Depression is the result.

Because the symptoms of depression are gradual, students sometimes don't know what's happening to them. Often it is a friend, co-worker, or family member who recognizes the symptoms of depression. The key to coping with depression is to get help. That's important particularly because what might seem like mood or common depression may be the precursor to the more serious form of clinical depression or even suicide. What are the signs and symptoms of depression? The symptoms of depression can vary quite a bit. Here are some common ones:

depression
A physical disorder, rooted in brain chemistry and genetics, and an emotional and environmental disorder, caused by stressful life events.

- A loss of interest in activities that once made you happy

- Physical aches and pains

- Appetite changes

- Excessive and quick weight loss or gain

- Fatigue

- Lack of motivation

- Feelings of hopelessness, sadness or despair

- Sleep disturbances (either insomnia or the desire to sleep excessively)

- Strong feelings of guilt, worthlessness, or low self-esteem

- Strong feelings of anxiety

- Trouble concentrating

- Thoughts of death or suicide (seek help immediately!)

Mood-Altering Alcohol and Drug Usage

The use of alcohol and other mood-altering drugs in college is an important public health and educational concern. Surveys consistently find college students have the highest rates of substance use, and recent studies have suggested that rates of drug and alcohol abuse are high among college students with as many as two out of five students abusing, not simply using, either alcohol or drugs.

Which of the following contains the most alcohol—a 4-ounce glass of white wine, a 10-ounce wine cooler, a 12-ounce draft beer, or 1 ounce of whiskey? Each of these contains about the same amount of alcohol, the most widely used

SUGGESTIONS FOR DRINKING SENSIBLY

1. Sip drinks with food or eat a good meal before you drink.

2. Limit your ready (refrigerated) supply of alcohol.

3. Alternate between alcoholic and nonalcoholic beverages.

4. Switch to beverages with a lower alcohol content.

5. Avoid situations in which you'll be expected to drink heavily.

6. Choose a designated driver.

7. Respect other people's decisions not to drink.

8. Act responsibly if you are the host or hostess of a party.

9. Set a limit to the amount you will drink and stick to it.

10. Space your drinks—it takes about an hour and a half for your body to metabolize a drink.

11. Sip, don't gulp.

12. Identify your reasons for drinking—get help if you need it.

psychoactive drugs
Chemicals that affect the mind or behavior.

drug on any campus. College students use alcohol to celebrate, reduce tension, relieve depression, intensify pleasure, enhance social skills, and change experiences for the better. Moderate amounts of alcohol work well in doing all of these. Larger amounts tend to decrease its benefits, however. Alcohol use and abuse alters attention span, memory, judgment, self-control, emotions, and perceptions of time and events. For underage students, it's illegal.

How much is moderate? How much is too much? No one really knows. That's because the amount varies from person to person, depending on genetics, health, sex, weight, and age. Nonetheless, most people define moderation as no more than two drinks per day for an average-sized man or no more than one drink per day for an average-sized woman.

As the drug of choice of most college students, it's not surprising that alcohol takes a direct route (no detours) to your brain. This means that an empty stomach absorbs 20 percent of alcohol molecules almost immediately. One minute after taking a drink, then, and particularly on an empty stomach, you feel the buzz you associate with alcohol.

If all goes according to plan, the route alcohol takes through your brain is orderly and well timed. When alcohol reaches your brain, it first sedates the reasoning part of your brain. Thus, judgment and logic quickly fall prey. As a result, you find yourself in situations you'd ordinarily avoid or doing things you would not normally do if you weren't drinking. Next, alcohol affects your speech and vision centers. Third, it attacks your voluntary muscular control, sometimes causing you to stagger or weave as you walk. Loss of vision and voluntary muscular control cause drinking and driving to have dire consequences. Finally, alcohol strikes respiration and cardiac controls. Eventually, the brain is completely conquered, and, if you're lucky, you pass out before you drink a lethal amount. If you drink so fast that the effects of alcohol continue after you are no longer conscious, you die. That's why you sometimes hear of students dying during binge drinking contests.

Suppose you avoid drinking contests but you do overindulge. What's the worst that could happen to you? Guilt, shame, poor grades, addiction? Yes, all are possible. But, if you drink sensibly, you can avoid all of these.

For some students, alcohol is not enough. They need more to fuel their party. As a result, they turn to psychoactive or prescription drugs. Use of **psychoactive drugs** often results in either physical addiction or psychological dependence. Addiction happens most often with drugs that cause withdrawal symptoms like vomiting, diarrhea, chills, sweating, and cramps. Such drugs include tobacco, amphetamines, barbiturates, heroin, and cocaine. All psychoactive drugs can lead to psychological dependence, the feeling that you need a drug to stay "normal" or "happy." All lead to long-term symptoms and potential for dependence and organic damage.

Prescription drug abuse is a growing trend on many campuses. Students use these drugs not only to "get high" but help them concentrate when cramming for papers or tests. They self-medicate for anxiety or depression and even to enhance their stamina when playing sports. Like psychoactive drugs, the misuse of prescription drugs causes future social and health problems.

Well-being Assessment

activity 4

Complete the following table to assess your health and well-being. Use the scale:

Almost always = 3

Sometimes = 2

Rarely or occasionally = 1

Never = 0

	3	2	1	0
I can cope with daily situations.				
I have already made some friends at my college.				
I have at least one person with whom I can freely discuss my feelings.				
I consider myself to be a happy person.				
I am emotionally comfortable with my sexuality and current sexual practices.				
I do not use drugs, alcohol, food, or buying things as a way to manage stress.				
I recognize feelings of sadness, depression, and anxiety, realizing that they are almost always temporary.				
I try to associate with people who have a positive outlook on life.				
I am satisfied with my life.				
I know how to identify the stressors in my life.				
I know how to protect my time and psychological space by saying 'no' to others' requests of me.				
TOTAL EACH COLUMN				
If your total is less the 28 you may want to consider a behavior change in this dimension.				
I care about other people.				
I'm involved in at least 1 college/university or community group/club.				
I know how to stay out of abusive relationships.				
I have friends from diverse cultural backgrounds.				
I am happy with my social life.				
I do not drive after drinking or get into a car with a driver who has been drinking.				
I have effective communication skills.				
I make and sustain close friendships and relationships.				
I am comfortable with others who are different than me (e.g., race, culture, religion, sexual orientation etc.)				
TOTAL EACH COLUMN				
If your total is less the 28 you may want to consider a behavior change in this dimension.				

I seek out and access resources when I recognize the need to do so.			
I know how to adapt to change.			
I can effectively manage my time.			
I take time to focus on attainment of personal goals.			
I know how to make decisions.			
I know how to set and reach goals.			
I can listen objectively to the ideas of others before coming to my own conclusions.			
I pursue challenging interests.			
I use new information to re-evaluate my judgment and opinions.			
I make good use of my free time.			
I make it a point to familiarize myself with local, national, and international news.			
I achieve many of the goals I set for myself.			
I like to learn new things.			
TOTAL EACH COLUMN			

If your total is less the 32 you may want to consider a behavior change in this dimension.

Safer Sex

No information about wellness is complete without information about safer sex. While many students think of safer sex as preventing an unplanned pregnancy, safer sex also protects against **sexually transmitted disease (STD).**

The advent of antibiotics once reduced the number of cases of STDs in the United States; but STDs become more widespread each year. This reemergence finds its roots in three factors. First, birth control pills replaced condoms as the preferred method of birth control, and birth control pills do not prevent STDs. Second, people thought that if they caught an STD, antibiotics would cure it. Third, the sexual activity of people with an expanding number of partners increased. Fourth, even though the risk is much lower than that of anal or vaginal sex, oral sex, often considered safe, can result in the transmission of HIV and other sexually transmitted diseases. Antibiotic resistance has made curing certain STDs harder to treat. And there are no cures for viruses, such as hepatitis and HIV.

So, how do you avoid STDs? Obviously, you have choices. One is abstinence. Another is safer sex (using condoms or dental dams). The enemy of the first is your innate sex drive. The enemy of the second is fear of embarrassment for several reasons. First, neither you nor your date may be planning on having sexual relations, and asking a date about protection may seem like some sort of verbal commitment to have sex. This is easily solved. No matter your gender, you need to be the one who is prepared for safer sex. Second, even if you feel a sexual encounter is soon to happen, how do you ask about protection or sexual history? After all, you don't want to seem too frank or unromantic.

The answer may not be the one you want. You may just have to take a chance. However, what you need to ask yourself is what you're really willing to risk—being momentarily uncomfortable or putting your health in jeopardy?

If you think you have an STD, you need to see a doctor immediately. If begun early, treatment is effective; if delayed, the disease becomes more perilous. A code of ethics requires that doctors guarantee confidentiality to their patients, so this shouldn't be a factor that keeps you away. However, if an STD is diagnosed, your sexual partners will be contacted. Ideally, you should contact them yourself.

Some suggestions for talking about safer sex are as follows:

1. Ask good-naturedly, "Do you have anything to tell me?" This question is open-ended, and if your date is as bright as you think, he or she might very well take the hint and tell you what you need to know.

2. If your date answers "I love you," be happy about it. You could respond with something like, "I'm crazy about you, too." A minute later, add, "Do you have anything *else* to tell me?"

> **sexually transmitted disease (STD)**
> Any disease transmitted via contact of the skin or mucus membranes of the genital area, semen, vaginal secretions, or blood during intercourse.

3. If your date says, "Like what?" you can beat around the bush one more time and say something like, "Well, I'm sure you weren't waiting for me all your life locked in a closet. I don't know everywhere you've been . . ."

4. If you're uncomfortable with that, or if you want to be more straightforward, you can say something like, "As far as I know I'm perfectly healthy. Have there been any problems with you I should know about?" Saying that you are healthy invites reciprocity in self-disclosure.

5. Once your date says he or she is free of STDs, you might pursue it by mentioning your ideas about prevention. You can say something like, "I've brought something (referring to a condom or dam), and I'd like to use it" or "I practice no 'glove, no love.'"

6. Or you can say something like, "I know this is a bit clumsy . . ." (you are assertively expressing a feeling and asking permission to pursue a clumsy topic; your date is likely to respond something like, "That's okay" or "Don't worry, what is it?") ". . . but the world isn't as safe as it used to be, and I think we should talk about what we're going to do."

activity 5 | Safe(r) Sex

GROUP APPLICATION: Choose a Challenge involving safe(r) sex (e.g., asking a partner about STDs, wondering if you have an STD, unplanned pregnancy, using protection, talking to medical professionals about STDs). Create a role play to show how the 5C process (Define the **C**hallenge; Identify the **C**hoices; Predict the **C**onsequences; **C**hoose an option; **C**heck your outcome) could be used to address it.

   Did the role play help you solve a problem you face? If so, how? If not, what do you do now? Use the 5Cs again to help you resolve this situation.

Staying Safe

On a college campus, the office of campus security or campus police exists to protect you. Like city or state police, campus police enforce campus rules and regulations and maintain order. They work to stop crimes and to protect campus buildings and property as well as students and faculty. Like calling 911, calling your campus security's phone number brings help quickly. Knowing this number by memory or placing it on a quick dial feature of a telephone helps insure your safety.

One crime that occurs often to college students is date rape, or acquaintance rape. According to the National Crime Victimization Survey (2000), 62 percent of all female rape victims knew their assailants and women in their late teens are four times more likely than the general population to be victims of rape. Date rape is sexual assault; it includes a wide range of behaviors including touching or penetration of another person's genital or anal area without the permission of that person.

Date rape can happen for any number of reasons and is often rationalized away by statements like, "s/he led me on," or "I was too drunk to know what I was doing." Of the contributing factors, alcohol and, increasingly, drugs like Rohypnol (more commonly known as "roofies") are the most prevalent. Date rapes happen on first dates, second dates, after a sexual encounter has happened between a couple, and whenever a man or woman says "No" and the message is not heard. Education is the key to stopping date rape.

Before a date . . .

1. **Know your sexual self.** How do you feel about sex? What role do you want it to play in your life?

2. **Plan before you party.** How does alcohol affect you? How much does it take to alter your decision-making capability?

3. **Talk it out.** Discuss gender roles, sex, and date rape with friends. Challenge stereotypes.

On a date . . .

1. **Be true to yourself.** Trust your instincts.

2. **Open your ears.** Listen actively to your date. Hear him or her. Do you know what's being said? If not, ask.

3. **Express yourself.** Say what you want or don't want, and say it with emphasis. Acting sorry or unsure sends mixed messages and only confuses your date.

If you have further questions or concerns, contact your campus security office or counseling center. Either one can provide you with the time, in-depth information, and personal attention that issues associated with this complex topic deserve.

To keep yourself safe in other ways, follow some commonsense suggestions. Remember the three *P*s of safety: *P*repare, *P*lan, and maintain *P*rivacy. Knowing and following these suggestions provide no guarantee of safety but make you less of a target.

1. *PREPARE*

   a. Walk with your head up and your eyes on the people around you.

   b. Have your keys ready for your front door or car.

   c. Drive with car windows up and doors locked; likewise, keep windows and doors of your apartment or house locked. Use dead bolts, if possible.

   d. Stay in the light. Park your car under lights, stay in illuminated areas, and keep a bright light near entrances and doorways. If you must travel in dimly lit areas, get someone to go with you. Never walk alone in the dark.

   e. Check the rear seat of your car before getting into it.

   f. Use ATMs (automated teller machines) only if they are located in highly public locations, check transactions before you leave, and put your money away before leaving the machine.

2. *PLAN*

   a. Establish signals and arrangements with others in your apartment building or neighborhood.

   b. Shout "Fire!" not "Help!" or "Rape!" People crowd around fires but avoid violence.

   c. Do not roll your window completely down or get out of your car in the event of an accident or car trouble. Instead, roll down your window just enough to hear and stay put until a police officer arrives. Even then, ask for identification before you leave your vehicle.

   d. Travel with a cell phone.

   e. Aim blows at an assailant's nose or the tops of the feet.

   f. When in doubt, make noise.

   g. If you're attacked, make noise and run away.

   h. If you're alone in your room or home and someone tries to break in, try to get out first and then call 911. If you can't get out, make noise as you call 911.

i. If someone grabs you by an article of clothing, try to slip out of the clothing. Run away, screaming.

j. Decide NOW what you will do if you get in trouble.

3. **Maintain PRIVACY**

a. If you are a woman, list only first initials in any directory, on your mailbox, or door. Don't list your address.

b. Never allow a stranger into your apartment or house without checking identification.

c. Do not pick up hitchhikers, even if they're women.

d. Be careful what you tell about yourself to the strangers you meet in day-to-day living.

e. Don't share your PIN (personal identification number) for an ATM with anyone.

f. If you are using an ATM, shield your actions on the numbered keys with your free hand.

Maintaining Safety Online

Social networking sites exist to help you do just that—network socially. But while the sites can increase your social life and friends, they also can increase your risk. Worst-case scenarios include being stalked, having your identity stolen, or having your computer hacked. The Federal Trade Commission suggests these tips for socializing safely online:

- Think about how different sites work before deciding to join a site. Some sites will allow only a defined community of users to access posted content; others allow anyone and everyone to view postings.

- Maintain control over the information you post. Consider restricting access to your page to a select group of people (e.g., friends, family, and other people you personally know).

- Keep your information to yourself. Don't post your full name, Social Security number, address, home or cell phone number, or bank and credit card account numbers—and don't post other people's information, either. Be cautious about posting information that could be used to identify you or locate you offline. This could include the name of your school, clubs, and where you work or hang out.

- Make sure your screen name doesn't say too much about you. Don't use your name, your age, or your hometown. Even if you think your screen name makes you anonymous, it doesn't take a genius to combine clues to figure out who you are and where you can be found.

- Post only information that you are comfortable with others seeing—and knowing—about you. Many people can see your page, including your parents, your teachers, the police, the college you might want to transfer to next year, or the job you might want to apply for in five years.

- Remember that once you post information online, you can't take it back. Even if you delete the information from a site, older versions exist on other people's computers.

- Consider not posting your photo. It can be altered and broadcast in ways you may not be happy about. If you do post one, ask yourself whether it's one your family would display in the living room.

- Flirting with strangers online could have serious results. Because some people lie about who they really are, you never really know who you're dealing with.

- Be wary if a new online friend wants to meet you in person. Before you decide to meet someone, do your research: Ask whether any of your friends know the person, and see what background you can dig up through online search engines. If you decide to meet them, be smart about it: Meet in a public place, during the day, with friends you trust. Tell a friend or family member where you're going, and when you expect to be back.

- Trust your gut if you have suspicions. If you feel threatened by someone or uncomfortable because of something online, report it to the police and the social networking site. You could end up preventing someone else from becoming a victim.

activity 6

Staying Safe on Campus

Visit the campus security office's website and your college library website, and gather information on each of the following topics in terms of your college or the area of the town it is in. When you return to class, divide into groups and give each group one topic to share information about. Ask groups to use the 5C approach to discuss the topics and how they can best be handled on your campus. Make class presentations.

- Environmental safety
- Incidental crime (robbery, etc.)
- Sex crimes
- Emergency weather
- Terrorist or shooting attacks
- Parking/driving issues
- Civility in classrooms and other meetings
- Safety of online identify

chapter review

Respond to the following on a separate sheet of paper or in your notebook.

1. What's the difference between a controllable and an uncontrollable crisis? How should you react to each?

2. Identify one situation in which stress is a problem for you and for which a solution is within your reach.

3. What have you learned about the role diet plays in stress management? Does your diet help or hinder your management of stress? Why?

4. What do you do to relax? Is this a positive or negative coping strategy? If positive, how could you maximize it? If negative, how can you change it?

5. What is the relationship between your stress level and exercise habits? Do you use exercise to cope with stress? If so, how?

6. Do you have a strategy for alcohol consumption at parties? If so, what is it? Does it work for you?

7. Consider making sex safer by discussing protection with your partner. In addition to the suggestions offered by the text, create three alternative approaches to this discussion.

8. Access your campus security's website and get a copy of the emergency procedures or protocols for your campus. Do these make you feel safer? Why or why not?

9. Examine your Facebook or MySpace site. Have you eliminated chances that you will be unsafe there? How?

did you decide?

Did you accomplish what you wanted to in this chapter? Check the items below that apply to you.

Review the *You Decide* questions that you identified at the beginning of the chapter, but look at them from a new direction. If you didn't check an item below, review that module until you feel you can confidently apply the strategies to your own situation. However, the best ideas are worthless unless they are put into effect. Use the 5Cs to help you decide what information you found most helpful in the chapter and how you plan to use it. Record your comments after the statements below.

☐ 11.1 I understand my stress factors.

_____

_____

☐ 11.2 I know how to cope with stress and crisis situations.

_____

_____

☐ 11.3 I have a plan to be more physically fit.

_____

_____

☐ 11.4 I know what to do I if I am having a health problem.

_____

_____

☐ 11.5 I know what is important in practicing "safer sex."

_____

_____

☐ 11.6 I have a strategy for staying safe.

_____

_____

perspectives

Dr. Sanford C. "Sandy" Shugart serves as the fourth president of Valencia Community College, one of the nation's largest two-year colleges and the second largest producer of graduates in the country. In addition to Dr. Shugart's role as president, he is a published poet and songwriter. The following excerpt comes from his 2000 commencement speech at Valencia.

After reading the passage, answer the following questions:

1. Shugart says that community college is the dominant mode of education in America? Why do you think this is so?
2. This address was given in 2000, a decade ago. Is it equally true today? Why or why not?
3. What do you see as the main idea of the last three paragraphs?
4. What effect does this article have on you?
5. What are the four lessons that faculty learn from community college students? Which of these do you think applied most to your life? Using the 5C approach, describe a decision you made in terms of these one of these four lessons.

   A. What was your **C**hallenge?

   B. What **C**hoices did you have?

   C. What would have been the major **C**onsequence(s) of each choice?

   D. What **C**hoice did you make?

   E. Do you think this choice was successful? How did you **C**heck it ?

My favorite day, most of the faculty's favorite day, in the academic calendar is the day of graduation. And not just because there are a few of you we won't have to see at 7:30 on Monday morning.

This is what we live for. Oh, not the actual ceremony. But all that it represents. Here in this room are some 500 of you. You represent some 3500 graduates this year. The latest in a line of 48,000 graduates from Valencia Community College.

And each of you has a powerful story. A story of dreams delivered, obstacles overcome, hard lessons learned, new friendships formed, new faith found, higher goals set, new passions discovered (a few of them, we hope, intellectual).

If you had some outside guest speaker here, I suppose he would feel compelled to deliver the standard commencement formula address:

Which is—advice.

But you see, an outside speaker doesn't know what we insiders at Valencia Community College know. We have a great secret. And I'm going to share it with you now:

The secret is this . . . you cannot imagine how much we admire you.
And you wouldn't believe how much we learn from you.
Do you find that farfetched? I assure you, it's true.
And I think I know why it's true.

This is where America goes to college. That's right—the American community college is now the dominant mode of higher education in the nation. It is where well over half of all Americans—Americans of every type, mind you—choose to start college. It is the envy of the industrialized world and is rapidly being duplicated in places as far away as Australia,

Britain, the Persian Gulf, the Far East, and South Africa.

Because this is where America goes to college, we get a cross-section of all the personal stories Americans have to tell.

Second, because we are committed to small classes, close contact with the best teaching professors, and a premium on your success—we get to know you and your stories up close, personally. And your stories are powerful testimony to the strength of the human spirit, the value of the mission to which we have given our lives, and the power of the institution we love—Valencia Community College.

So what is it we learn from you? What lessons have the students taught the teachers?

I'll mention only a few of the many things we could say, the many gifts you have given us.

First—it isn't so important **when** you bloom, only **that** you bloom.

Here in the room is a multitude of stories of "late bloomers." People whose early experiences of schooling and life might have suggested they had little potential and should limit their dreams and goals. But later in life—in your mid-twenties, mid-thirties, mid-forties and beyond, you discovered the courage to raise your aspirations and go for the best you could be.

Many of our finest students with the highest grade point averages and the most thorough mastery of their subjects are these late bloomers.

And we learn that in some area of our lives, we are late bloomers, too. You give us the courage to reach out and try new things, raise our aspirations, and risk looking foolish or failing in some new worthy endeavor.

Second—you remind us of **the power of persistence.**

Most of you have been here more than the two years the catalog might describe for a full-time student. The average time to graduation is more like three years. And many of you have been slogging your way toward your goal, let's face it, since the earth began to cool!

But the point is, you are here!! Your persistence has paid off. And it pays off with a bonus. Not only have you achieved this goal, but now you are stronger and more able to tackle your next goal with that same tenacity.

The marvelous poet Rainier Maria Rilke says, "Endurance comes from . . . enduring." You have become a person of endurance. It is a powerful character trait.

Third—**genius wears many faces.**

There is a terrible myth circulating in our culture that says that talent is a rare thing. Nothing could be further from the truth.

Scarcely any of us uses even a fraction of the gifts God has given us.

No, there is no shortage of talent. Opportunity, confidence, faith in ourselves, discipline to pursue our goals—these things may be in limited supply, but not talent.

Jefferson used to say, "Geniuses will be raked from the coals." He knew even in the eighteenth century that if our democracy could extend opportunity to the masses, we would discover true genius was much more amply supplied than anyone might guess. We learn this every year. A professor faces a new class. Behind any of those faces may lie a truly fine mind and the capacity to go further and achieve more than anyone would guess. And you can't tell from the faces which ones these are. Every year we are humbled to discover this truth from our own students.

Fourth—and I'll finish with this—we learn that **serving is always an essential part of living. . . .**

Students, already juggling enormous demands from school, family, career, and life issues—still find time, indeed make it a priority, to serve others. It's not something you say you will do later, when you're past all of this. It is a habit and commitment cultivated now, wherever you are.

This common habit of service is most impressive to us. It reminds us that we were born into a universe where giving is woven into the warp and woof of creation. Giving and serving are the style of creation, the natural way, a part of the design of creation. Our media gives so much attention to just a handful of people, really. People whose lives are largely a pathetic, selfish disgrace. Who have shaped their whole existence around receiving, acquiring, accumulating.

Let's face it, they give no Oscars for integrity.

But from you we learn that it is they who are living against the grain of creation. And it is the person whose life is a pattern of service and giving who is living a whole, fulfilling life and is really headed somewhere that matters. . . .

We, in turn, thank you for all that we have learned from you.

reflecting
on decisions

Now that you've read this chapter, how does what you learned affect your choices about physical and mental health and safety?

IT'S GOOD FOR YOU
TO BE GOOD

Recent research studies say that people who give social support to others have lower rates of mortality than those who do not—even when controlling for socioeconomic status, education, marital status, age, gender, and ethnicity. Furthermore, volunteering leads to improved physical and mental health. Volunteers have greater longevity, higher functional ability, lower rates of depression and less incidence of heart disease. As little as two hours of volunteering a week results in health benefits. "Civic engagement and volunteering is the new hybrid health club for the 21st century that's free to join," says Thomas H. Sander, executive director of the Saguaro Seminar at Harvard University. For information about service, visit the office in charge of campus organizations and ask about organizations that have service as part of their mission. Or, you can visit http://www.nationalservice.gov.

< CHOOSING TO SERVE

R E V I E W

Skim the notes you made throughout the chapter. How does the content fit together? What information is still unclear? Were your learning goals met? Can you answer the review questions and define terms?

< CHOOSING TO BE AN ACTIVE LEARNER

CHAPTER **TWELVE**

Exploring Career Options and Opportunities

What do you want to be when you "grow up"? You've probably heard that question many times. Think as far back as you can remember into your earliest years of childhood. What did you want to be then when you grew up? Why? How has that changed?

YOU DECIDE

To *wonder* means to think or have curiosity about. Things and ideas you wonder about often mask a need for a decision. Check the items below that apply to you.

In terms of my education and career, I've been wondering . . .

☐ 12.1 How do I decide on a major?

☐ 12.2 What's the difference between a Certificate and an Associate's and a Bachelor's degree?

☐ 12.3 How do I choose courses for each semester?

☐ 12.4 What career skills might I need?

Each of these decision points corresponds to the numbered modules that follow. Turn to the module for immediate help.

CHOOSING TO BE AN ACTIVE LEARNER >

SURVEY

Before reading this chapter, prepare for learning. Purposefully skim the title, introduction, headings, and graphics. As you survey, decide what information you already know and what information is new to you.

QUESTION

Change each section's heading into a question. This forms your learning goal for reading.

READ

Read the section without marking. Reread and mark key information that answers your question.

RECITE

Stop after each section and make sure you understood the content. Organize or summarize content and make notes.

The drive to choose a career starts early. Even before you were born, your family may have been planning your future. As you grew, adults asked, "What do you want to be when you grow up?" As you played, you may have pretended to be a police officer, a doctor, or a teacher. When you started to work, you probably had a variety of jobs—which may or may not have reflected what you wanted to be.

What's the difference between a job and a career? A job is work you do for a set amount of money. A career is a lifetime journey of making choices about your knowledge, skills, and experiences in the context of the opportunities available to you.

The U.S. Department of Labor reported that the average person holds approximately 11 jobs by the age of 42. Whether or not your collection of jobs becomes a career—or just a lot of disconnected jobs—depends on you and the decisions you make along the way. Your career comes from a series of related jobs in the same field. Thus, a career is not just a goal you attain in the future. Your career is a lifelong learning trip as you develop your knowledge, refine your expertise, and choose experiences that reflect your interests, values, and goals.

Students come to college with diverse job and career experiences. Students who have been out of high school for a while may already have had a career, or at least a job. They may be back in school to train for a new career, one that will be better in terms of interest, pay, or stability. Other students are recent graduates. Most of these students will have had "jobs"—flipping burgers or selling clothes at the mall—but not careers. A few students will have worked throughout high school and beyond with a clear and focused career direction. Perhaps they volunteered or have already worked in a job that matches their career goals. Such students are ahead of the game. Some students know that they want to pursue their educations but are not sure what they want their majors to be. They may be undecided about what fields they will ultimately work in. Some students may feel completely undecided without a clear idea of what major is right for

them. None of these situations is unique, and none is ultimately correct or better, as long as you know where you stand and are ready to take positive action to move forward—to whatever that might be.

Whatever your situation, this chapter will help you clarify your goals for college and career and discover resources that will help you achieve them.

Choosing a Major

Today's workers often change careers—not just jobs—many times in their lives. So how important is the major you choose? Well, that depends on whom you ask and what your goals are. If you plan to become a nurse or a paramedic, you should major in nursing or allied health sciences. If your goal is to become a general building contractor, majoring in construction management would be a good idea. In other words, if your career goals directly translate into a specific major and career, then you should probably major in that subject. But if your goal is to transfer to a four-year college to get a degree that will open doors for you in any number of careers, your degree options are likewise wide open. Here are some other suggestions to help you choose a major that's right for you.

Guidelines for Choosing a Major

Think about yourself. Consider your aptitudes, abilities, interests, needs, and values (see Chapter 2) in terms of career choices. For instance, what are (or could be) your strengths? Some careers require extensive time or lifestyle commitments. How would that fit into your personal, family, and other values? What personal traits do you have that make you suitable (or unsuitable) for a particular career?

Picture your ideal working environment. Do you want to work inside or outside? Do you prefer urban or rural areas? Do you like to work with people, information, or things? If you want to work with people, what age group would you prefer? Look for majors that reflect your choices.

Pay attention to what you enjoy. What are you passionate about? What courses, activities, topics, and people interest you now or have in the past? Why? What majors and careers offer those same kinds of interests?

Don't confuse your hobbies with your career. Maybe you do love music, but you don't sing well enough to be a professional and you don't want to teach. You can always sing in community groups and other places without making a career of it. You might enjoy cooking or reading, but you can't imagine wanting to do either professionally as a chef or an editor.

Research the career you want. Check out the government website for the *Occupational Outlook Handbook* (OOH) (http://www.bls.gov/OCO/). The website describes itself as "a nationally recognized source of career information, designed to provide valuable assistance to individuals making decisions about their future work lives." Revised every two years, the OOH identifies educational/training requirements, what a worker does on the job, and typical working conditions for the job. It also projects expected demand for the job and salaries by state. Search for other Web resources. For example, search using *What can I do with a degree in XXX?* (Substitute the degree you are considering for the XXX.) Look online for professional organizations related to your career choice. The content of their websites will generally describe what professionals do, required job skills, standards or certification requirements, and current trends. Try to research as many resources as possible. You are researching your future.

Weed out what you don't want to do. Get your college catalog and look through the majors and curricula. There will be many majors that don't fit your interests. For instance, perhaps you have no interest or skill in art. That leaves out many choices and majors from art history to graphic design. Or, maybe you faint at the sight of blood or find medical environments stressful. If so, a health care major may not be a good choice.

Avoid stereotypical thinking. Some careers (e.g., horticulture, industrial management, or funeral services) may not be as familiar to you as others (e.g., nursing, education, business). As a result, you might discount some careers that, upon further thought, would be good ones for you. Thus, as you look through your catalog's course options, take a second look at those majors that you don't know much about.

Look at the big picture. Some students find the right major in their last term. They think twice about it because a different major will take another semester or two in college. So if you graduate at the age of 25 and work until the age of 64, you have 40 years to work at a career you don't like. If you spend an extra year in college, you could work in a career you love for 39 years. How do you want to spend your life?

Read job descriptions. Check job descriptions in your local paper if you plan to stay in the area. Check job descriptions on Internet sites (e.g., Careerbuilder.com, Monster.com, Yahoo!, HotJobs.com) if you can be more flexible. Look for those jobs that make you think, "I'd like to do that." As you read, take note of what they require in terms of degrees and experience. This helps you make more informed choices about majors, internships, and other career options.

Talk to others. Many college faculty have had work experiences prior to teaching. Your campus career center is another resource you shouldn't forget. Both faculty and career center counselors can give you insider insights based on their career experiences. They may also be able to refer you to people who are currently working in the career you are considering. They can answer your questions and also serve as contacts for future job opportunities. Finally, you can always talk to other students about their career interests and work.

Finish your degree. Many employers hire workers with degrees, not necessarily a degree in specific areas. Employers often want to see that you had the perseverance to complete something. They'll often train you to do what they need. Just because you have an associate's degree in nursing doesn't mean that you wouldn't be good in business.

Don't be afraid to change your mind. Some people stay in majors because that's what they said they were going to do. Sometimes they worry more

Build a career out of something you enjoy.

about what they'll tell others than what they really want to do. Don't be one of them. When people ask, simply reply, "I thought I knew what I wanted to do, but I changed my mind."

Keep your eyes open. Your first, or even second, job may not be your dream job. But, they may give you skills and information that qualify you for jobs you never even imagined. Unless you're psychic, there's no way to know what the future holds. You can prepare for the future by taking advantage of as many opportunities as are available to you to learn.

Considering Majors

Using your institution's college catalog, your Challenge is to find two majors that you would consider. If you are planning to pursue a Bachelor's degree, you may use a catalog from a school you have under consideration. Use the 5C approach to identify Choices and determine Consequences for each major. Discuss these with an advisor before you complete the final two Cs.

Degree Options

Career decision making often involves finding the degree or program at your college that will take you where you want to go. On most campuses, you can choose between an Associate of Arts (AA), an Associate of Science (AS), and an Associate in Applied Science (AAS) degree, all of which are two-year degree programs, or a certification program which may have varying time periods for completion.

Community colleges often provide the greatest range of options for associate degrees. Such degrees usually can be completed within a couple of years. Associate degrees vary by institution. You may find anything from animal health technology to travel and tourism. An Associate of Arts (AA) degree allows you to transfer to a four-year degree program. An Associate of Science (AS) degree generally leads to a work career rather than to completion of a Bachelor's degree. AS degrees do require general education courses such as English, math, science, and social science but emphasize practical applications in career-specific areas. An Associate of Applied Science (AAS) degree focuses on the knowledge a student needs to succeed in a particular job. A Bachelor's degree is a four-year degree from a college or university.

Certificate programs are not degree programs, but they ensure that someone has met qualification standards in terms of knowledge or skill. Although many certification programs may require basic academic skills or other coursework prior to enrollment, they focus more on career-specific content. Some certification programs have corporate (e.g., Novell Network Engineer) or national (e.g., American Sign Language Interpreter) certification. Other programs—such as child care or business—provide institutional certification for program completion. Four-year colleges as well as community colleges offer certification programs.

Several states also allow community colleges to offer some four-year degrees. Sometimes, but not always, more coursework and higher degrees result in higher paying, higher status jobs and careers. Of course, not all satisfying careers come with high salaries. For instance, neither social workers nor teachers make a lot of money even though many of them have graduate degrees. Still, both are important professions that add to the quality of people's lives. You have to balance the extra time and cost of a four-year degree with how much you will earn and—most importantly—how much you will enjoy the career you choose.

If you are thinking about a four-year degree, there are some items you need to consider. First, where will you go? Obviously, you need to know that the major you seek is offered at the school you choose. But, just as important, you need to know that the major comes from a division in the school which is **accredited**, or recognized as maintaining standards requisite for its graduates to achieve credentials for professional practice. If you cannot find this information on the school's website, you need to ask.

accredited

Institution recognized as maintaining standards requisite for its graduates to achieve credentials for professional practice.

Second, plan ahead to be sure that your credits will transfer and apply to the major you want. To do so, find out if your college has an **articulation agreement,** which is an agreement between two institutions to accept credits of equivalent courses for transfer, with the four-year college you want to attend. If your college does not have an articulation agreement, it is up to you to contact the registrar of the degree-granting institution to learn what you need to do to make sure that your credits will transfer.

Third, it's also important to know if there are any other requirements you need to have to be accepted at the new institution. This could include a minimum GPA or standardized test score, completion of specific coursework, audition, development of a portfolio, personal interview, or other criteria. Identify these criteria as soon as you decide which institution you hope to attend. Otherwise, you may find that you've taken courses that do not transfer or that your GPA is not high enough for admission. Keep in mind that minimum qualifications for entry may be just that: minimum. Some programs do have minimum qualifications, but choose the best. So while the minimum GPA might be 3.2, those students that are getting accepted might have a 3.5. Thus, you need to determine if the program you want limits enrollment to only the best.

If you plan to transfer credit, you will need to have a copy of your **transcript** sent to the school you are transferring to. Get a copy sent to yourself as well. When it arrives, don't open it. An unopened copy keeps it "an official copy." When you visit your new school, take your copy of the transcript (just in case the school's copy failed to arrive) and a copy of your current school's catalog. This will help advisors at your new school make informed assessments about what you've done and what you still need to do.

It's not too early to think about graduate school, especially if you're thinking about a career like medicine or law. The academic record you're building now will, in part, determine your future acceptance to such programs. You want your grades to be an asset, not a liability. Graduate schools are most interested in the grades you receive within your major, because those courses will be most relevant to graduate school coursework; however, your total GPA is also important to maintain.

> **articulation agreement**
> An agreement between two institutions to accept credits of equivalent courses for transfer.

> **transcript**
> List of courses taken, grades and credit received, and quality points given.

Examining Courses

Using your catalog, compare the kinds of programs and degrees (e.g., AA, AS, AAS, Certificate programs) offered at your college. What coursework, if any, do they share? Why do you think those courses have commonalities? Is there coursework that you think you'd particularly enjoy? Are there courses you'd like to avoid? Now use the 5C process to create a short list of possible majors.

How do I choose courses for each semester?

Scheduling Coursework

OK. You're thinking about different careers. You're comparing different degrees. You haven't decided what you really want to do, but you need to schedule classes for the next term. What do you do now? Luckily, college faculty and other academic staff provide a wealth of information that can help you make major choices and career decisions.

Seeing Advisors and Career Counselors

At some colleges faculty advisors help students with scheduling and career questions. Special staff advisors may be available for students who are undecided about their majors. Other colleges have departmental advisors as well as advisors for undecided majors. Career counselors serve many of the same functions as advisors. But while their expertise may provide all sorts of information about school and also work concerns, remember that it is ultimately you who are responsible for the courses you take and the grades you make.

If you don't have an assigned advisor, get one by going to enrollment services or the admissions office and asking for one. If you have one, consider that person to be your ally and mentor. Take the opportunity to get to know your advisor and familiarize him or her with your goals. Check in often.

Because of their past experience and knowledge with college policies, programs, and courses, advisors are experts on what you should take. But they can't help you unless you are ready for their help. When you go to see them, come prepared with ideas and questions about the majors and degrees you are considering. Then you can ask advice about choosing courses that overlap several different majors while still gaining insight into career-specific courses.

For instance, you might be interested in computers as a career but don't want to take the math needed for computer science majors. In that case you may want to pursue coursework and a major that will build your computer skills while preparing you in a more general way for the work world. In this case, you could list the careers (e.g., business, digital media) or settings (law firm, hospital, school) you think you would enjoy and bring this to your advising appointment. Faculty members or advisors can provide the names of faculty in each academic discipline you are considering. By meeting with those instructors, you learn more about potential majors before you enroll in the courses.

Colleges also have career counseling services. They, too, can tell you about your college's courses, degrees, and programs. They know how those might transfer to four-year colleges or translate into career opportunities. They also keep track of labor demands and salary trends. This means that they know what careers will be in demand in the future. They can tell you how much you can expect to be paid.

Career counselors often network with local and other employers. They can help you connect with the people you need to know in order to take the next step in the career you want. As a result, many career offices also help you get internships while you're in school. Internships let you try out career interests as well as gain knowledge and experience. Internships can provide valuable work experience while you are still in school and they always look good on a résumé. Most important, career counselors provide you with the tools and resources you need for making career choices in the future.

Semester Scheduling for Undecided Majors

If you are unsure of your major, you can often choose courses that fit several different majors. Depending on the majors that interest you, you may be able to do this for the first term or two. For instance, you might be looking at first-year requirements in majors as diverse as business administration, dental hygiene, or criminal justice (a four-year degree).

After analyzing each one (see Table 12.1), you realize:

- English is needed in all curricula. Taking English 101 or 102 would be a good choice.

- College Math is required in Dental Hygiene. It is also one of the choices for math in Criminal Justice. College Math is the prerequisite course for the Algebra required course in Business Administration. Taking Math 121 and 122 meets the needs of all three majors.

- Biology is required for Dental Hygiene. By choosing it, you also meet the science elective for the other two majors.

Table 12.1 Sample First-Year Curricula

Business Administration		Dental Hygiene		Criminal Justice	
Business 101	3	Intro to Allied Health	3	Criminal Justice 107	3
Econ 121	3	English 101, 102	6	English 101, 102	6
English 101,102	6	College Math 121, 122[4]	6	College Math 115, 116[4] or	
Algebra 155, 156[3,4]	6	Biology 101, 102, 121	8	College Math 121, 122[4]	6
Science Electives[1]	6	Speech for Non-Majors 161	3	Science Electives[1]	6
Speech for Non-Majors 161	3	Intro to Psychology 100	3	Intro to Psychology 100	3
General Ed. Electives[2]	9	General Ed. Electives[2]	3	Sociology 101	3
				General Ed. Electives[2]	6
TOTAL	**33**	**TOTAL**	**32**	**TOTAL**	**33**

[1] Choose from Biology, Physics, Botany, Zoology, Chemistry, Geology, Astronomy.
[2] Choose from Art, Foreign Language, Psychology, Sociology, Music, Economics, History, Geography, Speech.
[3] Prerequisite courses are College Math 121, 122.
[4] Math 090 or a passing score on the Math Placement Test is a prerequisite of all math courses.

- Speech for non-majors is required in Business Administration and Dental Hygiene and satisfies the general education elective for Criminal Justice.

- Taking Introduction to Psychology fulfills the Dental Hygiene and Criminal Justice requirement and serves as a general education elective in business.

You could also decide to take one of the introductory courses (Business 101, Introduction to Allied Health, or Criminal Justice 107) in place of one of the elective courses. Although the course you choose might not apply toward all of the degrees, it would help you decide what major you want to pursue.

Creating an Educational Plan

semester system
Typically a 15- or 16-week term.

quarter system
Typically a 10- or 12-week term.

At some point, you will choose a major. Then you need a plan for completing it. Degree programs—for both two- and four-year degrees—list courses by term. Colleges that use a **semester system** generally list courses for fall and spring semesters. Colleges using a **quarter system** list courses for three quarters. Summer schedules are generally quite different varying from intensive one-week classes to classes that meet throughout the summer and everything in between. Courses can also be taken online or by correspondence. The educational plan you create will contain all of the courses for your degree, but not necessarily in the neatly listed curriculum found in your catalog.

For instance, due to work, family or other commitments, you may need to take fewer than 15 hours a semester. Thus, you might decide to take nine hours in regular semesters and not take any coursework in summers. At that rate, a 60-hour program would require about seven semesters. Or, perhaps your degree requires four math courses starting with calculus as the first credit math course; but you're not ready for calculus. You may need to take a preparatory math course first. Although some students think prep courses delay their graduation, the truth is that prep courses help to ensure graduation by creating a more solid foundation for future coursework. Other prerequisite courses (typically college algebra and trigonometry) will need to be scheduled first. Because the courses must be taken in sequence, you might need additional semesters to complete the math requirements. The plan you create should fit your needs.

A plan is just that—a plan. It helps you determine what you need to do, but it is not set in stone. Changes in your life or a lack of course availability can alter the details. That's one reason that meeting your general education requirements first is a good idea. Still, having a plan helps you see what you need to do to stay on course to reach your goal.

Creating a Tentative Schedule and Educational Plan

PART 1:   Tentative Schedule

Using the majors that you thought of considering in Activity 2, list the courses that you could take next semester. Make a tentative schedule with a rationale of how the courses that you chose fit into each curriculum.

PART 2:   Educational Plan

Choose the degree program that you think is your top choice. Using your college catalog and the form below, create an educational plan for the courses by term. Provide a written rationale for the number of courses you plan to take each semester (e.g., prerequisite courses, other commitments).

FALL 20____	
Course	**Credits**
TOTAL CREDITS:	

SPRING 20____	
Course	**Credits**
TOTAL CREDITS:	

FALL 20____	
Course	**Credits**
TOTAL CREDITS:	

SPRING 20____	
Course	**Credits**
TOTAL CREDITS:	

GROUP APPLICATION: Compare your semester schedules and educational plans. What can you learn from looking at other students' schedules and educational plans?

Planning for a Career

Sometimes even a college degree doesn't seem to be enough today. How can you lay the groundwork for the world of work while you're still getting used to college? This may seem an overwhelming task when you first think about it. It's really not, however.

Start by assessing your strengths. Once you know what these are, you can build on them. For instance, you can tap on-campus resources to develop your career skills. In today's competitive job market, you need to have every advantage you can. When you apply for a job, everyone will have some degree and varying levels of experience. You need to make the experiences you have stand out in ways that appeal to future employers. Making conscious decisions about the job skills you want is not only smart. It pays off in future job searches.

❯ Workplace Skills

Over 20 years ago, the U.S. Department of Labor authorized the Secretary's Commission on Achieving Necessary Skills (SCANS)—a list of foundation skills and workplace competencies that are still valuable in today's workplace. SCANS divides foundation skills into three groups. These are *basic literacy skills* in language and math; *thinking skills* such as creativity, problem solving, and decision making; and *personal qualities* such as responsibility and self-management. It divides workplace competencies into five groups: resource management (e.g., time, money, people, things); interpersonal skills (e.g., teamwork, tolerance of diversity, leadership); information management skills; organizational management; and technology (computer) skills.

Lists like SCANS are available on the Internet. You might look at the Job Skills Checklist at the Purdue Online Writing Lab (http://owl.english.purdue.edu/owl/resource/626/01/); or Job Skills Inventory at the University of Minnesota–Duluth (http://careers.d.umn.edu/inventories/skills_test_intro.html). You can use these in several ways. First, look at the list and check off the skills you already possess. Second, think about how your coursework helps you refine and develop skills. For instance, which courses provide ways for you to increase writing skills? Which ones help you develop creativity or problem-solving skills? Which ones require group projects that foster interpersonal skills? Which ones involve computer or other technology use? Rather than taking these skills for granted, collect specific examples of ways in which you demonstrate such skills in a portfolio. You can use these later to market yourself when you apply for jobs.

If you find your expertise lacking in any area, look for specific ways to develop that skill or competency. For instance, if you want to develop speaking skills, take a speech course or audition for a campus play. If you aren't satisfied with the quantity and quality of your leadership experiences, start a study group or run for an office in a campus organization. Or, if you want to increase your tolerance for diversity, join clubs or organizations that involve diverse people or attend campus programs and functions that focus on diversity. Again, document what you learned for future reference in job applications.

Opportunities in Campus Organizations

Have you ever heard, "Lead, follow, or get out of the way!" Colonial American patriot Thomas Paine wrote these immortal words to the New England citizenry about the fight for independence. They are equally true for you as you struggle to find your future. Whether as a leader or follower, joining a campus organization provides ways for you to add to your career skills.

The first step in any organization is membership. Joining campus organizations (e.g., Culinary Student Association, Future Teachers, Criminal Justice Organization, Peace Initiative, Chess Club) often gives you a chance to talk to students, meet faculty advisors, and learn more about the careers they reflect. Regularly attending meetings and other organization events lets you know what the group's mission is, who the officers are, and what their responsibilities and duties involve. You hear issues discussed. You gain an education that is outside the classroom. Once you've gotten a good idea of what the organization is about, you can then think about taking a leadership role.

So, how do you become a leader? One way is to start small. You could chair a committee or lead a group project. Or, you can ask officers what you can do to help. Most officers appreciate members who are willing to arrive early and arrange chairs, distribute materials at the meeting, or clean up after the meeting ends. So, volunteer!

At the same time, participate in meetings and look for ways to contribute. For instance, if you are good with computers, offer to develop the organization's website. If you like graphic design, offer to create fliers for advertising group meetings or projects. Or, suggest a fund-raiser or service activity and offer to organize it.

Many students think there are few chances for leadership roles on a college campus. After all, each organization only has a limited number of officers. And if you're new to a school, how would you ever get enough people to vote for you? The truth is that few people run for office in an organization, because everyone assumes that getting elected is impossible to achieve. All organizations need people who can take charge and be responsible. So, identify two or three offices that you would like to hold or that you think might contribute to your personal skills and competencies. Talk to the officers that currently hold those positions, or ask the group sponsor or advisor for more information. By learning firsthand about their experiences, you can decide if you want to follow in their footsteps.

Service Learning and Volunteerism

Do you ever wonder what your college courses have to do with real life? Have you ever felt like what you're learning is too abstract and theoretical? Would you like to help others but wonder what one person can really do? Perhaps you should look into the options for service learning or volunteerism at your college. Many campus organizations provide service to your campus or local community. While the goal is to provide assistance to others, these volunteer experiences can supply a valuable service to you as well.

Volunteer experiences build the skills you want to develop. For instance, you may learn teamwork by being part of a group that builds a house for Habitat for Humanity. Or, you might chair a fund-raiser and learn how to manage time, money, materials, facilities, and people.

Volunteer experiences also provide ways for you to sample careers before investing an entire degree in them. For instance, you might be thinking about a career in teaching. Volunteering as a tutor for a campus Big Brother/Big Sister organization can help you decide if you have the right stuff.

Volunteer experience may open an avenue of interest you've never even considered. For instance, perhaps a campus religious organization sponsors conversational English sessions for international students. Although you've never traveled out of the country, your participation may lead you to consider careers in international business, travel, communications, or teaching.

In addition, some colleges also offer service learning courses that apply course information to volunteer opportunities. For instance, students in a freshman composition course might volunteer to work with senior citizens and then write essays about their experiences. Students in a nursing course might volunteer to provide educational programs on healthy choices to high school students. Students in a horticulture program might help a neighborhood start a community garden.

The opportunities for service—and learning—are endless. What good can one person do? Actor Whoopi Goldberg once said that if every American donated just five hours a week, it would equal the labor of 20 million full-time volunteers. Even if you contribute an hour a week or a few hours a semester, it all adds up and makes our world a better place.

Networking

You've probably heard the phrase, "It's not what you know, it's who you know." To some degree, that has merit. While you may still have to have a degree or certification to get into the career you want, it may be the people you know that help you get a job in that career. A first step is to network with faculty and advisors. Tell them about your goals and interests. Ask about internships—both paid and unpaid—as well as opportunities to shadow someone on the job. These allow you to meet and work with career professionals. Such contacts may be worth more than any amount you might be paid. Joining campus organizations that are affiliated with your fields of interest is another way you can learn about professionals and meet people who will be your colleagues. You might also consider joining some professional online communities. For example, LinkedIn (www.LinkedIn.com) is a professional network of members in over 150 industries and 200 countries. Joining this network allows you to find, meet, and interact with professionals in the careers you want to pursue. You can find, be introduced to, and collaborate with qualified professionals that you need to work with to accomplish your goals.

Finally, remember that networking is not just simply getting people to know you. It's about developing mutually beneficial relationships and finding ways in which both you and the people in your networks can help one another. It's a two-way, not one-way, street.

Continuing Education

Learning doesn't end when you get your degree or certification. It may not seem like it now, but in practically no time, you'll complete your education at your college and then . . . keep learning. Your college education prepares you for whatever you encounter. That doesn't always mean that you'll know all that you need. It does mean that you'll know what you need to know. You'll recognize your need for additional information, training, and experience. Continuing education may come from conferences, on-the-job training, online workshops, professional organizations, or keeping up with the latest trends in the news or on the Web. In a perfect world, your employer might pay for such education. But in today's world, employer funding is less common than it used to be. Keep in mind that your professional development benefits you and your future goals. A lack of funds doesn't have to keep you from continuing your education. For instance, you might not be able to afford an expensive conference; but you might find free online workshops that meet your needs. Lifelong learning is part of every career. You can decide now that it will be part of yours.

So, whether you keep up on the latest research in industry publications and journals, attend seminars and conferences, or take additional coursework in a classroom or online, your journey will continue. You now have the tools you need—personal desire, the ability to identify what you know and what you don't know, and a decision-making process.

Using the 5Cs to Research Options for Your Career Plan

Use the 5Cs—Define the **C**hallenge; Identify the **C**hoices; Predict the **C**onsequences; **C**hoose an option; **C**heck your outcome—to plan your career.

1. Use your responses to Activity 1 of this chapter to identify the Choices you are considering.

2. Research the Consequences for each option by using the *Occupational Outlook Handbook* (http://www.bls.gov/OCO/). Determine type of degree, salary trends, working conditions, and demands for each option. Find information about the career using any three of the following: identification of relevant job skills, specific service learning opportunities at your college, internships at your college, professional organizations, networking opportunities, volunteering possibilities, LinkedIn, interview with faculty or professional in the field.

3. Next, given the information you have, explain which option you would now Choose. How will you apply this information to your career planning?

4. Describe how you would Check the outcome of your choice.

GROUP APPLICATION: Share your findings with others in your group. What can you learn from their research strategies and results? What can you learn from the way they made decisions about their careers?

chapter review

Respond to the following on a separate sheet of paper or in your notebook.

1. Which tips for choosing a major did you find most valuable? Why?

2. What are the differences among associate's degrees, bachelor's degrees, and certificate programs? What kinds of degrees and programs are offered at your college?

3. In terms of the majors you are considering, what kinds of workplace skills do you think are most important to develop while you are in college? In what areas of SCANS do you find them?

4. How can service activities or volunteer projects affect your career goals?

5. According to a survey at George Mason University, lifelong learning is part of every career. What does this mean? Does that finding encourage or discourage you? Why?

did you decide?

Did you accomplish what you wanted to in this chapter? Check the items below that apply to you.

Review the *You Decide* questions that you identified at the beginning of the chapter, but look at them from a new direction. If you didn't check an item below, review that module until you feel you can confidently apply the strategies to your own situation. However, the best ideas are worthless unless they are put into effect. Use the 5Cs to help you decide what information you found most helpful in the chapter and how you plan to use it. Record your comments after the statements below.

☐ 12.1. I understand the process of deciding on a major.

_____

_____

☐ 12.2. I know the difference between a Certificate and an Associate's and a Bachelor's degree.

_____

_____

☐ 12.3. I can knowledgeably choose courses for each semester.

_____

_____

☐ 12.4. I know what career skills I might need.

_____

_____

perspectives

Below you will read excerpts from a high school commencement speech made by Pulitzer Prize–winning cartoonist and author Doug Marlette. Marlette started his career in cartooning on the campus paper at Seminole Community College.

After reading the article, answer the questions which follow:

1. Marlette says that he was not one of the smart or popular students in high school. How do you think this affected him as an adult?

2. List the components Marlette sees as the keys to success. Which do you think you possess? How do you know?

3. What do you see as the main idea of the speech?

4. What effect does this speech have on you?

5. Examine the advice Marlette gives graduates. Using the 5C approach, identify one of them that could result in a decision about your future.

   A. What is your **C**hallenge?

   B. What **C**hoices do you have?

   C. What is the major **C**onsequence(s) of each choice?

   D. What would be the best **C**hoice?

   E. How could the outcome of the decision be **C**hecked?

Now there's something about the commencement address that brings out the pompous and pretentious in all who deliver them. . . . For all I know, by the time I'm done I'll be speaking with a British accent.

But don't worry, this is not a self-help commencement talk. For one thing, selves are not that easy to help. Selves, as you will discover, take time and hard work. I should know. I was a loser in high school. With grades, with girls, with sports. I did not excel. I stayed home and drew. *Mad Magazine* was my inspiration. I once concocted a parody of the popular Batman TV show called "Ratman," which featured several of my teachers at school. My friends laughed at "Ratman" but one said scornfully, "You spent your weekend doing this?" Yes, I was a geek, a dweeb, a dork, a tool. I still am, but for a cartoonist that's a job description. . . .

And I'm here to tell all my fellow dweebs and losers that your day will come. . . . Things change. You change. Baby fat melts away. Faces clear up. There is hope. And today is the beginning, Square One, for all of you. Commencement. Today the graduating class of 2005 says "Dude, whassup, yo?" to the real world. . . .

Plato and Aristotle asked: "How ought one to live?" Kierkegaard put it another way: "What must I do to be saved?" Today higher education asks: "How did you do on your SATs?" I'm not going to tell you what I made on my SATs but let me put it this way: none of your places at Princeton would have been threatened. I know it's hard to believe but in real life nobody cares what you made on your SATs. I'm not saying it doesn't matter how you scored—those fat and skinny envelopes from the spring attest—but I want to help put SATs and tests in general in perspective.

A few years ago I was at a dinner in New York with a bunch of people who were getting something called the Golden Plate, an achievement award for doing well in their fields. Some were celebrities—Barbara Walters, Calvin Klein, Colin Powell—others were less well-known, but had done things like discover the planet Pluto. Oprah emceed. I was the least famous person there. The idea was to get a bunch of "achievers" together and bring in four hundred high school National Merit Finalists from around the country for three days of schmoozing with the accomplished. The idea, I suppose, was that achievement was contagious, like pink eye. . . .

At a black-tie dinner where we collected our Golden Plates the final night I was seated between the soap star Susan Lucci and the Pulitzer Prize–winning poet James Merrill. The next morning at breakfast I was discussing the event with a Nobel Prize–winning physicist from Stanford who had discovered the subatomic particles called quarks. What would a cartoonist and a physicist have to say to each other? The Nobel Laureate asked me, "Would you have been invited to something like this when you were in high school?" I laughed and said, "No, I wasn't a very good student." He shook his head and said, "I didn't even finish high school." I was stunned. "You're kidding." "I had to get my high school equivalency later," he confessed. Then, looking around us, he said, "I wonder how many of the others invited here were National Merit Scholars in high school." What he was hinting at was the puzzle of human personality, the mystery of success, late-blooming talent and confidence, the ineffable qualities of character, drive and ambition, qualities that are often key components of achievement and are sometimes even galvanized by those early high school humiliations.

Since I seem to have fallen into the trap of all commencement speakers and started to give you the advice I promised I wouldn't, what-the-hey, let me finish before the British accent kicks in. Here's my advice:

- Don't get caught downloading music.

- Don't e-mail anything you wouldn't want forwarded.

- Practice, practice, practice. It's hard to get worse at something if you practice. But talent is not enough. Talent is not creativity, just as a seed is not a crop. You have to till the soil, plant the seed, work it, water it, harvest it. Creativity is hard work.

- Don't worship celebrities. With the fall of communism the only ism left to worry about is showbizm.

- Read. Reading is active. TV, movies and video are passive. Reading engages your imagination. Video substitutes for your imagination. Reading takes you into life, while television distracts you from life.

- Recognize political correctness for what it is: a bureaucratic substitute for thinking. It evolved out of a righteous impulse to rectify historic wrongs—racism, sexism, various forms of bigotry—but it has morphed into a Stalinist means of suppressing free speech. It thrives on campuses and in the human resources departments of large corporations. It's a way for businesses to pretend to have consciences. It's cheaper to install handicapped parking spaces and make employees watch films on sexual harassment and attend sensitivity training sessions than to pay them decent wages. . . . Repent of labels, the sophisticated name-calling we dispatch so easily—manic-depressive, bipolar, OCD, ADD—to summarize and pigeonhole and reduce the complexity of human beings to a sound-bite. Such labels dehumanize people and enslave us to stereotypes and limit us with reduced expectations, all defined by the word "can't."

- Be suspicious of experts. Especially those promiscuous dispensers of labels and meds. Question authority, including your own. But always trust your own experience and instincts over the experts. . . . Strive for excellence. But don't condemn yourself when you fall short. High expectation without condemnation. . . .

- Be competitive, but remember, envy is not competition. The word "competition" derives from the Latin *con,* which means "with" and *petere,* which means "to strive." Competition: to strive together. Competitors are in secret alliance, not to do each other in, but to bring out the best in each other.

- Don't do drugs. I know I sound like the mom in "Almost Famous," but she was right. Anybody can do drugs. It takes no special talent to get drunk or get high. I worry especially about children of privilege like you, and the secret guilt you may feel about your advantages. You may drug yourselves to level the playing field, to dumb yourselves down. Don't. Life's a gift. Don't anaesthetize yourself to it. Feel life in all its pain and mystery. If you can't feel pain, you won't feel joy, either. There's plenty of time to be comatose, like for the rest of eternity.

- Above all, remember: You are not your résumé. External measures won't repair you. Money won't fix you. Applause, celebrity, no number of victories will do it. The only honor that counts is that which you earn and that which you bestow. Honor yourself. And despite all I've said about the authorities, honor your parents. You will eventually realize that there are no grownups. . . . But you will learn in time that this is a good thing. If we didn't insist that you do as we say, not as we do, civilization would crumble. . . . In fact, a pretty good definition of maturity is knowing how immature you are. A pretty good definition of sanity is knowing how crazy you are. A pretty good definition of wisdom is knowing how foolish you are.

reflecting on decisions

Now that you've read this chapter, how does what you learned affect your decisions about your major and future career?

VIRTUAL VOLUNTEERISM

As a busy college student, you may not always be in a position to volunteer when organizations need help. Your college may not offer service learning courses or, if it does, they may be in courses that you don't need. Or, you may not know which organizations even need volunteers. Luckily, there is a quick and easy way to find volunteer experiences that meet your needs. Volunteermatch.org lets you search by city or zip code for opportunities to serve. You can even find virtual opportunities (e.g., e-mail pen pals, grant writing, researching topics, writing thank-you notes) to serve. Use the 5Cs to select three local and two virtual opportunities that interest you and that meet your schedule demands. While there is no substitute for actual work experience, this is a close second. And virtual experience demonstrates your ability to work in an online digital environment.

◀ **CHOOSING TO SERVE**

REVIEW

Skim the notes you made throughout the chapter. How does the content fit together? What information is still unclear? Were your learning goals met? Can you answer the review questions and define terms?

◀ **CHOOSING TO BE AN ACTIVE LEARNER**

glossary

A

abilities Capabilities that result from aptitude combined with experience

academic calendar Calendar of the school year starting in August or September rather than in January; shows information such as registration and drop dates or exam periods

academic freedom Freedom to teach or communicate even ideas or facts that are unpopular or controversial

accredited Institution recognized as maintaining standards requisite for its graduates to achieve credentials for professional practice

active listener A student who consciously controls the listening process through preplanned strategies

adjunct Part-time faculty

adult One of the three inner dialogue voices, the part of you that thinks analytically and solves problems rationally

advisors Persons who provide information and advice on a range of topics including college policies and course schedules

aptitudes Inborn traits or talents

articulation agreement An agreement between two institutions to accept credits of equivalent courses for transfer

asynchronously Hybrid course content delivered not at the same time

attractive distracters Incorrect choices on objective tests that seem plausible

B

backward planning Setting goals by starting with an end goal and working backward

body language Nonverbal communication

bookmark To mark a document or a specific address (URL) of a Web page so that you can easily revisit the page at a later time

browse Follow links in a Web page, or explore without specific direction, as the spirit moves you, until you find what you want

budget A plan for the management of income and expenses

burnout Physical or emotional exhaustion

C

chart Information presented in columns and rows

child The part of you that wants to have *fun* and have it *now*

citing Telling the source of information

closure The positive feeling that occurs when you complete a task

college catalog Book describing services, curricula, courses, faculty, and other information pertaining to a postsecondary institution

college work-study programs Federally funded job programs for students who can prove financial need

Cornell notes Page divided vertically into two sections with right side (about two-thirds of the page) for class notes and left column for recall tips you create afterward

course management system An electronic message center that serves groups with similar interests; software used by faculty and students to deliver online learning (e.g., Angel, moodle, Blackboard)

critic Role that suggests that you are unworthy or incapable

D

depression A physical disorder, rooted in brain chemistry and genetics, and an emotional and environmental disorder, caused by stressful life events

discretionary costs Nonessential items over which you have discretion, or choice

diversity Variety in the academic environment as the result of individual differences

download To copy data (usually an entire file) from their main source to your own computer or disk

E

eating disorder Any of various psychological disorders, such as anorexia nervosa, bulimia, or chronic dieting, that involve insufficient or excessive food intake

environmental preferences Physical surroundings that are most comfortable for you

ethics Standards of behavior that tell us how human beings ought to act in certain situations

expenses The amount of money or its equivalent that you spend during a period of time

F

5Cs Five-point decision-making process

formal outline Main points arranged vertically first using Roman numerals and indented capital letters, and then Arabic numerals and lowercase letters to sequence supporting ideas

G

GPA Grade point average

H

hybrids Courses that are a combination of face-to-face and online content and/or distance learning

hyperlink A piece of text or a graphic that serves as a cross-reference between parts of a document or between files or websites

I

idea mapping Graphical picture you make of main ideas and details

income The amount of money or its equivalent that you receive during a period of time

informal outline Same idea as formal outline, but uses spacing as you like and special markings you choose (e.g., all capital letters, dashes, stars)

intranet Internal network

L

labeling A note that identifies important information, usually written on the side of a page

learning style The mix of attributes that describe the ways that you best acquire and use information

locus of control A person's expectations about who or what causes events to occur

long-range goals Goals that take a long time, even a lifetime, to accomplish

M

map A graphic representation of main ideas and details

memory blocks Sudden losses of memory for a specific piece of information

mentors Wise and trusted counselors or teachers who advise, instruct or train a student outside a regular classroom

mid-range goals Goals that serve as a checkpoint on the way to achieving long-term goals

mnemonics Set of techniques for improving your memory skills

N

narrative text Readings that tell a story; narrative text can be both fiction and nonfiction

netiquette Abbreviation for Internet etiquette

nondiscretionary costs Fixed expenses over which you have no discretion, or no choice

nutrition The process by which you take in and use food and drink

O

objective test A test in which you select an answer from several choices provided by an instructor

P

plagiarism Stealing another person's work and presenting it as your own

preview Reading a chapter's introduction, headings, subheadings, boldfaced terms, and summary before a full reading of the content

priorities The people or items that you feel are most important to you

procrastination Delaying or putting off assignments or other activities

psychoactive drugs Chemicals that affect the mind or behavior

Q

quality points Numerical value assigned to each letter grade from A to F when given as the final grade in a course; used to calculate grade point average

quarter system Typically a 10- or 12-week term

R

relaxation A positive feeling created through the loosening of muscles

relevance Importance to your topic

retention When students stay in school until they meet their goals or finish a degree or program

S

search engine An Internet program that searches documents for specified keywords and returns a list of the documents where the keywords were found

self-talk The internal communication that you have with yourself; can be positive or negative; affects time management and self-confidence

semester system Typically a 15- or 16-week term

sexually transmitted disease (STD) Any disease transmitted via contact of the skin or mucus membranes of the genital area, semen, vaginal secretions, or blood during intercourse

short-term goals Goals that can be achieved in a relatively short amount of time

skim Read quickly for key ideas

S.M.A.R.T.E.R. Acronym for the necessary parts of a goal: Specific, Measurable, Achievable, Relevant, Time-Sensitive, Evident, and Recorded

SQ3R An active reading strategy developed by Francis Robinson consisting of five steps: Survey, Question, Read, Recite and Review

strategic planning A design that gathers, analyzes, and uses information to make decisions

stress The nonspecific response of the body to environmental or emotional demands

study group Two or more students who work together to learn information

studying The purposeful acquisition of knowledge or understanding

subject directory A set of topical terms that can be browsed or searched by using keywords

subjective questions Prompts which require you to write answers in essay or paragraph form

suspension Prohibition from enrolling in coursework

syllabus Outline of course content for a term

synchronously Hybrid course content delivered at the same time

T

tactile/kinesthetic Sense of touch

taxonomy A list of ordered groups or categories that lets you identify differences and similarities among the groups

technology Computers and the digital resources accessed by them

transcript List of courses taken, grades and credit received, and quality points given

V

values Personal beliefs and standards expressed in the topics and activities that are important to you

visualization Creating mental visual images of achieving a goal

W

websites Sites (locations) on the Web owned by a person, company, or organization that have a home page, the first document users see when they enter the site, and often additional documents and files

Web pages Specially formatted documents that support links to other documents, as well as graphics, audio, and video files

references

CHAPTER 2   Greenburg, D. & O'Malley, S. (1983). *How to Avoid Love and Marriage*. Philadelphia, PA: Running Press.

CHAPTER 3   Gardner, H. (2006). *Multiple Intelligences: New Horizons in Theory and Practice*. New York: Basic Books.

CHAPTER 4   *101 Goals in 1001 Days*. http://101goalsin1001days.com/.

Ambler, G. (2006). Setting SMART objectives. *The Practice of Leadership,* March 11, 2006. Retrieved from http://www.thepracticeofleadership.net/2006/03/11/setting-smart-objectives/.

Rotter, J. (1966). Generalized expectancies for internal versus external control of reinforcements. *Psychological Monographs* 80, 1–28.

CHAPTER 6   Ebbinghaus, H. (2010). *Memory: A Contribution to Experimental Psychology*. Translated by Henry A. Ruger & Clara E. Bussenius (1913). New York: Nabu Press.

CHAPTER 7   Tomlinson, L. M. (1997). A coding system for notemaking in literature: Preparation for journal writing, class participation, and essay tests. *Journal of Adolescent & Adult Literacy* 40(6), 468–476.

CHAPTER 9   Arringon, M. (2006). YouTube's magic number—$1.5 billion. *TechCrunch,* September 21, 2006. Retrieved from http://techcrunch.com/2006/09/21/youtubes-magic-number-15-billion/.

CTIA US Wireless Quick Facts (2009). Retrieved from http://www.ctia.org/media/industry_info/index.cfm/AID/10323.

Facebook statistics retrieved from http://www.facebook.com/press/info.php?statistics.

Google corporate information retrieved from http://www.google.com/intl/en/corporate/facts.html.

McGee, M. (2010). By the numbers: Twitter vs. Facebook vs. Google Buzz. *Search Engine Land,* February 23, 2010. Retrieved from http://searchengineland.com/by-the-numbers-twitter-vs-facebook-vs-google-buzz-36709.

Number of Cell Phones in Use (2002). Retrieved from http://hypertextbook.com/facts/2002/BogusiaGrzywac.shtml.

Step Zero: What to Do before Searching. Retrieved from http://webquest.sdsu.edu/searching/stepzero.html

CHAPTER 11   Eating disorder statistics retrieved from http://www.mirasol.net/eating-disorders/information/eating-disorder-statistics.php.

National Crime Victimization Survey retrieved from http://www.icpsr.umich.edu/icpsrweb/ICPSR/series/00095.

Sarros, J. C. & Densten, I. L (1989). Undergraduate student stress and coping strategies. *Higher Education Research and Development* 8(1), 47–57.

Sleep in America Polls retrieved from the National Sleep Foundation, http://www.sleepfoundation.org/category/article-type/sleep-america-polls.

CHAPTER 12   Number of jobs held, labor market activity, and earnings growth among the youngest Baby Boomers from a longitudinal survey summary (2008). Retrieved from the Bureau of Labor Statistics, http://www.bls.gov/news.release/nlsoy.nr0.htm.

credits

Photo Credits

Text Credits

CHAPTER 1 From Mark David Milliron, LEARNING ABSTRACTS, April 2004, Vol. 7 #4. © 2004 Mark Milliron. Used with permission. http://www.letssaythanks.com/Home1280.html 5C process adapted from: *Risks and Rewards of Entrepreneurship*, EMC Publishing, Saint Paul, MN. CHAPTER 2 The Maxed-Out Tech Student's Guide to Mastering Communication Skills by Patrick Amaral, *Graduating Engineer*, 3/9/98. © 1998. Used by permission. CHAPTER 3 "Olson looks for career in education," Morgan Muhlenbruch, *The Logos*, www.niacc.edu. © Morgan Muhlenbruch. Reprinted by permission of the author. CHAPTER 4 http://101goalsin 1001days.com/step-1/© Philip Berry. Used with permission. CHAPTER 6 Enhancing Students' Notetaking through Training and Evaluation Norman A. Stahl, James R. King and William A. Henk *Journal of Reading*, Vol. 34, No. 8 (May, 1991), pp. 614–622 International Reading Association Changing Landscapes by Evelyn L. Kent, Modesto Junior College, *Community College Times* CHAPTER 7 "Following Your Own Unique Path" by Robert DuBois. © 2008 Robert DuBois. Used with permission. CHAPTER 8 Test Anxiety Scale reproduced from Sarason, I.G. (1980), Test Anxiety: Theory, Research, and Applications.

Reprinted by permission of the author. List describing common question words in essays, examples of how they might be used, and strategies for responding to them. *Adapted from Jeanne Schumm, University of Miami; Miami, Florida* "Lack of sleep, may lead to lack of future" by Mary Allen, GCC Voice, 3/21/07. © 2007. Used with permission. CHAPTER 9 Are you ready to be a distance learner? Quiz used courtesy of Florida Distance Learning Consortium. © 1997–2010. The Internet: A Friend Made to Look Bad by Richard Okagbue Copyright 2002 Richard Okagbue. Reprinted by permission of the author and Metropolitan Community Colleges. CHAPTER 10 Fairy tale becomes reality: Credit disenchantment *ACCENT*, Austin Community College, Vol. 5, #2, Oct. 2002. © 2002. Used with permission. CHAPTER 11 Daily Wellness Log. © 2009 Tristan J. Loo. Used by permission of the Self Improvement Association. Common STDs from: http://www.gallupcpc.com/COMMON%20STD%20CHART.htm. My Favorite Day Dr. Sanford C. "Sandy" Shugart. Commencement speech given at Valencia Community College, 2000. © 2000 Sanford C. Shugart. Used with permission. CHAPTER 12 Perspectives article used courtesy of Florida Distance Learning Consortium. Copyright © 1997–2010.

index

Notes

Notes

Notes

Notes

Notes

Notes

Notes

Notes

Notes